LANGUAGE, LABOUR AND MIGRATION

Language, Labour and Migration

Edited by
ANNE J. KERSHEN
Centre for the Study of Migration
Queen Mary and Westfield College

Ashgate

Aldershot • Burlington USA • Singapore • Sydney

Published by
Ashgate Publishing Ltd
Gower House
Croft Road
Aldershot
Hants GU11 3HR
England

Ashgate Publishing Company
131 Main Street
Burlington
Vermont 05401
USA

Ashgate website: http://www.ashgate.com

British Library Cataloguing in Publication Data
Language, labour and migration. - (Studies in migration)
   1. Migrant labour - Social aspects - Congresses 2. Immigrants
   - Language - Congresses 3. Immigrants - Employment -
   Congresses 4. Language and culture - Congresses
   I. Kershen, Anne J., 1942-
   306.4'4'089

Library of Congress Catalog Card Number: 00-132604

ISBN 0 7546 1171 X

Printed in Great Britain by
Antony Rowe Ltd, Chippenham, Wiltshire

Contents

PART TWO: LABOUR 119

List of Figures

List of Tables

Contributors

Paul Bailey is Reader in East Asian History at the University of Edinburgh. His publications include *China in the Twentieth Century* (1988), *Reform The People* (1990) and *Postwar Japan* (1996). He is currently writing a book-length manuscript on Chinese workers in France during the First World War.

Alice Bloch is Lecturer in the Department of Social Policy and Politics, Goldsmiths College, University of London. Her recent publications include an edited collection, with Carl Levy, *Refugees, Social Policy and Citizenship in Europe*, Macmillan, 1999.

Ian Duffield teaches in the Department of History, University of Edinburgh. He has published extensively on convict transportation and on African Diaspora History. Among his 1990s publications are: Jagdish S. Gundara and Ian Duffield (eds), *Essays on the History of Blacks in Britain*, Aldershot, Ashgate, 1992; Ian Duffield and James Bradley (eds), *Representing Convicts*, London, Leicester University Press, 1997 and 2000. He is also founder and principal researcher of the International Centre for Convict Studies, University of Tasmania (Hobart). A former president (1994–97) of the British Australian Studies Association, he is one of the three current editors of its refereed journal, *Australian Studies*.

Anne J. Kershen is Barnett Shine Senior Research Fellow and Director of the Centre for the Study of Migration at Queen Mary and Westfield College, University of London. She has published widely and is the author of *Uniting the Tailors* (1995); co-author of *Tradition and Change: A History of Reform Judaism in Britain 1840–1995* (1995) and editor of and contributor to, *London the Promised Land? The Migrant Experience in a Capital City* (1997) and *A Question of Identity* (1998). She is currently working on a study of the way in which politics impact upon the lives of the poor and the way in which the poor affect the course of politics.

Tony Kushner is Professor of History and Director of the Centre for the Study of Jewish/non-Jewish relations at the University of Southampton. He is the author and editor of 10 books, the latest co-authored with Katherine Knox, *Refugees in an Age of Genocide: Global, National and Local Perspectives During the Twentieth Century* (1999).

Shompa Lahiri is Research Associate at the Centre for the Study of Migration, at Queen Mary and Westfield College, University of London and has published articles on South Asians in Britain and British policy towards Indian Princes. She is the author of *Indians in Britain: Anglo-Indian Encounters, Race and Identity* (1999) and is currently working on a study of ethnic minorities in the criminal justice system.

Mahmood Messkoub lectures in economics at Leeds University Business School. He has also taught and researched at Queen Mary and Westfield College, University of London and the Institute of Social Studies at the Hague. His current research interests are in the interface between population studies and economics, particularly in the areas of migration and population ageing.

Wayne Parsons is Professor of Public Policy at Queen Mary and Westfield College, University of London and a graduate of the University of Wales. He was born in Cardiff and is the product of a diverse Celtic background. Amongst his publications are *Keynes and the Quest for a Moral Science* (1997), *Public Policy* (1995), *The Power of the Financial Press* (1989) and *The Political Economy of British Regional Policy* (1988).

Bronwen Walter is Senior Lecturer in Geography at Anglia Polytechnic University, Cambridge. She has a long-standing research interest in Irish migration to Britain, particularly in the experiences of Irish women in the diaspora. She is co-author of the 1997 report for the Commission for Racial Equality, *Discrimination and the Irish Community in Britain*.

Veronica L.C. White is Specialist Registrar in Respiratory Medicine and TB Research Fellow at the Barts and London NHS Trust. She is currently researching an MD on 'Barriers to the Effective Management of Tuberculosis in the Bangladeshi Community of East London' and is a contributor to the Royal College of Physicians Medical Masterclass.

Preface

The Centre for the Study of Migration was established in the autumn of 1994 at Queen Mary and Westfield College, University of London, in order to provide a focal point in London for those concerned with the study of the movements of people locally, nationally and internationally. One of the major attributes of the Centre is its multi-disciplinary nature and its intention to promote the interaction of all those engaged in the study of migration. One way of achieving this aim has been through the mounting of conferences which explore specific themes through a variety of lenses. To date three conferences have been held each of which has been followed by the publication of a selection of essays, some of which were given as papers at the conference, others specially commissioned. The first two conferences spawned *London the Promised Land? The Migrant Experience in a Capital City*, published in March 1997, and *A Question of Identity*, published in November 1998 – each edited by myself.

The third conference, held in November 1998, was on the theme of 'Language and Labour' and this volume is the outcome, once again a collection of conference papers with some additional, specially commissioned chapters which expand on the theme. As befits the Centre's *raison d'être* the contributors represent the diversity of fields engaged in the study of migration at the dawning of the twenty-first century, these include economics, geography, history, medicine, political science and sociology. All are engaged in extending their, and our, awareness and knowledge of the complexity of the everyday issues that confront the immigrant – the need to communicate and the need to work.

I should like to thank all those who have contributed to this volume and who have borne my appeals, now sent through the miracle of modern technology – the email – for copy and adherence to house style. I should also like to thank the members of the Centre's Steering Group, most particularly its current Chair, Professor Philip Ogden, and Professor Sheila Hillier who so ably helped chair the conference which provided the material for this book. My thanks also to my colleagues in the Department of Politics: Departmental Secretary Jasmine Salucideen; Eilis Rafferty and the staff of QMW Library.

A very special thank you to the Centre's Research Associate, Dr Shompa Lahiri, to Professor Ken Young, to Lord Levene, Chairman of the Centre's Advisory Board and the Advisory Board members. Most particular thanks to Martin Paisner without whose concern and support much of the Centre's work could not take place. Finally, as always, my deepest thanks to my husband Martin for his love and support when the going gets tough.

Anne J. Kershen
Director, Centre for the Study of Migration
Queen Mary and Westfield College
University of London
Spring 2000

1 Introduction

ANNE J. KERSHEN

Language and Labour,[1] the ability to communicate and the facility to provide for dependants and self as a result of personal – physical or mental – work are two essentials of civilised society; equally as important to the native resident of a nation-state as to settlers from beyond its boundaries. For immigrants however these two pillars of survival are, all too often, far more difficult to support. In order to communicate with the majority community some, if not total, fluency in the tongue of the receiving society will be required, whilst levels and availability of immigrant employment will be reliant upon the economic barometer, contemporary labour requirements and the influence of racism and negative stereotyping. This volume sets out to explore the experiences of migrants, some voluntary others not, as measured by the words of its title. What role has language played, and does it play, in the integration process? How important is bilingualism and where should the emphasis lie, on the acquisition of the majority tongue, with the goal of eventual monolingual fluency, or on the retention of mother tongue whilst acquiring that of the receiving society? For some, such as the Bangladeshi community in late twentieth century Britain, the 'People's right to use and maintain their mother language is a prerequisite',[2] for others, such as the British Jewish community of the late nineteenth century, the need for their Eastern European coreligionists to eschew Yiddish in favour of English was paramount. But does an inability to verbally communicate with the receiving society automatically preclude employment? In other words can an immigrant, deficient in the majority language, get a job? How serious a handicap is majority language deficiency? Further, if jobs are available to incomers, what form do they take, what kind of labour is on offer? Are there any opportunities for the unskilled labourer, the indentured worker or the enslaved black mariner to escape the shackles of exploitation and join the ranks of the upwardly mobile? And, can the stigmas and stereotypes attached to those alienated by reason of sound of voice or low level of employment, ever be eliminated? The chapters in this book set out to examine and respond to these, and other such, questions.

Before briefly exploring the core themes of the book, a note of linguistic explanation. In this volume the noun 'language' will be used in several forms. As describing a means of communication, as denoting the language of a particular community or country – thus enabling the incorporation of dialects and vernaculars – or to signify the style and use of words, as for example the languages used by proselytising missionaries in the nineteenth century or that used by those communicating on the Internet in the twenty-first century. The word 'labour' has already been used in its verbal form to describe physical exertion, as illustrated in Eric Hobsbawm's early 1960s publication, *Labouring Men*.[3] In this work Hobsbawm focused not only on those who laboured, as members of the working class(es) but, additionally, on the conditions that activated their responses, thus combining the active with the passive. At the same time E.P. Thompson in his seminal work, *The Making of the English Working Class*,[4] was bringing to our attention those labouring men whom he considered to be the 'losers of history'. Some of those losers, such as Paul Bailey's First World War indentured Chinese labourers, Shompa Lahiri's Indian lascars and Ian Duffield's Black African slave mariners, find their way into this book, rescued from invisibility as a result of diligent archival research.

In its noun form the word labour has, as Robin Cohen highlights, two senses,[5] as a collective noun, for example 'migrant labour', or 'industrial labour' and as an abstract, as in the title of another of Hobsbawm's books, *Worlds of Labour*.[6] When in operation as a noun to describe a group of workers, the word both takes on, and bestows, a (lower) class value. In whichever form the word appears, it remains the one most frequently applied to the majority of those who move from one place to another, either within or beyond national boundaries, to achieve economic advancement. It is applied equally to those who have chosen, and those who have been forced, to become part of that collective of labour that has fed, and continues to feed, the requirements of communities, nations and organisations eager to grow rich on the backs of exploited and majority language deficient immigrants and refugees.

Language

The chapters included in this section embrace themes which are central to any debate on the role of language in the migrant experience. It has to be universally acknowledged that language and identity are entwined. For immigrants whose skin colour and physical characteristics are no different to that of the majority society, language and voice are the first means of identifying difference. In her chapter on 'Language and Racialisation', Bronwen Walter illustrates the way in which the Irish voice and syntax have been the catalyst for racism and negative stereotyping, 'to the uninformed all Irish accents are the same, and lower class'. Thus language is used not only as a means of separating the alien from the mainstream but, in addition, as a means of establishing class. Even the Huguenots, positively stereotyped as the 'profitable strangers' suffered criticism from members of the receiving society for the 'great noise and croaking of the Froglanders'.[7] Criticism can also come from within the same ethnic or national group. Anne Kershen describes how, at the end of the nineteenth century, Yiddish speaking immigrants were at the receiving end of snobbism from their British coreligionists, whilst Sylheti speaking Bangladeshis are considered inferior by the more educated élite of their native country. The spoken and written foreign tongue not only identifies the 'alien in our midst' it can also, sometimes mistakenly as Tony Kushner explains, spotlight the enemy. German refugees in Britain seeking sanctuary from the evils of Nazism were warned 'not to read German papers in public' and 'not to speak German in the street'. Thus, in order to remain invisible a policy of silence is adopted by those whose voices identify them as other.

Language not only works as a negative means of identification, it can also be used as an aid to the construction and confirmation, and in some instances the reconstruction, of ethnic identity. Wayne Parsons, in his chapter on Cyber-Cymru, combines one of the oldest of languages, Celtic, with the most modern of technological advancements, the Internet, to demonstrate how, in North America, Welsh-Americans are reclaiming their ethnic identity and rediscovering the language of their forefathers. Using the World Wide Web they are opening up the frontiers of diasporic awareness, reconfirming their roots, which for some have been submerged under decades of acculturation, by means of a virtual reality which, it has to be said, uses as its dominant tongue, the language of the Web, English. The construction of a national/ ethnic identity through the dominance of language is now written into the history of the Bangladeshi people, and plays an important part in their diasporic self-evaluation process. Kershen explains how the struggle for Bangladeshi independence began over the language issue and how, consequently, Bangladeshis choose to identify themselves by their language – as Bengalis – rather than by the name of their nation-state.

As a number of chapters illustrate, language deficiency frequently acts as a catalyst for tension and racism, imposing behavioural pressures on the immigrant. It encourages conformity and invisibility. However, at times, as Kushner and Veronica White show in the case of Belgian refugees to Britain during the First World War and late twentieth century Sylhetis in London's

East End, lack of fluency in English can elicit sympathy for those considered unfairly treated or those unable to communicate their health problems. But the plus side of language deficiencies are rare, as the norm for those who suffer from this condition is loss of self-respect and feelings of insecurity, emotions common to the Huguenots in the late eighteenth century and more recent Irish arrivals. In fact, recent medical research has shown that amongst elderly immigrants to Britain who have not mastered the native tongue the resultant feelings of isolation have produced the depressive condition known as SAD (symptoms of anxiety and depression).[8]

A number of chapters illustrate the way in which migrants deficient in a minority language have adopted both positive and negative strategies to cope with the disadvantages that ensue. The most obvious route to overcoming the problems of weakness in the primary language is through education. Whilst 100 years ago, as Kershen demonstrates, it was left to the immigrant community to provide pedagogic bridges between Yiddish and English, through trade unions, charitable organisations etc., in the multi-cultural twenty-first century the state takes a far more dominant role, cooperating with ethnic minority groups to ensure that mother tongue teaching, viewed as a vital step on the road to bilingualism and the acquisition of the majority language, is available to all those, especially schoolchildren, who need it. In her chapter on health advocacy, White leaves us in no doubt as to the dangers to health of illiteracy and inarticulacy in English. Adequate verbal communication is deemed vital to the health of the patient. She quotes one American physician as commenting that, 'What the scalpel is to the surgeon, words are to the clinician ... the conversation between doctor and patient is the heart of the practice of medicine'.[9] White, a senior hospital registrar and thus at the grass roots, describes the way in which health advocates in hospitals in East London have to some extent overcome the communication barrier, facilitating the ethnic patient/doctor relationship and consequently reducing the dangers of misdiagnosis and inappropriate medication. However, not all strategies have been, or are, as constructive. Kershen, Kushner and Walter all highlight the way in which the racialisation of language has reinforced the ghetto mentality and encouraged immigrants to adopt policies of silence as a means of acquiring invisibility.

Labour

As noted above, the word labour as it appears in this book provides a vehicle for the actual and the abstract, the individual and the group. It embraces the willing and the unwilling, the hopeful and the hopeless. The chapters which appear in the section headed Labour, similarly to those which appear under Language, demonstrate that time has not reduced the hardships undergone by 'strangers' seeking employment. Duffield in his chapter on African slave mariners of the eighteenth and nineteenth centuries describes all too painfully the inequities suffered by Black slave labour. Though their situation was not without a glimmer of light – patience and providence could buy freedom – the value of the 'invisible' slave seaman was such that sale and resale, as a commodity on the stock market, took place irrespective of the individual's legal status. It was not only the enslaved that were subjected to inhuman treatment, both Bailey and Lahiri describe how indentured labour, Chinese and Indian, were dehumanised – the former often by their own government for political gain. Victims of racial stereotyping and exploitation, their varying skill levels were used as tools in the cruel battle for survival and economic reward.

Just as those condemned by their language deficiency adopted strategies of survival so did those whose labour made them appear docile, malleable and exploitable. Lahiri recounts how strikes were organised by lascars who refused to be exploited by their employers. She also explores the 'subtle manipulation' of the missionaries by lascars who were prepared to accept charity yet determined not to succumb to conversion to Christianity. The latter was a strategy adopted by pauper Jewish immigrants in London's East End. They metaphorically closed their ears to the religious tracts and chants of the London Society for Promoting Christianity amongst the Jews, whilst accepting the food and warmth of the mission halls.[10] Other strategies for survival were adopted by Duffield's protagonist Olaudah Equiano who, 'eventually accumulated … the £40 to buy his freedom' and by Chinese workers who took industrial action to protest against the 'breaches in contract, the dangerous nature of their work and the harsh treatment … received'.

As noted, hardship and exploitation is not the preserve of migrants of the past. As we enter the twenty-first century the problems facing immigrants and refugees who seek to provide for themselves and their families continue. Alice Bloch describes how refugees in the London Borough of Newham, one of the poorest in Britain, in spite of their education and ability, have been unable to find employment commensurate with their qualifications. One of the major barriers being the level of language skill and the 'Catch 22' of a training scheme which requires full-time attendance, thus denying access to employment which might support until work becomes an option. Those without an academic background suffer still more; lack of awareness or understanding of what training is available reduces the scale of opportunity . However, Bloch reveals that, even if training is undertaken, job opportunities for refugees in Newham are few. She argues in favour of a receiving society which, instead of marginalising new arrivals, takes advantage of what they have to offer and uses a system of 'fast-track conversion' courses to enable both established community and incomers to benefit.

Not all the problems of migration and settlement are immediate, some accrue over the years. This is particularly evident in a post-modern world which has an increasingly large ageing population. Whilst longevity is, for the most part, to be desired, it brings with it economic pressures. Theoretically the pension system should be able to provide a safety net for the elderly. However, as is becoming apparent in a number of European countries, this situation is rapidly reaching crisis point. Mahmood Messkoub provides evidence that it is the elderly members of ethnic communities – particularly those from Bangladesh, Pakistan and Somalia, that will be affected worst of all. They joined the labour market later than the indigenous workforce and have been in receipt of lower wages, thus they can expect to receive little more than the basic state pension, one which, not having kept pace with inflation, provides its recipients with an income on, or just above, the poverty line. With the constant need to send remittances home there has been little or nothing over for the poorer immigrants to put by for their old age.

Conclusion

The chapters in this book have been compartmentalised in order to prioritise their dominant theme. However, it is immediately obvious that such a division is purely academic. Bloch's refugees suffer as much from language deficiency as unemployment. Jewish tailors, Sylheti leather workers and Chinese indentured labourers were, all too often, the subjects of labour exploitation as a result of their language deficiency and dependency on those who could interact with the receiving society's employers. As much, if not more, exploitation was carried out by co-nationalists and religionists as by members of the majority community. Duffield's 'Black Labourer' overcomes his disadvantages and finds his 'voice' and subsequently uses language, in the context of the written word, to inform others of the experience of one, among many, Black slaves.

The chapters that follow explore the themes of language and labour as they impact upon the lives of migrants. The compilation of works from authors representative of different disciplines, including one, Veronica White, whose experience comes as much from the shop – or ward – floor as from the world of academe, is indicative of the breadth and importance of the two pillars in determining the direction and fortunes of those who have moved from home to 'somewhere else', though often not sure where that elsewhere will be. What is clear is that in the century ahead migrants will need to communicate – face to face or through virtual reality – in whatever is the dominant language[11] whilst at the same time keeping hold of their perceived (if not always real) identity through the retention of mother tongue. At the same time, even though the methods and levels of exertion may be subject to flux, some form of labour will be required in order to ensure the survival of 'Those that will work; those that cannot work and those that will not work'.[12]

Notes

1 The different interpretations of the word 'labour' and their application in this volume will be dealt with below.
2 S. Alladina and V. Edwards (eds), *Multilingualism in the British Isles 1*, Harlow, Longman, 1991, p. 2.
3 See E.J. Hobsbawm, *Labouring Men*, London, Weidenfeld and Nicolson, 1964.
4 E.P. Thompson, *The Making of the English Working Class*, London, Victor Gollanz, 1963.
5 R. Cohen, T*he New Helots: Migrants in the International Division of Labour*, Aldershot, Avebury, 1987, p. xiii.
6 E. Hobsbawm, *Worlds of Labour*, London, Weidenfield and Nicolson, 1984.
7 Robin D. Gwynn, *Huguenot Heritage*, London, Routledge and Kegan Paul, 1985, pp. 118–19 as quoted in Michael D. Keating, 'The Huguenots as Exemplary Incomers: Did the Huguenots Set the Agenda by Which Future Incomers Have Been Measured?', unpublished MPhil dissertation, University of London, 1998, p. 66, n. 172.
8 Ellen Silveira and Ahmed Abdullahi, 'Report into the Health and Social Circumstances of Somali Elderly People in Tower Hamlets', Royal Free Hospital and London Hospital Medical College, 1993.
9 S. Woloshin, N.A. Bicknell, L.M. Schwartz et al., 'Language Barriers in medicine in the United States', *Journal of American Medical Association*, 1995, 273 (9), pp. 724–8.
10 For details of Christian missionaries working within the Jewish immigrant community of London see T. Endelman, *The Jews of Georgian England 1714–1830*, Ann Arbor, University of Michigan Press, 1999, pp. 71–4.
11 At present English is the language of the information superhighway. It is the medium through which different nationalities can communicate without a broad linguistic knowledge. If this remains the case one is left questioning whether in the decades ahead bilingualism will come to mean simply a spoken and written knowledge of English plus the official (and perhaps dialect) of the individual's nation-state. For further thoughts on this see, Krishna Dutta, *Times Higher Educational Supplement*, 23 April 1999, p. 26.

12 These are the lines that appeared on the frontispiece to the social investigator Henry
   Mayhew's volumes of *London Labour and London Poor* which were first published in
   1862.

PART ONE
LANGUAGE

2 Mother Tongue as a Bridge to Assimilation?: Yiddish and Sylheti in East London

ANNE J. KERSHEN

Language is one of the main pillars of civilised society; a landmark in its evolution. It is the gateway to all levels of day-to-day interaction in the public and private spheres, to intellectual and cultural development and to furthering our understanding of the ways in which humankind functions. As much as it produces union and community it separates, creating invisible barriers, alienating outsiders whose otherness is manifested by language. Thus, it is not only outward appearance which labels the alien in our midst, so too does speech; as Alladina and Edwards record:

> The outsider, the immigrant and the oppressed have been repeatedly marked and condemned, first for not learning English and second for not learning the right kind of English.[1]

Over the centuries immigrants to London with little or no English have been consigned to linguistic ghettoes. This chapter sets out to examine the way in which two immigrant groups, who occupied the same space, though at different times, have reacted to the problems of majority language deficiency. That space is Spitalfields – the traditional first point of settlement for incomers to London – which lies to the east of the capital, at the western end of the London Borough of Tower Hamlets. The two groups under the microscope are the Eastern European Jews who arrived in this country during the last decades of the nineteenth century and the Bangladeshis – more specifically those from the region of Sylhet – who arrived almost 100 years later. In exploring their experiences of linguistic separation and assimilation several questions arise. Firstly, how did each group perceive the role of language? Was it as a means of communication, as a source of national pride, as a weapon for alienists and racists or as a vehicle for assimilation? Secondly, were the

11

problems of linguistic disability resolved by the adoption of a policy of bilingualism – through the retention of mother tongue parallel with the acquisition of the majority language? Or by eschewing the past and eradicating difference, through the exclusive use of majority language and the exclusion of mother tongue? The one a policy of separation yet integration, the other one of total assimilation. In seeking the answers the chapter exposes linguistic social divisions, illustrates changing attitudes to multilingualism and locates the place of language on the political agenda of local community groups.

Before proceeding it is important to identify certain linguistic terms and their correlation to the status of the two groups under discussion. Firstly, what do we understand by the term *mother tongue*? In most situations the expression is interchangeable with *vernacular* and describes the everyday speech of a group, community or nation. Thus, although Yiddish has never achieved 'national' status it was the 'language' of Jews (excluding the minority bourgeoisie) in nineteenth century eastern Europe. It was the written and spoken medium of their daily interaction at home and at work, though not of their prayer, which was classical Hebrew. Yiddish was both mother tongue and vernacular. However, as will be explained below, the same cannot be said of Sylheti, the medium of conversation used by the majority of Bangladeshis living in the region of Sylhet and of 95 per cent of those living in the London Borough of Tower Hamlets. Sylheti may well be the vernacular, the spoken everyday tongue,[2] but it is Bengali that is considered the Sylheti people's mother tongue; the national taught, and official, language of Bangladesh. In any discussion of Bangladeshis in Britain and the place of mother tongue we have to be aware of the parallel usage of the informal spoken tongue (Sylheti) and that which is the formal spoken and written language (Bengali).

Secondly, Yiddish and Sylheti speakers have frequently been stigmatised as of low social class. At the end of the nineteenth century Eastern European intellectuals and members of the Anglo-Jewish establishment regarded Yiddish in pejorative terms, as a *jargon*, not a language: in 1883 the *Jewish Chronicle*, the organ of British Jewry, highlighted the need for teachers in the Jews' Free School to 'understand the Jargon';[3] whilst British government colonial officials and, post 1947 and then 1971, their Pakistani and Bangladeshi successors, devalued Sylheti giving it the status of a 'dialect', a distinction which some linguists argue does not exist.[4] Whilst the intricacies of these linguistic debates must be left to the experts, it is important for the purposes of this study to note the social perceptions of those with the power and influence to determine the role of mother tongue/vernacular in the immigrant experience.

Yiddish

Yiddish is the language of the deracinated, synonymous with diaspora and fusion, representing a synthesis of the distant and recent past. It is a language without a national base or an official role,[5] arguably a language of weakness.[6] It is a language which, through its dynamism, reflects the geographic dispersal of its speakers. Yiddish is more than one thousand years old, originating between the ninth and twelfth centuries[7] along the banks of the Rhine, in the region of Loter,[8] an area which incorporated Cologne, Maine and Metz. In its earliest form it was a combination of Hebrew, Loez[9] and German, written in Hebrew characters.[10] From the thirteenth century onwards, as western European persecutions took a hold, Jews migrated eastwards, Yiddish absorbing elements of other languages as they progressed. In what is known as the period of 'middle yiddish' (between 1500 and 1750), a flourishing literature emerged, laying the foundations of a tradition of prose and poetry which to this day commands respect.

By the nineteenth century the majority of European Jews were to be found in Russia and Russia-Poland, within the Pale of Settlement.[11] 'Modern' or 'new' Yiddish had taken on a different, more lowly mantle. The Jewish orthodoxy considered it inferior, a 'low language' as compared to Hebrew, the 'high language' of religion. For the Jewish intellectual and politicised élite, Yiddish was the language of the uneducated and socially subordinate Jews of the ghetto, no more than a 'jargon destined to disappear ... a dead language',[12] a language of function. But that function had to be acknowledged, for it was the route to the acquisition of the majority language and, in the eyes of Jewish socialists, to fellowship with all the oppressed and exploited East Europeans under Tzarist rule. As would be recognised more generally by educationalists in the late twentieth century, literacy in mother tongue was considered by the radicals to be the first step towards articulation and literacy in the majority (in this instance Russian) language. As early as the 1880s a British government schools inspector working in Spitalfields revealed that, 'It is found that the children whose language is foreign often attain finally a higher standard of English speech than the children handicapped from birth by learning a vulgar and slovenly English'.[13] However, it took almost 100 years before this educational truth was translated into pedagogic application. Now, as we enter the twenty-first century, bilingualism is accepted as being 'beneficial in general cognitive development'[14] and, as we will see below, within the London borough of Tower Hamlets, mother tongue classes are now available for children for whom English is a second language. Though in the last quarter of the nineteenth century socialist activists in Russia were most unlikely to have been aware of the findings of that British schools inspector, they were forced to acknowledge that in spite of their own disregard for Yiddish, and their preference for Russian, 'mother tongue' was a more effective vehicle with which to launch a propaganda campaign. They had no option but to, 'avail themselves of so powerful a tool as the living tongue [Yiddish] of the folk masses in order to penetrate the very depths of their life and emotions'.[15] Thus, even in the region in which, in reality, Yiddish was the majority language, moves were underway to bridge the gap, to eschew the language of the *stetl* and substitute the language of the state in the cause of politics and ideology.

With the exception of intellectual refugees escaping the restrictive Russian regime, Eastern European immigrants arriving in London from the 1870s onwards cared little for politics and ideology, their priorities were domestic and economic security. Arriving at the Port of London they carried with them the visible and mental baggage of the Diaspora; the stench of steerage travel; poverty; a preparedness to work as long and as hard as was necessary for survival; a language which both identified them as other and separated them from the native workforce and the hopes and dreams which had been a part of the Jewish Diaspora since biblical times.[16] These new arrivals were mainly 'greeners' who fuelled the swelling pool of semi- and unskilled exploited labour in London's East End and provided ammunition for anti-alienists keen to control the entry into Britain of pauper aliens.

Bridge Building or Social Control?

The very 'alien' nature of the Eastern European immigrant presence wrought similar reactions from sections of Jewish society – the Anglo-Jewish establishment and Jewish refugee intellectuals – which in all other ways were polarised. The visible concentration of a large number of impoverished aliens in close proximity to the heart of the metropolis and their perceived, if not always real, demands on the labour and housing markets, unnerved a recently emancipated[17] Anglo-Jewish establishment which considered its constituents to be 'Englishmen of the Mosaic persuasion'. They were embarrassed, if not ashamed, of their newly arrived indigent and foreign-looking coreligionsts who, by their concentrated visibility were furthering the cause of anti-alienism. There were some English Jews, such as Morris Joseph, Senior Minister of the West London Synagogue of British Jews, who considered it no less than the 'Russo-Jewish immigrants' ... duty to leave behind them the ideas and habits that were tolerated in Russia'.[18] Others, amongst them members of the Cousinhood (the leading families of Anglo-Jewry), reacted in a more positive vein by developing different methods by which the process of 'ironing out the ghetto bends' could be advanced as rapidly as possible.[19] A major objective was the eradication of the language of the Pale. Evidence of the low regard in which British Jewry held Yiddish became increasingly overt. In 1880, the 'organ' of British Jewry, the *Jewish Chronicle*, reviewed Yiddish plays with an obvious disdain; the reviewer noting that they were '… performed in the *Judisch Deutsch* dialect, a language which we [British Jewry] should be the last to encourage any efforts to preserve'. At this early stage there was even a reluctance to use the more commonly descriptive title 'Yiddish' as the means of identifying the mother tongue language.

The 1891 Decennial Census figures confirmed what had become visibly obvious, that there had been a significant increase in the number of Eastern Europeans resident in England and Wales, the reported total had risen from 14,549 in 1881 to 45,808 in 1891;[20] Eastern Europeans now represented one-sixth of the alien population of Britain. With the British economy in decline and unemployment on the rise support for anti-alienism strengthened. As part of British Jewry's response, in 1892, the Russo-Jewish Committee[21] sponsored a series of Free English Evening Classes. The aim of the classes was to 'impart a knowledge of the English language, habits and usages, to adult Russian Jews and Jewesses'.[22] Nightly attendance was at times as high as 500, though 'not the same persons attended regularly'; significantly students were 'five-eighths male and mostly under thirty'.[23] Anglo-Jewry urged immigrants of all ages to eschew Yiddish, 'that miserable jargon which is not a language at all' and learn English. Both young and old were targets for change, and if the task was too arduous or impossible for the older generation then they were instructed to ensure that their children grew up 'to be identified as English',[24] by speech as well as behaviour.

As current evidence has shown, it is much harder to re-educate adults, particularly if their entry level of literacy in the mother tongue is poor. Therefore it was towards the children of the immigrants that the most powerful thrust of Anglicisation through the teaching and learning of English was directed. The policy of schools established by the Jewish establishment[25] to educate their poorer, and often foreign, coreligionists was one which would ensure that students would graduate (aged 12 to 13) thinking and speaking as Englishmen. Yiddish, the language Moses Angel, headmaster of the Jews' Free School in the East End of London, considered 'unintelligible', was discouraged from the day a child started school. In some instances children who spoke Yiddish were made to stand on a stool in the centre of the classroom as a punishment, an approach reminiscent of the 'Welsh Not', the sign Welsh children were made to hang around their necks at school if they committed the misdemeanour of using the 'old [Celtic] language'.[26] For the children of the Eastern European immigrants their first day at school often coincided with the first time they heard English spoken. The vernacular of the Eastern European household at the end of the nineteenth century was Yiddish and its continued domestic use was viewed as a major obstacle to proficiency in the majority language. Samuel Montagu, Member of Parliament for Whitechapel, went so far as to ask pupils at Jews' Free School to 'refuse to learn Yiddish from their parents'.[27]

In spite of the desire to eradicate Yiddish from the immigrant world, for practical reasons, both at schools and in the home, Yiddish was to be a vehicle for Anglicisation. Teachers in Jewish primary, and English Board, schools had to use Yiddish as the initial means of communicating with their pupils, some of whom may only have arrived in the country just days before starting school. For teachers at Christ Church School in Brick Lane this meant learning Yiddish. How else would they interact with their Jewish pupils who, by the late 1880s, made up almost 95 per cent of the student population of the board school? (At the end of the twentieth century teachers at the same school had to learn Bengali and Sylheti in order to communicate with the children of the latest immigrant community.) Within a short while the children of the immigrants had learnt English, and learnt it well. It became their main language, used to converse with parents in the home, to interact with English children in the streets and, as they grew older, in the workplace and at leisure. Parents accepted that learning English was a necessary, and willing, step their children took on the road to becoming accepted as Englishmen and English women even if they themselves continued to use the 'jargon', on occasions much to the displeasure of their offspring as the following quotation illustrates:

> Imagine, even when we go with our father to buy something in a store ... he insists on speaking Yiddish. We are not ashamed of our parents ... but they ought to know where it's proper and where it's not. If they talk Yiddish among themselves at home, or to us, it's bad enough, but among strangers and Christians?[28]

The above quotation appeared in an American/Yiddish newspaper in the early 1930s, however it expresses only too well the sentiments of the children of (persistently) Yiddish-speaking parents in England as is confirmed by the memories of a child growing up in Manchester during the first decade of the twentieth century: 'Yiddish was frowned upon ... it was kind of degrading to speak Yiddish.'[29]

The other impetus for Anglicisation came from the radical Jewish intelligentsia and trade unionists (Jewish and English). If the future was to be one in which workers stood shoulder to shoulder against the forces of capitalism and exploitation then there would have to be brotherhood not separation. A prerequisite for worker unity was vocal communication, if not for all, then for the majority. However, for all but '... the gifted minority [that] went on to the *Yeshiva*[30] for intensive Talmudic study'[31] standards of education for Jews in the towns and villages of eastern Europe were low. Boys received religious education (in classic Hebrew[32]), at least until the age of 13, the age of *barmitzvah*,[33] and some basic secular education provided by poor teachers in poor conditions. Women received little or no secular or religious teaching – one explanation for their poor attendance at the Free English Classes was, that as they were illiterate in their mother tongue it was very hard for them to learn to read and write in English; this an example of the universal problem of teaching a second language to those illiterate in their mother tongue.

With little education and few, if any, skills, the immigrant arrivals of the last decades of the nineteenth century had little choice but to take whatever work was on offer. In an economic environment which had seen a huge expansion in consumer spending amongst the skilled working and lower middle classes during the second half of the century it was the industries which had grown in response to the new markets which supported, and exploited, immigrant labour. For Eastern Europeans, not renowned for their physical strength,[34] those industries included clothing,[35] cabinet making and other small-scale trades. The willingness of the alien to work for the lowest of wages, in the worst conditions, for the longest hours i.e. to conform to the definition of sweated labour,[36] led refugee socialist intellectuals and leaders of English tailoring trade unions to recognise that if change was to be brought about the exploited Jewish workers would have to learn the language of the majority society and develop basic literacy skills; if illiterate in their mother tongue then that inadequacy too would have to be addressed. It was a recognition which preceded by some 15 years the establishment of the Free English Classes.

One of the earliest pioneers of trade union organisation amongst the Jewish tailors of the East End of London, was the 'founding father of Jewish socialism', Aaron Liberman. An intellectual who regarded Yiddish as an inferior medium of communication, in 1876 he founded the Hebrew Socialist Union in Spitalfields. The title of the organisation, and its stated intention to 'spread Socialism among Jews as well as non-Jews ... to unite all workers in the fight against their oppressors ...'[37] is indicative of the man's linguistic bias and his ideological direction. In spite of the concession made by writing the rules of both unions in Yiddish as well as Hebrew, Liberman's inability to appreciate the immediate economic and cultural needs and preferences of the workers in the East End resulted in the collapse of the main Socialist Union and its tailoring offshoot. Three years later another organisation, the Jewish Workers' Union was established in East London with an impressive pedagogic programme, to set up a library and teach its members to read and write in English and Yiddish. Within a few months however the combination of worker disinterest and an inability to pay the weekly fees resulted in the union's collapse.[38]

It was concern about the immigrants' presence and their impact on wage rates that finally persuaded the exclusivist English, Amalgamated Society of Tailors (AST) that it was in the best interests of its members to organise the sub-divisional East End Jewish tailors and admit them to the union via a specifically designated 'Jewish' branch. It was hoped that through organisation the deleterious effect on incomes which resulted from deskilling and undercutting might be reversed. Standing in the way of organisational fellowship was the illiteracy – in both Yiddish and English – of the tailors. In 1884 the AST reported that the secretary of its newly established Jewish branch was providing lessons in Yiddish speech and accounting.[39] As the trade unionist and journalist Joseph Finn recorded, somewhat despondently, in the first socialist Yiddish newspaper to be published in Britain, the *Polishe Yidel*, 'few [of the immigrants workers] can read an English newspaper, they know no English nor do they want to learn to read or write in Yiddish'.[40] Twenty-two years later, little had changed. In 1906 Moses Sclare, secretary of the Leeds Jewish Tailors', Machiners' and Pressers' Trade Union, giving evidence to the Truck Committee revealed that, not only were the 'majority of the members unable to read ... but many of the masters were illiterate'.[41] Indeed fluency in Yiddish was to prove of vital importance to trade union leader Jacob Fine in his dealings with employers as late as the 1930s.[42] In fact, it was the trade union of which Jacob Fine was Secretary, the United Ladies' Tailors' Trade Union, based in the East End of London, which, until its amalgamation with the National Union of Tailors and Garment Workers in 1939, always published its annual report in Yiddish and English, a clear indication that those early arrivals clung to the *mammaluschen* (mother tongue) for as long as possible.

It was obvious to those who supported its usage, as well as to those who did not, that Yiddish was the vital medium through which to build bridges between alien and English workers and the means to facilitate and accelerate the assimilation of the aliens in their new homeland. The Yiddish press, anarchist and moderate, operating on a variety of agendas, encouraged and cajoled: the *Polishe Yidel*, published for a short period during 1884 and its successor, *Der Arbeiter Fraint* (*Workers' Friend*) – an anarchist newspaper which intermittently appeared between 1885 and 1910 – kept their readers informed as to current political events in Britain, albeit with an extremist bias, and regularly called upon their readers to, 'unite internationally and with the Christian workers fight the general enemy'.[43] Other journals avoided radical politics, the *Yidisher Telefon* provided local and national news and gossip, the *Yidisher Velt* offered literary excellence whilst seeking to Anglicise its readership through its Yiddish pages and the long-lived *Yidisher Zhurnal* played its role in building the bridges that brought the immigrant closer to the English way of life. So too did Yiddish theatre. The first performance in London took place in 1886. Yiddish theatre reached its peak in the first decades of the twentieth century and then faded as did the Yiddish speaking generation. Yiddish theatre embraced a spectrum which covered traditional Eastern European drama through to the equivalent of rowdy and low-humoured East End music hall. Somewhere in between were Yiddish translations of classics by Shakespeare and Ibsen, specially written plays which portrayed the immigrant experience in England, even opera. Performances of these were not always as sophisticated as might have been hoped, a 1912 production of Rigoletto, though considered by the *Jewish Chronicle* to have been, 'A notable operatic triumph', suffered by nature of a translation into Yiddish that was 'less than eloquent' and 'an orchestra that was a tad too small'.[44]

Gradually the Eastern European immigrants of the 1870s, 1880s and 1890s became Anglicised. Their Yiddish conversations, journals, theatre, trade union reports and posters, began to incorporate the language of the receiving society. Announcements of trade union activities, strikes and meetings whilst still appearing in Hebrew now carried transliterations of words such as 'strike', 'secretary' as well as those of the names of institutions, organisations and streets which played important roles in the life of the immigrant community. The Anglicisation of words such as 'trade union' spelt out in Hebrew characters rather than the Yiddish/German equivalent *vereingt*, signalled a determination to use mother tongue characters to help create the bridge between the two cultures and the means of narrowing the linguistic lacuna between groups with common interests. English usage might sometimes have become confused, as occurred in the example given by Sholem Aleichem whose mother went to the 'chicken to salt the kitchen',[45] but, as was to become evident in the Eastern European experience and, as will be illustrated below, is being repeated in that of the Bangladeshi community one hundred years on, language is a vital link between communities, particularly those which are ethnically separate yet geographically close. How rapidly that link is forged and how securely those bridges are built depends on both native and newcomer.

Sylheti

Sylheti is a 'language' of place, its eponymity ensuring it is associated as much with the land as with the people of that land. (It is perhaps necessary to indicate at this point that I have chosen to use the noun 'language' in this instance because of the importance of 'language' in the context of the fight for Bangladeshi independence and the subsequent issues surrounding the role and place of Sylheti within the newly created state. I will revert back to using the nouns 'dialect' and 'vernacular' below in order to retain thematic continuity.) Unlike Yiddish, which immediately calls to mind diaspora and deracination, Sylheti is governed by tangible boundaries and a positive spatial history.[46] Sylheti is the dialect, Sylhet is the homeland.

Sylhet lies in the northeast corner of Bangladesh, 200 miles from Dacca the capital and 300 miles from the Chinese border. It covers an area of some 4,785 square miles and has a population numbering some seven million,[47] the majority of which are Sylheti speaking. The economy of the region is tied to the production of tea in the uplands and rice on the flat and is blessed and cursed by rain which fertilises the crops and destroys people, homes and communications – rainfall measures between 150 and 200 inches per annum. Though there is a minority educated élite, the major part of the population ranks amongst the least urbanised, poorest and most illiterate in the modern world.

For almost 200 years, from 1765 until 1947, Sylhet was part of India, thus part of the British Empire. Linguistic and physical links were set in place over the centuries. As Rosina Visram and Caroline Adams both have described,[48] in spite of Sylhet's distance from the coast, the tradition of Sylheti men finding employment as lascars on board British ships sailing from Calcutta predates colonisation. Subsequent interaction between British government officials, local landowners and peasants resulted in the gradual, almost imperceptible, absorption of English words into the Sylheti vocabulary. 'Chair' and 'table' became as much a part of the everyday lives of those who remained in the villages of Sylhet as of those in England. After partition in 1947, when the region became part of East Pakistan, language played an increasingly important role in the destiny of the people. It was an issue which was to spread, as the Sylhetis themselves spread, 'across seven seas and thirteen waters' to Britain and to the area of highest concentration of Sylheti speaking Bangladeshis in Britain, the Spitalfields district of Tower Hamlets.

Though the Sylheti presence in East London dates back to the eighteenth century it was not until the 1950s and 1960s that it became visibly significant. In spite of the difficulties experienced by East Pakistanis in obtaining passports for the United Kingdom, during the 1950s young men began to find their way to Britain. To a destination which they believed would, after a short period of very hard work in the sweatshops of London's East End, enable them to return home as 'rich men of high status'.[49] Their arrival coincided with, and enabled, a transition in the labour and production practices of the Jewish tailoring and furrier workshops of Spitalfields. Jewish sons and daughters no longer saw their future in the rag trade, the route to upward socioeconomic mobility was now through the professions – medicine, law and accountancy. However, by the late 1950s, a new source of employers (exploiters) and unskilled and semi-skilled labour was set to take over garment manufacture, now geared more to the production of leather garments than tailored clothes. Mainly non-Sylheti speaking entrepreneurs took over the running of the workshops whilst Sylheti labour carried out the various sub-divisional processes. The integration of Pakistani immigrants into the traditional economy of the immigrant East End provided a late twentieth century example of the transitional interaction of two ethnic minority groups, Jews and Asians, within the mainstream economy. The manufacture of clothing was not the only trade which benefited from, and attracted, the young men of Sylhet. Indian curry houses, so much a feature of British life at the end of the twentieth century, were just beginning to become familiar faces on the high street, these too provided employment, however harsh and poorly paid, for the illiterate and non-English speaking new arrivals.

Whilst there was a level of native/immigrant economic integration, significantly between workshop masters and their wholesale and retail customers,[50] there was little need for linguistic intercourse between the workshop hands and non-Pakistanis. Very few of the men from East Pakistan who came over in the 1960s 'bothered with English', particularly 'if they worked in the London sweatshops or restaurants',[51] it was not a necessary prerequisite of employment, in fact quite the reverse. Within the workshop, or in the restaurant kitchens, the linguistic interaction that did take place was between Bengali speaking employers and their Sylheti-speaking sweated labour. Then as now, deficiency in the language of the majority community facilitated the exploitation of labour.

The recession of the late 1960s and early 1970s, allied to the Immigration Act of 1971, slowed down, almost to a halt, the immigration of young men from Sylhet. In London, financial inadequacy and the demanding regularity of remittances to Bangladesh destroyed the myth of return. Sojourners became settlers and young men's ghettoes were gradually transformed into family based communities. The process of reunification of immigrant men with their wives and children began; in some cases taking over 20 years to complete. Some men decided to maintain one family in the *desh* (home) and raise another in the *bidesh* (the foreign land), bringing over new, younger and stronger wives to London. It hardly needs stating that very few of the women, and only a tiny minority of the children, that made the journey from east to west spoke, read or understood English. Levels of literacy in Bengali were little better, with no more than 35 per cent of the population in Bangladesh estimated to be literate.

The Bangladeshi community of Spitalfields gradually spread out from the spine of Brick Lane to the surrounding areas, over-spilling into Mile End, Poplar and even Bow.[52] By 1981 there were some 10,000 Bangladeshis resident in Tower Hamlets; by the close of the twentieth century that number is expected to have risen to between 50,000 and 60,000. As the community expanded so did their problems. Shortages of housing and employment, the eternal diasporic condition, were aggravated by problems of language. The need for the old, but more especially for the young,[53] to communicate with the majority society at school, at work and for their medical needs, was becoming an increasing problem. For Jews 100 years before it had been a relatively simple matter, or at least was perceived as such by those coreligionists and political and labour activists eager for the aliens to become Englishmen and Englishwomen – Yiddish had to be eschewed in favour of the majority language. For Bangladeshis it was not that easy, be it mother tongue or vernacular, neither were to be eschewed, thus the debates had to centre around trilingualism rather than bilingualism. At the same time it had to be remembered by those outside of the community that, for Bangladeshis, language had to be equated with politics, cultural independence, identity and nationhood.

For Bangladeshis language was a core issue in their fight for nationhood and an independent identity. The battle began in 1952[54] when the Pakistani government announced its intention to make Urdu, not Bengali, the official language of *all* (including East) Pakistan. The bloody civil war that followed culminated in the creation, in 1971, of Bangladesh, a state whose official language was designated to be Bengali.[55] A language which had gained its formal status by the shedding of blood should have been regarded as inviolable and yet, only a few years after the civil war ended, a further tussle over language emerged. This time the demands were for Sylheti to be given the status of 'a language in its own right'.[56] Some went so far as to call for devolution and independence for the region of Sylhet. Once more language was at the heart of debates on identity and sovereignty. The reaction of the Bangladesh government and educated élite was reminiscent of that of the Anglo-Jewish establishment the century before. Sylheti was no more than a regional dialect, one associated with poverty and illiteracy, a language common to 'low-class Mohammedens'[57] – its speakers became the recipients of negative stereotyping. The Bangladesh government adopted a policy of language suppression.[58] Any elevation of the Sylheti language was deemed politically unacceptable. Sylheti was given the stamp of the vernacular, perceived as a means of conversation which had no accompanying literature. Ignorance about the existence of a written form of Sylheti – Sylheti/Nagari – is not uncommon amongst those living within the region as well as those beyond it. Rod Chalmers has traced the written history back to the fifteenth century, its main use being to record religious poetry. A rich language with an alphabet of 34 letters as opposed to the 50 of Bengali, Sylheti/Nagari is judged as easy to learn. The written history came to a halt in 1971 when, following the civil war with West Pakistan, all the Sylheti/Nagari printing presses were destroyed.[59] Even those reporting to the British government's Home Affairs Committee for the *Report on Bangaldeshis in Britain*, which was released in 1986, were under the impression that Sylheti had always been a spoken dialect.[60] Thus when, during the 1970s, the problems of language communication in Tower Hamlets became a local issue it was not just a question of the role of mother tongue in the migrant experience but rather a politicised debate about which of the two mother tongues should take priority.

A Bridge, But to Where?

Whereas the Jewish community of Tower Hamlets had been encouraged to learn English at the expense of Yiddish, the Bangladeshi community and its leaders were determined to retain their cultural, and newly acquired national identity and transmit this to their children – some British born – through the Bengali language. The first mother tongue classes for Bangladeshis in Tower Hamlets were organised by a non-Sylheti speaking immigrant, Nurul Huque, in the mid-1970s.[61] The classes given were in Bengali not Sylheti. This decision not only acknowledged the superior status of Bengali, but in addition pragmatically recognised that there would be little mileage in promoting the teaching of a low grade vernacular for which there appeared to be no available literature. Logically, Bengali was the only 'mother tongue' that could be taught. At the same time it was obvious that Tower Hamlets education services would not be able to cope with an expanding young Bangladeshi community which was unfamiliar with the English language. What was denied by the Anglo-Jewish establishment of the 1880s was now accepted by communal activists and local government officials in the 1980s; mother tongue was an essential element of the education process for children from minority backgrounds, both as a mean of retaining their ethnic cultural identity and as the vehicle for fluency in the language of the majority society.

During the first half of the 1980s language came to play an increasingly important role in the communal politics of Tower Hamlets's Bangladeshi population. In 1983 the Council put in place an initiative to improve local educational resources, this included support for mother tongue classes in local community schools such as Huque's. At the same time, the battle to achieve recognition for Sylheti as a 'language' which was taking place in Bangladesh found its way onto the streets of Spitalfields. Demands were made for local Sylheti speaking people, irrespective of their academic qualifications or ability, to be given preference over Bengali speaking teachers from beyond the community when mother tongue teachers were being selected. The protagonists believed that in this way Sylheti would be upgraded. A local forum for debate was BENTH (Bangladeshis' Educational Needs in Tower Hamlets), one of a number of communal organisations[62] which sought to represent the demands of the Bangladeshis to government bodies such as ILEA. However, in common with other community groups, BENTH was far from a homogenous entity. Supported mainly by young activists it was riddled with acrimonious internal political divisions. The battle lines became clearly drawn. On the one side was the professional Bengali-speaking élite, on the other, local Sylheti speaking workers. As one hundred years before, the intra-ethnic divide was one of socioeconomic class and status. For a while it looked as though the pro-Sylhetis would be victorious. A report produced at the time by Greg Smith suggested that they had the upper hand.[63] However, true to local tradition[64] internal divisions let to the collapse of BENTH in 1985 and with it the death of the pro-Sylheti campaign, one which never again took centre stage. Shortly afterwards the decision was taken that *the* mother tongue taught to local Bangladeshi children would be Bengali, in fact there was 'a strong level of demand amongst parents for tuition in mother tongue to be available in the mainstream school curriculum'.[65] For diaspora Bangladeshis a national language which had cost the blood of their kinfolk, and which was the source national identity, was one which demanded acceptance beyond the narrow confines of the immigrant ghetto.

Almost fifteen years on, what is the current state of play? A draft report prepared by Tower Hamlets Council in 1998 acknowledged that nearly 80 per cent of those living in the borough with a 'home language' other than English spoke Benglai/Sylheti (the difference even now not clearly defined). In the document the Council emphasised the benefit of bilingualism and biculturalism for the local community as a whole and the importance of developing mother tongue alongside English. In addition, the Council stated its intention to 'offer pupils the opportunity to read and enjoy literature in their mother tongue'.[66] Current policy for children between the ages of 5 and 11[67] is to instruct Sylheti speakers to learn Bengali, the tuition to be provided by teachers with an 'A' level qualification in Bengali, obtained either in Bangladesh or Britain, with some experience of teaching.[68] This is carried out in supplementary classes, organised jointly by local community organisations and the LEA, which run for approximately two hours at the end of the school day. A directory published in 1997 lists 46 separate projects running Bengali mother tongue classes as well as one offering both Urdu and Bengali, one offering Bengali/Arabic and three others offering Chinese, Cantonese and Vietnamese.[69]

According to Ayub Ali, Head of Mother Tongue Teaching for Tower Hamlets Council, the role of Sylheti in the mother tongue war is no longer a political issue. Bengali is now the accepted mother tongue, viewed by parents not simply as a pathway to education but, more importantly, as a means of 'inducting a new generation to their own culture'. This is confirmed by interviews recently carried out by the author with a number of Bangladeshi graduates and undergraduates, all of whom said that their parents had encouraged them to learn 'proper Bengali', in order to 'understand their culture and not forget their roots'.[70] All those questioned insisted on being known as Bengali as opposed to Bangladeshi, thus highlighting language as the heart and soul of their identity. The young people believed that the need to respect their roots was directly linked to the issues of the 1960s/70s civil war, one which was fought on the language issue, 'as kids [we] feel it is our duty to learn Bengali and grow up appreciating why'.[71] They also admitted that there were pragmatic reasons for the learning of Bengali, ones which confirmed the illiteracy of their parents. These included learning Bengali in order to communicate in writing with officials and family in the *desh*.

In spite of parental determination that their children become fluently bi- or trilingual, knowledge of English being deemed essential for social and economic mobility on the threshold of the twenty-first century, some 40 years after the cohorts of young men arrived, Sylheti remains the domestic vernacular of the Bangladeshi community of Tower Hamlets. Many of those early male arrivals 'lacked any interest in learning English', and failed to attend what English classes were on offer. Even if there had been a willingness learn, paucity, or total lack, of education back in Bangladesh would have made it very difficult for them to 'know how to learn'.[72] And though some men have absorbed English through interaction with the native community at work, socially and in the hospitals,[73] doctors' surgeries and local welfare offices, few of their womenfolk have followed suit. One young interviewee revealed that though her mother had lived in England for 30 years she spoke no English. As she explained, there had been no need, father and the other male members of the family had always acted as interpreters.[74] This evidence highlights another facet of Bangladeshi culture, the role of women within its society. As James Lloyd Williams, an English teacher and resident of Bangladesh for 25 years sees it, Bangladeshi men have shown a reluctance to permit their women the 'freedom to absorb western culture'.[75] Women play a subservient role, their needs secondary to those of their men folk. All too frequently when wives attended English classes their husbands had 'put a stop to it'.

Amongst the elders of the Bangladeshi community, within the extended nuclear family, in the sweatshops of Brick Lane and thousands of Indian curry houses, Sylheti remains dominant. In spite of this English has found its way in, as it did under colonial rule, often through the kitchen and workshop door. As the young generation import English into the home, parents are overhead using English, sometimes unconsciously: 'I often hear my mother on the phone and though she is speaking Sylheti, she uses English words such as "shops", "road" or "friend", without realising it.'[76] In a multicultural society, even without imposed pressures from an élite, language transference and leakage takes place. Both by the code-switching of occasional words and by the prolonged use of the majority language for purposes of communication outside the home environment. This reality leads one to question whether the English language will absorb Sylheti words as it has done Yiddish. For example in a report which recently appeared in *The Times* the word chutzpah (cheek) was used to describe someone's audacious behaviour without any accompanying translation or italisation.[77] In the multilingual environment in which today's schoolchildren are growing up, the 'playing' with, and adoption of, words from minority languages is an established fact.[78] Perhaps in years to come it will not be just Yiddish words which have an accepted place within the English language but those originating from Punjabi, Urdu, Bengali and Sylheti,

Cantonese and Chinese languages/dialects, to name but a few.

Two separate ethnic minority groups, occupying the same space, at either end of the twentieth century. Eastern European Jews and Bangladeshis, people who believed that their opportunity for socioeconomic advancement lay on the gold paved streets of East London. Outsiders whose otherness was identifiable as much by speech as by appearance.[79] What forces determined the way in which their deficiency in majority language was to be overcome? What part has mother tongue played? That of a clearly defined bridge to assimilation, acculturation and Anglicisation or, the guardian of a specific ethno-cultural identity which, in addition, could operate as a vehicle for the acquisition of the majority language – a necessary accoutrement for those in the *bidesh*?

Though attitudes towards the place and function of mother tongue have been very different it should not automatically be assumed that there are no common denominators linking the two subjects of this study. Not only were Eastern European Jews and Bangladeshis alienated from the host community by language difference but, in both cases, their ability to acquire the basics of that majority language was hindered by its being written in Roman characters – unlike those of their own which were in Hebrew and Indic. Religious differences too separated and reinforced the use of the minority tongue, both written and spoken. Working conditions provide further examples of shared experience, Jews and Bangladeshis found employment in the sweatshops of the East End. In both cases labour exploitation was carried out by fellow countrymen, though the reactions of one group to the sweating system was very different to that of the other. Finally, within both immigrant communities, the lowest levels of mother tongue literacy and majority language literacy and articulacy were to be found amongst the older female population – perceived as having a purely domestic role. However, recent research has proved that in the case of the Jewish community this was not always the case. Jewish women carried out a diversity of economic activities, some of which necessitated their interaction with the majority community and required, at the very least, a basic knowledge of English.[80] This suggests that, in some ways, the bridge between mother tongue and English may have been an easier one for women to cross in the late nineteenth century than it has been for their ethnic minority sisters 100 years on. Finally, if we are to reach any conclusions as to the linguistic policies that have operated in Spitalfields it is necessary to consider the socioeconomic and political imperatives that determined actions and reactions at either ends of the century.

Mother Tongue and Education

It has been established that those who have not enjoyed the benefits of education as children do not 'know how to learn' as adults. Thus any use of mother tongue as a means of achieving bilingualism has to be dependent on some basic learning when young. For the male Eastern European Jewish immigrants the foundations were laid in childhood; religious requirements ensured basic literacy in classic Hebrew.[81] That learning could subsequently be put to work when it came to reading Yiddish. The bridge to English was thus negotiable, though exhaustion from the long working day in the sweatshop sometimes made the journey less attractive. For the untutored Jewish female, literacy was the exception rather than the rule, many were denied the opportunity to read, though for the female immigrant bilingual conversation improved with length of settlement.[82] For Muslim Sylhetis religion neither played, nor plays, a necessary part in developing literary abilities. The Koran is written in Arabic, although Bengali versions – for the educated minority – are available, but the teaching of the Book is by rote[83] and thus literacy is not a prerequisite. Neither has there been an established Bangladeshi élite insistent upon the eschewing of mother tongue and its replacement by English. Minority group political pedagogic pressures now operate in the reverse direction, concerned with the promotion of the official language of Bangladesh and the reinforcement of an ethnic – Bengali – identity rather than its denial.

Mother Tongue and Labour

What part has the workforce played in strengthening or weakening the linguistic bridge? As illustrated above, the international spread of socialism and the belief in the benefits of worker unity resolving the problems of exploitation and capitalism acted as the incentive for Jewish refugee intellectuals and Jewish socialists both to tolerate Yiddish and to encourage those for whom it was mother tongue to learn English. At the same time English trade unionists and political radicals recognised that the bond formed by a common language could only act positively in the struggle to end the evils of sweating. The emergence of new unionism at the end of the 1880s was evidence that those previously considered unorganisable, the unskilled, seasonal and casual workers – and this included Jewish tailors, cabinet makers and shoe makers – could play a constructive role in redressing the status quo. It is difficult to gauge the exact level of success in terms of increased labour literacy in relation to their union organisation but where interaction took place, at trade union assemblies, strike meetings and political rallies[84] union advancement occurred and language absorption and increased fellow feeling followed.

By comparison to the indictments placed at the thresholds of the Eastern European workforce Bangladeshis suffer little. They are rarely criticised for taking the jobs of Englishmen, racist accusations are directed at domestic targets, at Bangladeshi families being awarded larger and more up-to-date council housing. As one critic accusingly queried during the 1993 local council elections, 'Why should they [the Bangladeshis] get all the best flats with all the new showers?'[85] Many Indian subcontinent employers ensure that their labour force has little contact beyond the local working community. On the side of labour, there is little evidence of older workers aspiring to learn English or of any incentives to self-organise. A survey carried out in 1985 revealed that Bangladeshi workers in the clothing trade believed fluency in English was not essential, even a knowledge of Bengali was deemed no more than 'helpful'.[86] The report also exposed the total disinterest shown by the exploited Sylheti workers in trade union membership.[87] Ten years on, in a climate of falling membership and disillusionment with trade unionism, the clothing section of the GMB had made virtually no inroads into the Sylheti speaking sweatshops of Spitalfields,[88] neither had the Bangladeshi clothing workers established ethnic trade unions as had their Eastern European counterparts one hundred years before. The difficulties of trade union organisation amongst a semi- and unskilled casual labour force are reinforced by illiteracy. 'There is no point in distributing trade union literature to workers who cannot read in their own, or any other, language ... we do not have any Sylheti speaking officials to make verbal contact.'[89] Thus the low level of wages and poor conditions of employment are sustained, with little protest forthcoming from the workers, many of whom are illegal immigrants or dependent upon welfare benefit to supplement a less than minimum wage. There is no portal through which external forces can gain entry and promote the cause of majority language literacy and articulacy as a means of alleviating labour exploitation.

Mother Tongue and the Media

The main avenues of mass communication for the immigrant population of Spitalfields at the end of the nineteenth century were the Yiddish press and the Yiddish theatre. Those male members of the community who could read Hebrew fluently, could read Yiddish, and thus be kept informed of events taking place on the broader local and national political canvas. The contributors to the short-lived *Polishe Yidel* made sure that their readership were kept informed of the passage of the 1884 Reform Bill[90] – though few were directly affected by it – whilst 28 years later the *Arbeiter Fraint* encouraged Jewish tailors to retain their membership of the English trade unions as well as providing regular, if somewhat tendentious, reports of the wave of strikes that crossed Britain and of syndicalist activities in America and France. In the theatre positive steps were taken to enable Yiddish speakers to come to terms with the life and culture of western society through dramatic representation.

At the end of the twentieth century the ethnic media has a far wider span. In East London alone there are eight or nine Bengali and Bengali/English newspapers, a range of available Bengali and Bollywood videos and films, as well as two Bangladeshi radio programmes and the newly opened (November 1999) Bangla TV channel. This volume is not all it might seem. None of the above are in the Sylheti language, thus only a minority of the elders are able to take full advantage of what is on offer. The 'Bollywood' films are in Hindi, a language with which the younger members of the community are now becoming conversant. Thus in many ways, for those with little or no Bengali, the ethnic media offers less today for the non-English, non-Bengali speaking immigrants of Spitalfields than it did yesterday. Even so, multiculturalism and multilingualism dominates. Bangladeshis are able, and encouraged, to remain close to the music, art and food which forms part of their perceived identity, one proudly advertised by the Bangladeshi Festival that was held in East London during the summer of 1998. There are even attempts to restore regional identity by bringing back Sylheti-Nagari. James Lloyd Williams is working at reproducing poetry and prose in order that the 'present generation of Sylhetis will want to rediscover their own heritage, culture, history and written language'. He has produced a small volume of poetry in Sylheti/Nagari, Bengali and English, the latter so that those in the *bidesh* might 'have at least a small taste of the rich heritage of Sylhet'.[91] This is not as simple as it might appear, for those unable to read, be it Bengali, Sylheti/Nagari or English, are dependent on the literate minority for a taste of that heritage.

Mother Tongue and Politics

For Eastern European Jews entering Britain at the end of the nineteenth century, at a time of increasing anti-alienism and jingoism, the acquisition of English was deemed politically, as well as socially, vital by the Anglo-Jewish establishment which saw the continued usage of Yiddish as a loud speaker which broadcast the alien presence to the streets of East London. Even the Jewish member of parliament for Whitechapel, Samuel Montagu, who frequently championed the immigrant cause, was determined that the language of the alien be eradicated as rapidly as possible. Trade unionists, socialists and anarchists were convinced that a common language was an important weapon in the fight to eradicate exploitation and the power of capital over labour. Those were the exogenous forces, however the immigrants' ambitions to establish their home and Englishness in a society which offered citizenship and the possibility of future economic security, for their children if not themselves, with no formal restraints[92] must not be overlooked. For those with the tenacity and will to sacrifice, Spitalfields offered an opportunity to put down roots in a nation which was reputed to operate one of the most liberal immigration policies of the late nineteenth, early twentieth centuries.

For Bangladeshis the situation was, and remains, very different. The arrivals of the 1950s and 1960s came as sojourners, but even in the ghetto of temporary residence external forces were at play. The politics of the village were often played out in Brick Lane and Hanbury Street whilst contemporary economic and social conditions transformed sojourners into settlers for whom English and Bengali were both foreign tongues. There was no long-established community either to provide a nexus of charitable support or to insist that the recent arrivals become 'Englishmen' and 'English women'. The Bangladeshi community was left to come to terms with the complexities of understanding self-identity through a miasma of language difference and alienation operating in a supposedly multicultural society.

In addition to accommodating the impact of spatial transition was the need to absorb the politics of Spitalfields. This was indeed complex for added to the problems of communication was the subtext of Sylheti village politics undermining local Tower Hamlets issues. This situation, which has been dealt with admirably elsewhere by John Eade,[93] was of particular relevance within the context of the battle for language status. Even though the young activists failed to hold the day they displayed an uncommon vitality. Generally members of the Bangladeshi community manifested political apathy, but how much of this was the outcome of an inability to comprehend local and national political literature as opposed to general disinterest is hard to assess. The local Labour Party attempted to overcome the problem by orally translating party business and minutes into Sylheti prior to the commencement of meetings. Unlike the Jewish experience, total reliance had to be placed upon oral communication. Local ethnic associations and organisations were faced, and in a number of cases still face, the same problem. Here, Sylheti leapfrogs Bengali, as English is the medium used for recording organisational business.[94]

Now, as Spitalfields enters the twenty-first century, it has a vital and politically active Bangladeshi community with significant representation on the local council. However, it is a point of interest that in the general election of 1997, though a number of Bangladeshi candidates were fielded by amongst others, the Conservative and Liberal Democrat parties, the elected (Labour Party) member was Oona King, who though of ethnic minority background[95] had no Bangladeshi connection but was deemed the most acceptable candidate, thus proving that electoral voting patterns are determined more by political expediency than by ethnic empathy.[96]

Mother Tongue and Identity

In the case of both the Eastern European Jews and the Bangladeshis, the issue of the acquisition of majority language is one closely allied to perceptions of identity. For the British Jewish establishment the language of the alien acted as a beacon of difference, for the Bangladeshis it radiates nationhood. For Jews in the diaspora there have always been conflicts of identity, most particularly between religion and citizenship. For the majority of Jews in Britain at the end of the nineteenth century there was no discord, both immigrant born and English born observed Judaism whilst being, or striving to become, English. For a minority, the arrival of political Zionism[97] in 1897 posed a challenge which some have still not resolved. In this friction language plays no part, the official language of the state of Israel is *Ivrit*, or modern Hebrew. With the creation of the state in 1948 came the naming of the language, one which set out to 'separate from the Diaspora the language of the Diaspora'.[98] Yiddish acted as a bridge to *Ivrit* in the newly created political homeland of the Jews, by so doing playing the same role as it had for others in the diaspora for hundreds of years. For Bangladeshis language was, and is, synonymous with identity. The noun 'Bengali'[99] used today by the young to describe both their mother tongue and what they are, irrespective of where they are.

Conclusion

For more than 100 years, for diaspora travellers arriving in Spitalfields, mother tongue has been, and still is, a gateway to the future. For the Eastern European Jews it was most definitely a bridge to Anglicisation, acculturation and assimilation, to citizenship and a secular, national pride they had never previously possessed and which they eagerly grasped.[100] For literate Bangladeshis the bridge has a duality of purpose. It provides a gateway to the acquisition of the English language, something many of the older members of the community illiterate in their, now acknowledged, 'mother tongue' have been unable, and/or unwilling, to access. For the educated younger generation it provides both the mechanism for socioeconomic upward mobility and a medium for the re-enforcement of national identity through learning and culture. Does this mean that the illiterate are totally excluded? Many of the male elders have had to find their way, building fragile linguistic bridges from Sylheti, using spoken rather than written words to form a basis of communication with the majority society. Their female counterparts, often far more restricted than their Jewish sisters of 100 years ago, may not make the crossing. For although there is some evidence of women carrying out economic activity in the home[101] there is none which illustrates interaction with the majority society and thus little need to use any language but Sylheti. As one young Bengali girl explained, 'My mother used to speak English but she doesn't bother with it any more'.[102] Mother tongue has been, and remains, a necessary bridge in the immigrant journey, it is up to the migrant to determine where it should lead.

End Piece

The foregoing chapter has looked at the experience of two groups occupying the same space at different periods on the time scale, and their attitudes to, and use of, mother tongue. Yiddish was eschewed and had all but died out by the late 1950s. Recently it has enjoyed a renaissance, it has been brought back to life by intellectuals and academics who value its literature – its poetry, prose and drama. Courses held in the language are attended by as many non-Jews as Jews. Sylheti is the dominant vernacular of the people of that region both at home and in the diaspora. The children of that diaspora are convinced the language will survive. Can a language which is degraded in its country of origin as well as by many in the diaspora, is not taught at home or abroad and which has a barely accessible literary past, have a future? As standards of education in Bangladesh – Sylhet included – gradually improve and the children of the villages become literate and articulate in Bengali whilst their counterparts in Britain are brought up on English and Bengali, will Sylheti die? Or, will it survive as a spoken dialect, as has Swiss-German in relation to High German, being a language of ease and casuality? It has been said that, 'the death of a language equals the death of a culture';[103] thus if Sylheti dies then so does its culture, its history, myths and the Sylheti identity. James

Lloyd Williams is attempting to keep the Sylheti culture and identity alive. It remains to be seen whether the young Bengalis will follow suit and incorporate it into their bridge to the future.

Notes

I should like to thank Professor Ken Young, Professor Jenny Cheshire and my research associate, Dr Shompa Lahiri, for their comments on this chapter and Abdur Rafique and Ayub Ali for their help on matters relating to mother tongue and the British Bangladeshi community.

1   S. Alladina and V. Edwards, *Multilingualism in the British Isles, Vol. 1*, London, Longman, 1991, p. viii.
2   See below for history of Sylheti and its history.
3   *Jewish Chronicle*, 4 May 1883.
4   See G. Smith, *Language, Ethnicity , Employment, Education and Research: The Struggle of Sylheti-Speaking People in London*, CLE/LMP Working paper No. 13, Community Languages and Education Project, London, University of London Institute of Education, 1985, p. 14.
5   Although never a 'national' language, in 1906 the South African Parliament voted Yiddish a European language, but it was not until 1910 that the *Bund* (the Jewish socialist party) held an all Yiddish speaking conference. E.S. Goldsmith, *Architects of Yiddishism at the Beginning of the Twentieth Century*, Associated University Press, Cranbury, N.J., 1976, pp. 96 and 83.
6   See J. Fishman, *Yiddish: Turning to Life*, Philadelphia, John Benjamins Publishing Co., 1991, p. 83.
7   'There was no one-time act of birth': M. Weinreich, *History of the Yiddish Language*, Chicago and London, University of Chicago Press, 1973, p. 6.
8   The region of Loter is an internal Jewish designation, but can be equated with the region of Lorraine: Weinreich, op. cit., p. 332.
9   The Jewish correlates of Old French and Old Italian: Weinreich, op. cit., p. 100.
10 Ibid.
11 The Pale of Settlement was an area of some 362,000 square miles within which all but the bourgeois minority of the Jewish population of Russia and Russia Poland were required to live.
12 E.S. Goldsmith, op. cit., p. 72.
13 Quoted in G. Black, *JFS: the History of the Jews' Free School, London, Since 1732*, London, Tymsder, 1992, p. 127.
14 G. Smith, op. cit., p. 75.
15 E.S. Goldsmith, op. cit., p. 74.
16 For a late twentieth century approach to the diasporic experience, see R. Cohen, *Global Diasporas*, London, UCL Press, 1997.
17 Whilst the entry of a Rothschild into the House of Commons in 1858 marks a major step in the emancipation of the Jews in Britain, their *total* emancipation cannot be said to have taken place until 1871 with the passage of the Promissory Oaths Act.
18 A.J. Kershen and J.A. Romain, *Tradition and Change: A History of Reform Judaism in*

Britain 1840–1995, Ilford, Valletine Mitchell, 1995, p. 98.

19 Whilst organisations such as the Jewish Board of Guardians and the Russo-Jewish Committee attempted to help the indigent arrivals they also developed programmes of repatriation. At the same time clubs and organisations such as the Jewish Lads' Brigade were set up by the Anglo-Jewish establishment to facilitate the Anglicisation process.

20 *Decennial Census 1891*, PP 1893–4, CVI.

21 The Russo-Jewish Committee was established in 1881 in response to the pogroms that followed the assassination of Tsar Alexander II in that same year.

22 Quoted in L. Gartner, *Jewish Immigrant in England 1870–1914*, London, George Allen & Unwin, 1960, p. 239.

23 Gartner, ibid., p. 240.

24 *Jewish Chronicle*, 7 July 1905.

25 The Jews' Free School was founded in the East End in 1732 and between 1880 and 1900 educated one-third of London's Jewish children: in 1900 it had 4,000 pupils. See G. Black, op. cit. Other Jewish schools included the Westminster Jews' Free School, the Stepney Jewish Schools, the Metropolitan Jewish School and the Jewish Girls' High School.

26 See W. Parsons, 'Being Born Lost? The Cultural and Institutional Dimensions of Welsh Identity', in A.J. Kershen (ed.), *A Question of Identity*, Aldershot, Ashgate, 1998, pp. 25–59.

27 G. Black, op. cit., p. 126.

28 Quotation apears in N. Green (ed.), *Jewish Workers in the Modern Diaspora*, Berkeley, Los Angeles and London, University of California Press, 1998, p. 194.

29 R. Livshin, 'The Acculturation of the Children of Immigrant Jews in Manchester: 1890–1930', in D. Cesarani (ed.), *The Making of Anglo-Jewry*, Oxford, Blackwell, 1990, p. 82.

30 Rabbincal training colleges of higher education which were also hotbeds of radicalism.

31 A.J. Kershen, *Uniting the Tailors*, Ilford, Frank Cass, 1995, p. 6.

32 However, whilst the boys would be taught to read the Hebrew alphabet and language, few had any idea of the literal meaning of what they read.

33 Thirteen, when a Jewish male comes of age.

34 Whereas the muscular Irish immigrants found work in the docks and building industries.

35 In London's East End and in cities such as Leeds and Manchester the clothing industry included tailoring, cap making, slipper and shoe making – dressmaking (mass produced) was a section which developed during the early decades of the twentieth century.

36 For detailed description of the system of sub-divisional labour as experienced by Eastern European immigrants in London's East End in the years between 1870 and 1939 see Kershen, *Uniting...*, op. cit.

37 Ibid., p. 128.

38 Ibid., p. 11.

39 *Polishe Yidel*, 17 October 1884.

40 Ibid., 1 August 1884.

41 Quoted in Kershen, *Uniting ...*, op. cit., p. 11.

42 Ibid., p. 145.

43 *Arbeiter Fraint*, 18 March 1905.

44 *Jewish Chronicle*, 12 April 1912.

45 N. Green, op. cit., p. 193.

46 For histories see R. Visram, *Ayars, Lascars and Princes*, London, Pluto, 1986 and C. Adams, *Across Seven Seas and 13 Rivers*, London, THAP, 1987.

47 Choudhury, writing in 1993 put the figure at six million and Chalmers, writing in 1998

increased that number by one million. See Y. Choudhury, *The Roots and Tales of Bangladeshi Settlers*, Birmingham, Sylheti Social History Group, 1993 and R. Chalmers, 'Paths and Pitfalls in the Exploration of British Bangladeshi Identity', in Kershen, *A Question of ...*, op. cit., pp. 120–35.

48   See Visram, op. cit. and Adams, op. cit.

49   See A.J. Kershen, 'Huguenots, Jews and Bangladeshis in Spitalfields and the Spirit of Capitalism', in Anne J Kershen (ed.), *London the Promised Land? The Migrant Experience in a Capital City*, Aldershot, Ashgate, 1997.

50   When the author visited a leather garment workshop in the early 1980s the workshop master made it impossible for her to have any contact with the workshop hands.

51   Author's interview with James Lloyd Williams, 25 years a resident of Bangladesh and now running a Sylheti translation service in Bethnal Green, 15 July 1999.

52   For the problems of housing within the Bangladeshi community of East London see C. Foreman, *Spitalfields: a Battle for Land*, London, Hilary Shipman, 1989.

53   The 1991 decennial census showed that almost 50 per cent of the Bangladeshi community is aged under 15.

54   In November 1999 a group of Canadian Bangladeshi students appealed to UNESCO to make 21 February – the day Bangladeshis the world over remember those that died as 'Language Martyrs' – World Wide Language Day. UNESCO has subsequently agreed.

55   Although spoken by one-sixth of the world's population, Bengali is the official language of only one country, Bangladesh.

56   See Smith, op. cit., p. 37.

57   Ibid., p. 20.

58   Ibid., p. 69.

59   For history and explanation of Sylheti/Nagri, see R. Chalmers, 'Paths ...', op. cit. and R. Chalmers, *Learning Sylheti*, London, Centre for Bangladeshi Studies, 1996, pp. 4–11.

60   Chalmers, 'Paths ...', op. cit., p. 133.

61   Information from the author's meeting with Ayub Ali, Head of Mother Tongue and Study Support, London Borough of Tower Hamlets, 7 September 1999.

62   For a detailed account of the internal politics of the Bangladeshi community of Tower Hamlets, see J. Eade, *The Politics of Community*, Aldershot, Avebury, 1989.

63   Smith, op. cit., pp. 39–40.

64   A number of the early East End Jewish trade unions and societies collapsed due to internal differences – see W.J. Fishman, *East End Jewish Radicals*, London, Duckworth, 1975 and Kershen, *Uniting ...*, op. cit.

65   Smith, op. cit., p. 75. This ambition was achieved with the introduction of the new school curriculum in the 1990s when Bengali was listed as a national language which could be taught in secondary schools.

66   Draft document, 'Tower Hamlets Policy for Mother Tongue Teaching', undated, unpaginated.

67   Though some classes on offer are for those up to the age of 16.

68   Information provided by Ayub Ali, 7 September 1999.

69   *A Guide to Mother Tongue Classes and Supplementary Education*, London, Tower Hamlets Education, 1997.

70   Author's meeting with 10 Bangladeshi graduates and two undergraduates, 3 June 1999.

71   Ibid.

72   James Lloyd William, meeting, 15 July 1999.

73   See below, chapter 5.
74   Author's meeting, 3 June 1999.
75   James Lloyd Williams, 15 July 1999.
76   Author's meeting with young Bangladeshis, 3 June 1999.
77   *The Times*, 5 November 1999.
78   I am grateful to my colleague Professor Jenny Cheshire for pointing this out to me.
79   It should be noted that the Eastern Europeans, when they arrived in England were instantly recognisable by their dirty appearance and foreign clothes, Jews generally were caricatured as having hooked noses and dark swarthy looks. See C. Holmes, *Anti-Semitism in British Society 1876–1939*, London, Edward Arnold, 1979, pp. 114–15.
80   See R. Burman, 'Jewish Women in Manchester, c. 1890–1920', in D. Cesarani, op. cit., pp. 55–75.
81   In order to be recognised as having reached maturity Jewish boys aged 13 have to be *barmitzvah*. This requires reading passages of the *Torah* and *Talmud* in Hebrew from the scroll and prayer book.
82   The author's grandmother could not read or write, having come to England as a young bride, after many years in London however she was able to converse freely and thus enjoy the benefits of radio and television.
83   In common with so much of secular teaching in Bangladesh.
84   See Kershen, *Uniting ...*, op. cit., for details of these forms of interaction.
85   Derek Beackon, the only BNP candidate ever to be elected to a local council, was elected as a Poplar councillor in 1993 by disenchanted members of the native community who believed that Bangladeshis were being given the local government accommodation that they deserved.
86   Smith, op. cit., p. 36.
87   Author's conversation with member of clothing division of the GMB, 20 February, 1995.
88   See Kershen, *Uniting ...*, p. 190.
89   Member of the GMB clothing division to the author, 20 February 1995.
90   *Polishe Yidel*, July and August 1884.
91   James Lloyd Williams and Matiar Rahman Chowdhury, *Ten Sylheti Poems*, London, Sylheti Translation and Research, 1998 (unpaginated).
92   The Aliens Act, which was criticised by some for its ineffectiveness, was not passed until 1905 and even after its passage, Jewish immigrants retained freedom of speech, freedom to live where they wished and pursue what occupations they wished.
93   Eade, op. cit.
94   Meeting with James Lloyd Williams, 15 July 1999.
95   Oona King comes of mixed – African-American and Jewish – parentage.
96   See S. Saggar, *The 1997 General Election: ethnic minorities and electoral politics*, London, CRE, 1998.
97   Geoffrey Alderman suggests that the majority of working class Jews 'if not anti-Zionist ... were non-Zionist'. See G. Alderman, *London Jewry and London Politics*, London, Routledge, 1989, p. 74.
98   Weinreich, op. cit., pp. 311–12.
99   This within itself is confusing as there are many people from the Indian subcontinent, particularly from the region of West Bengal, who consider themselves Bengali yet have no association with Bangladesh.

100 Even though some of those early arrivals spoke little or no English they took a pride in being English – in the early 1900s naturalisation could be purchased for the princely sum of £7. Some Jewish residents of Leeds prided themselves on being Yorkshire men first and foremost!

101 Information from meeting with third year Bangladeshi students autumn 1999.

102 Meeting, 3 June 1999.

103 Prof. David Crystal, quoted in *Calabash*, London, Black Literature Development Project, 12, Autumn 1999, p. 3.

3 'Do Not Give Flowers to a Man': Refugees, Language and Power in Twentieth Century Britain

TONY KUSHNER

In *Square Fish*, an introduction to the United Kingdom for young refugees and asylum seekers of the 1990s, a guide is given to British etiquette:

> When you are talking to someone British you must ask 'How are you?' and they will then ask you. Whatever you do you are not supposed to say how you really are, for example 'Oh I am really ill today and I feel terrible'. You have to say 'I'm fine thank you'. In the UK people talk about the weather when they meet – this is seen as very polite and you can have a very long conversation about the weather!

Shoes, it adds, do not have to be taken off when entering a house, people should not be touched 'when you are talking to them unless you know them well' and, of course, one never gives 'flowers to a man'.[1]

This advice is at the level of the comic, the equivalent of Hoffnung's suggestions to tourists in Britain including the necessity, when entering a railway compartment, of shaking hands with all one's fellow passengers.[2] Less humorous were the 'lines of conduct' given by the German Jewish Aid Committee, a British Jewish organisation, to the refugees from Nazism in a widely distributed pamphlet *While You are in Britain* during 1939 and 1940. These were to be regarded as 'duties to which you are in honour bound':

> 1. Spend your spare time immediately in learning the English language and its correct pronunciation.
> 2. Refrain from speaking German in the streets and in public conveyances and in public places such as restaurants. Talk halting English rather than fluent German – and *do not talk in a loud voice*. Do not read German newspapers in public.

39

Finally, the pamphlet warned, 'the Jewish Community is relying on you'.[3] This chapter explores the changing patterns of expectations regarding refugees in relation to both learning English and in maintaining their 'mother tongue' language(s). Is learning English a necessity in the economic and social adjustment of the displaced or will it always be at the cost of undermining the culture of those who have already lost so much?

The Invisibility of Refugees

As the title of the German Jewish Aid Committee's pamphlet suggested, refugees from Nazism were not regarded by Jewish organisations that attempted to administer them as fixed additions to the British population. Indeed, it concluded by suggesting that they should 'regard this stay in England as a "mark time" period during which you are preparing yourself for your new life'.[4] The anxieties of the British-Jewish elite in this respect reflected government policies in the interwar period: Britain was not a country of immigration and, at most, it would be a place of transmigration rather than one of permanent settlement.[5] The construction of Britain as a homogeneous nation without an immigration tradition has continued since the Second World War. It is a myth that has been challenged, but not yet overcome, by either the presence of large scale movements from the British Commonwealth and elsewhere since 1945 or the development of historical writing devoted to those who came to the country before then.[6] But for those coming to Britain during the twentieth century an equally powerful romance has existed, the 'myth of return', which has been a critical factor in determining ethnic minority identities and patterns of settlement.[7] For refugees, however, the possibility of return has been even less realistic than others entering Britain more as a result of individual choice. Those refugees able to return 'home' have been the exception rather than the rule.[8] Most refugees in Britain have remained tolerated at best, or have been forced to move on through lack of opportunities or the inhospitality shown to them by state and society. It is partly the impermanence of refugees, their essential characteristic as people on the move, that explains why so little scholarly attention has been given to them. As the editor of the only journal devoted to the subject suggests, the work carried out has 'for the most part ... existed on the periphery [rather than] the mainstream of academic enterprise'.[9] In the words of a Bosnian refugee, Himzo Skorupan: 'this is the way things are: I am not really here, and over there, I am no more.'[10] Academics have been part and parcel of a world of neglect and marginalisation of refugees, refusing to confront people whose uncertain status and lack of belonging make them easier to ignore.

In popular anti-alienism, at least since the turn of the century, refugees have been seen as unwanted immigrants whose claims to be victims of persecution adds another layer of distrust to their general undesirability. 'Genuine' refugees are almost always in the past representing no challenge to the present as in the quaintly named 'Silk Quarter' property development of the late 1990s with its faint echoes of the Huguenots in partly gentrified Spitalfields. On the one hand, the exorbitant prices in the 'Silk Quarter' exclude the local working class Bengali population whose presence is no doubt an embarrassment to those trying to sell the attractions of the district, especially its closeness to the City of London. On the other, the idea of the Huguenots as model newcomers to the area who contributed quality and prosperity to it ignores the fact that many were not economically successful and that they too, like their refugee successors, faced local animosity when they first arrived.[11]

Similarly, the Home Office's White Paper, *Fairer, Faster, and Firmer: A Modern Approach to Immigration & Asylum* (July 1998), the basis for the Labour government's Asylum and Immigration Bill 1999 talks in self-congratulatory tone of Britain's past and its 'long-standing tradition of giving shelter to those fleeing persecution in other parts of the world, and refugees in turn have contributed much to our society and culture'.[12] In contrast, those seeking asylum today are more often than not, including in the White Paper, portrayed as 'economic migrants'. Ironically, however, work on migration, immigration and 'race' often ignores the presence of refugees. Thus the PSI survey, *Ethnic Minorities in Britain: Diversity and Disadvantage* (1997), which regards itself as the most comprehensive and wide-ranging ever undertaken, 'an invaluable source of reference, and no work on the subject that ignores it can henceforth be taken seriously', has no specific section on refugees or asylum.[13] Indeed, it hardly mentions refugees in Britain at all. Refugees, it must be acknowledged, do not fit easily into models of immigration and settlement. They also cross over the 'black/white' binary which permeates so much research and writing in the study of 'race' and racism. Yet rather than adjust such work at a theoretical and practical level the response of many academic disciplines, as well as state bodies, has been to pretend that they do not exist. In culture as a whole the marginality of refugees has led almost to an embarrassment in mentioning their existence. In John Simpson's anthology, *The Oxford Book of Exile*, they hardly merit inclusion, perhaps too depressing to be included in contrast to 'Bertie Wooster hunted down and exiled by his aunt'.[14]

Even in a period where multiculturalism and a commitment to diversity have gained wide acceptance across party politics and society as a whole, there is a desire for refugees to become invisible. In attempting to shame the Labour Home Secretary's asylum policies, an editorial in the left-liberal *Observer* could still state that refugees 'need to be dispersed around the country, rather than allowed to be concentrated in just a few London boroughs ... They need to be taught English and assimilated into local communities'.[15] Apart from querying such policies, this chapter will analyse the inter-relationship of refugees, language and power in twentieth century Britain. It will suggest that although refugees are indeed 'different', the approach of dealing with that difference by hoping it will go away is both naive and harmful to the dispossessed themselves but ultimately damaging to the receiving society as well.

Pre-1945 Refugees

The half million east European Jews who passed through Britain, some 150,000 settling, at the turn of the century are a useful starting point for the discussion of refugees and language.[16] Attacked as undesirable aliens by their opponents and defended as deserving recipients of an immutable right to asylum in Britain by their supporters, the group acts as a classic illustration of the fact that whilst not every economic migrant is a refugee, every refugee is an economic migrant. On the one hand, east European Jews were escaping popular violence and state oppression. On the other they were part of the global movement from the poorer parts of Europe to the west and north in search of greater economic opportunities. Though the anti-alienists desperately avoided using the word 'Jew' in their attacks on the newcomers for fear of being labelled violent antisemites, it was the *type* of immigration and not just the numbers involved that motivated their hostility. Cultural objections to the east Europeans underpinned the anti-alienists' arguments to whom the visibility of Yiddish language in making the East End 'the new Jerusalem' was perhaps the most significant.[17] Sharing some of the same cultural snobberies, as well as fearing for its own security, the British Jewish establishment set up a range of educational and cultural bodies to straighten out the 'ghetto bend' of its poorer, foreign co-religionists. In particular, Jewish schools, clubs and organisations, secular and religious, abhorred the use of Yiddish by the immigrants and their children, the latter often being physically punished for its everyday use.[18]

Recent literature has modified accounts written in the 1970s and 1980s which tended to portray the immigrants as passive victims of a policy of forced and brutal anglicisation. It has been pointed out that adult night classes in English were immensely popular and that parents were happy for their children to attend Jewish schools and clubs not unaware of the education they would receive. Learning English was seen as a way of getting on in the new country or even, as in the case of the world of Jewish radicalism, of uniting with the English working classes.[19] There is, however, a danger of going too far with this analysis forgetting the power relations that existed and the lack of choices faced by the immigrants. In a society where Yiddish language and accents were, in popular culture, as illustrated in cheap literature and the music hall, the butt of racist humour and, at a state level, linked to crime, disease and revolution, it is not surprising that many would feel ambivalent about its use.[20] Oral history of the children of the immigrants points to the huge embarrassment and anguish experienced by those whose parents could not master the English language. It led to generational tensions and rifts beyond the norm. One second generation Jew in Manchester recalled that his 'father couldn't speak English at all and I couldn't speak Yiddish ... I [c]ouldn't have a conversation with me father at all'.[21]

Lest this appear an ahistorical attack on anglicisation, its satirising by the Anglo-Jewish novelist, Israel Zangwill, in the 1890s, significantly written in Yiddish, illustrates contemporary concern from someone with a foot in the camps of both the settled community and the newcomers. Zangwill was partly brought up in the East End and then taught at the Jews Free School in Spitalfields:

> My brothers, sisters newly here,
> Listen to my wise oration,
> You can live without the fear
> Of hatred and repatriation,
> All you have to do, I bid,
> Is stop acting like a yid.

Language and intonation were particularly singled out for parody by Zangwill:

> Ei, ei, ei is so demeaning,
> English voices sing so sweet;
> Ei, ei, ei is so unseeming,
> Oi, oi, oi, an ugly bleat.
> Pom, pom, pom, is rude and crazy,
> Try instead Tra La or Daisy.[22]

It might be added as an aside that at this time of flux and uncertainty in British social and imperial history it was Jews, British born and foreign, who were often at the forefront of inventing traditional Englishness whether in the case of Sir Sidney Lee and the canonisation of Shakespeare and the creation of the *Dictionary of National Biography* (an ongoing project which has taken its first hundred years to acknowledge its own exclusionary nature, including the marginalisation of women and ethnic minorities) or the Hungarian Imre Kiralfy and his representation of English racial superiority through world fairs and exhibitions celebrating the monarchy and its imperial achievements. As Paul Greenhalgh says of the latter:

> It was as though his Jewish origins, in a country which was part of an unstable empire, had filtered through to the very core of his psychological make-up, to surface in a manic involvement with the empire of his adopted home. He had made himself part of a stable, powerful nation by lauding it in a way it had never been lauded before. By 1914, he was more responsible perhaps than anyone for the vivid and vulgar understanding the British population had of its foreign territories.[23]

By 1918 the thriving Yiddish culture of the East End of London and other areas of settlement across Britain was in near terminal decline. Unlike Paris or New York, it would not receive any significant regeneration through new arrivals from eastern Europe because of the near-totality of Britain's alien exclusion policies during the 1920s. Although Yiddish continued through literary publications, theatre and radical politics, as well as amongst an older generation who had never come to terms with the English language, by the 1930s there was a self-awareness within its younger practitioners that there was a conscious need to keep the language alive, echoing those that promote its revival at tertiary and adult education level more recently.[24] The only Yiddish weekly, *Di Tsait*, began to fade away in the interwar period, and was eventually published with some of its contents in English. Today, a sense of loss amongst younger generations with east European Jewish roots, intensified by a growing acknowledgement of the damage inflicted by the Holocaust, has highlighted the cultural loss resulting from the actions of the British Jewish elite at the turn of the century which attempted to act as power brokers and intermediaries between the state and the newcomers.[25]

The First World War itself acted as a catalyst of prewar tendencies so that communal organisations were set up to instil a greater sense of Jewishness amongst a younger generation who it was now believed were too concerned about their Englishness.[26] But the four years of the war had also seen a remarkable movement into Britain representing the largest refugee presence in the country's history – though one that has been almost totally neglected by historians. Some 250,000 Belgians entered Britain, most in the first months of the war. The speed of their arrival, however, was matched only by the pace of efforts to remove them so that by the time of the 1921 Census the number of Belgians born in Britain had only just increased over that in 1911.[27]

Hardly any area of Britain failed to be touched by the Belgian refugee presence. The concentration of 4,000 Belgians in Birtley, County Durham, which even possessed its own Belgian policeman, and in Earls Court Camp which 'became a Belgian village in miniature', were exceptional, but the existence of 2,500 refugee committees set up in the war gives an indication of their geographical spread across the country.[28] Even more remarkable, in the light of responses to earlier and later refugees, was the encouragement given by the British state for the maintenance of Belgian language and culture. The British government-sponsored handbook of 'suggestions and advice' to the refugees, circulated at the end of 1914, stressed that 'every Belgian must be a *good patriot* ... Indeed, nothing is more delightful than to find the characteristic life of Belgium reproduced in Great Britain'.[29] Rather than represent a new found love of pluralism, the encouragement of Belgianness by the state was opportunistic, similar to the sensitivity to the religious and cultural needs of the recuperating Indian soldiers in Brighton and elsewhere – these were transient guests who should return home with happy memories of their land of temporary exile.[30]

The Belgian authorities in Britain were happy to support such strategies. Asking where the refugees should fix their hopes, the Official Committee of Belgians provided a clear answer: 'On their country ... The time of refuge in Great Britain must prepare the Belgians for the heavy task which awaits them on their return. No one should think of avoiding this task, or should dream of settling abroad.'[31] In fact, many Belgians *did* desire to settle in Britain and their removal after the war was carried out with insensitivity and bureaucratic crudity by the state.[32]

The Belgians were thus in some ways exceptional – they had the sympathy of the British population to begin with, although this later declined. The Belgians, or at least their official representatives, also desired to maintain their language and culture, reflecting their status as temporary exiles rather than as permanent settlers. It is significant, however, that there was much greater state and popular support for the privileged, largely French speaking refugees and antagonism to the more rural Flemish speaking arrivals who were often treated as potential enemy aliens when their language was heard in public.[33] Indeed, the war experience, including that of exile, acted as a stimulus to the expression of Flemish nationalism. But refugees, if of the right class, if indisputably deserving of sympathy, and, essentially, if of a temporary nature, could be allowed, even be extolled, to continue to speak their own language. This was especially so if it was French which was less threatening and could indeed could be encouraged as an educational tool.[34]

The harsh removal of the Belgians after the war was indicative that the rediscovered concept of asylum in 1914 had been subject, once again, to amnesia. The 1919 Aliens Restriction Act failed to mention asylum for the persecuted and until the end of the Nazi era few refugees would be allowed to settle permanently in Britain even though the interwar period, and especially the 1920s, witnessed the largest presence of the forcibly displaced in modern world history up to that point in time. Fifteen thousand White Russians were allowed temporary entry, again reflecting their favourable credentials in terms of class and political leanings, but even they were largely encouraged, successfully, to re-emigrate to France where a large and thriving Russian exile community and culture developed in Paris. In addition, some 1,000 Ukrainian Jews, victims of pogroms, civil war and famine, were refused entry through the USA's new quota laws and dumped back in Britain at Atlantic Park near the railway town of Eastleigh.[35]

The Home Office and some sections of the British Jewish establishment were keen to make the life of these stranded refugee transmigrants at Atlantic Park as uncomfortable as possible so that they would be encouraged to return 'home' or continue their journeys to (what the refugees themselves believed) were less desirable places of settlement such as South America, Palestine or South Africa. A power struggle developed in the Jewish community over the approach to be adopted to the transmigrants, some of whom were trapped in Atlantic Park for the better part of a decade. The state was determined that they should not be allowed to settle in Britain but through the efforts of the local authorities and the Union of Jewish Women, the Ukrainian refugees were provided with language and other educational instruction. As temporary residents attempts at total anglicisation were limited, although cricket was encouraged as perhaps one of the least practical skills to enable the transmigrants to adjust in countries of re-migration. The chance to learn English was welcomed by many of the refugees, especially for those still harbouring hopes of entering the USA, but the library which was built up for them according to their requests reflected their complex identities: material was demanded in Hebrew, Yiddish, Russian as well as English. In this process the classics of east European culture competed for space on the library shelves alongside *Robin Hood and His Merry Men*.[36]

On the surface the Atlantic Park experience had much to commend it. The refugees themselves were not passive victims and were able to shape the cultural life of the camp, including in the language that was spoken and read there. Yet underneath a fundamental problem existed – the refugees were not at liberty to settle in Britain on a permanent basis. Some in the district have fond memories of their presence and learnt much from the refugees, including Russian, but the camp was designed to make that local impact minimal by ensuring that Britain was not to be their future home. The intention was the same, if ultimately on a larger scale, with those who came to Britain after the Nazi rise to power.[37]

This chapter has already touched upon the powerful attempts to suppress the use of German by the refugees from Nazism. For the older generation of refugees, most soon realised that as the Hungarian Jewish refugee, George Mikes, put it in *How to be an Alien*, attempts to imitate the English could lead to only one result: 'if you don't succeed in imitating them you become ridiculous; if you do, you become even more ridiculous.'[38] For the 10,000 refugee children who came in the year before the war, however, the pressure to conform meant that more acute problems emerged. As the historian and former child refugee, John Grenville, puts it,

> an intense feeling of insecurity [developed], which manifested itself by wanting to adapt as rapidly as possible … wanting to be accepted as totally English and losing one's German identity totally … to be more English than the English … to change one's name … to wipe out all traces of German and taking up English sports like playing cricket.

The result, as Grenville concludes, was that he felt himself playing a 'role and felt a little bit false and artificial'.[39] Even for adults, the pressure to become invisible was hard to avoid with all resultant problems. As Mikes put it: 'this whole language business is not at all easy. After spending eight years in this country, the other day I was told by a very kind lady: But why do you complain? You really speak a most excellent accent without the slightest English.'[40]

Post-1945 Refugees

Immediately after the Second World War, the British state proved again that it was capable of dealing with difference, including language, if other factors acted as compensation. Whilst Holocaust survivors were, with very few exceptions, kept out of the country, being regarded as unsuitable workers and racially undesirable, the government recruited massively from others in the displaced persons camps of the continent. The largest national group to come to Britain, numbering over one hundred thousand, were the Poles. As Robert Miles suggests, 'In planning for and affecting the resettlement of the Poles, the Labour government accepted that it constituted a population with a distinct history and culture, and considerable administrative effort and financial resources were devoted to the maintenance of a distinct Polish community'. Miles acknowledges that this went on alongside 'strong pressure to learn English and adapt to that strange abstraction that is the "British way of life"', but he adds that it 'provides a remarkable contrast to the way in which subsequent governments insisted upon "integration" when British subjects from the Caribbean and Indian subcontinent first arrived'.[41]

Various factors were at play in favour of the Poles. At a general level was British guilt at leaving the Polish nation to fall under the influence of Communism. More critically the dire shortage of labour made foreign workers essential but those recruited had to be of the 'right type'. The Poles met the criteria because of their anti-Communism and perceived racial suitability – especially in contrast to 'non-desirables' such as Jews and Afro-Caribbeans. Even when basic economic arguments could not be marshalled against the entry of newcomers, policy was still highly racialised in the selection of prospective immigrants. Moreover, rather than simply tolerating the Polish national-religious desire to promote their own language, state support had ulterior motives. Keeping alive an anti-Communist Polish culture served Cold War needs well, especially as it was hoped that the Poles might return to their homeland providing something of an echo of the treatment of the Belgian refugees in the First World War. Numbers and the importance of the Polish Catholic church in Britain ensured that for at least the second generation, Polish language and culture would be maintained. There was, however, as with all refugee movements, great pressure to disperse and assimilate the Poles in order to serve the needs of the British economy and to remove the possibility of 'ghettos' being created. Fifty years on, tension has developed between generations of Poles over the extent of anglicisation that has taken place. As one older former Polish refugee sadly reflects: 'the second generation doesn't seem to get very, or as, involved in the community – a lot of them have dropped out ... You see a Polish name ... but he can't speak Polish.'[42]

Much smaller numbers and greater pressure to assimilate meant that the Hungarians fleeing Communist oppression in 1956 failed on the whole to establish their own cultural forms in Britain. The government, along with the

Women's Voluntary Service and the British Council for Aid to Refugees, organised courses and publications on the 'British way of life'. These provided a ludicrously romanticised view of the country's history and customs: Britain as a homogeneous, pre-industrial rural idyll. With the sympathy for their plight abroad not being matched by their treatment in exile, many Hungarians left for larger refugee communities across the Atlantic.[43]

The government policy of forcing refugees to disperse in order to remove a potential source of racism became explicit from the 1970s until the 1980s when refugee groups including Ugandan Asians, Chileans and those from Indo-China came to Britain. The impact on refugees whose culture was particularly different, especially the Vietnamese, was profound. As Truc Long Pham, Regional Officer for the Vietnamese Settlement Programme in the southwest of Britain put it:

> The idea by central government was that if you settled people in small amounts in different areas they would be less of a draw on services. Also that if there were less people of their own culture, then the Vietnamese would have to settle more quickly into British culture. The mistaken thinking behind this is that you can take people and shape them into any culture you want, as if they were made of clay.[44]

The pressure to speak English put a great strain on the older generation, leading to conflict in groups where previously the old had been held in esteem and an undermining of their confidence: 'Gone is the time that people seek me out for advice and guidance ... Since birth, this is the first time that I witness such [a] humiliating reverse of order.'[45] Ultimately, dispersion was unsuccessful – most refugees continued to congregate in specific cities – but some refugees, often through reasons of poverty and dislocation, became isolated and cut off from the security of clubs and informal gatherings where they could speak their own language. As one Vietnamese refugee recalls:

> Life in England is very hard at first when the language problem is huge – you cannot listen to the radio, cannot read the newspapers, cannot watch the television, cannot talk to your neighbour and worst of all, there is no temple to go to, to soothe your soul. I was as good as deaf and dumb, or dead.[46]

Slowly in the late 1970s and 1980s, following developments in the educational world as a whole in Britain, attempts were made to provide support in refugee communities to promote bi- or multilingualism. Unfortunately, however, a lack of commitment to funding such positions, especially at a time of assault on local authority funding, has undermined the impact of this more sophisticated approach to dealing with the needs of refugees. Barry Cole is a headmaster in a London primary school which has had over a twenty year plus period refugees from Vietnam, Hong Kong, Ethiopia, Eritrea, Somalia, Sierra Leone, Zaire, Kenya, Sri Lanka, Bangladesh, Pakistan, India, Bulgaria, Albania, Chile, Turkey, Cyprus, Iraq and Colombia. Half of his present pupils are refugees or asylum seekers. He relates how, 'We have found it incredibly difficult to get interpreters and almost impossible, except in the most exceptional cases, to get other support with which to address the emotional needs of children who have seen close relatives shot or bombed [or] who have themselves been injured ...'. Some resources were found to start a new arrivals group and the results were 'excellent': 'A trained teacher of English as a second language works with the parents and a teacher works with the children. At the end of the session the two groups get together and the parents learn what the children learnt in school. This was a local authority inspired project and shows that creative thinking still exists in these beleaguered institutions.' Typically, Cole adds, 'the money has now run out and unless we can find alternative funding, the project will cease'.[47]

As this chapter has shown, state recognition that refugees often passionately desire to maintain their own culture whilst simultaneously wanting to become part of the new one – a process in which language is essential – goes back as least as far back as the arrival of the Belgians. The failure to support a more pluralistic approach reflects an unwillingness to accept that refugees are here to stay or if they are, that they must be pressurised into becoming less different. Unfortunately the pedagogic progress made during the 1980s when policies of dispersion and total assimilation were under attack has gone alongside not only the diminishing resources of local authorities and refugee organisations but also an attack on the concept of asylum, leading to a general undermining of refugee legitimacy. Detention of refugees, which serves to make them invisible from the population and also to deter would be entrants, has led to the isolation of asylum seekers from society as a whole. The 1998 White Paper *Firmer, Faster and Fairer* – moves back to a policy of dispersion which is not only likely to fail but to put pressure on refugees to regard their own cultural forms as inferior.[48] As a Chilean refugee expresses it, referring to the problems of rebuilding a life in exile:

> You have to learn how to live in a new culture and at [first] I felt so stupid without the language. I [no longer felt] an intelligent person, and this ... was a big humiliation. Th[e] impossibility to express your feeling, your thoughts, to

be constricted to basic words. So I studied English quite a lot but sometimes my mind was blocked, I couldn't learn because all the terrible things that happened in my country were living in me as a nightmare. I think during the first three years in England, I suffered each night with nightmares about torture.[49]

Refugees are ordinary people to whom something extraordinary has happened. Because of their experiences they may require support to help them come to terms with the trauma of the past. The legacy of oppression, however, has not stopped refugees from contributing to all aspects of their place of asylum if given a chance to do so. And yet in spite of this rich inheritance, politicians in Britain have tended to perceive refugees simply as a problem, especially if they congregate in the same location.

Conclusion

Much is often made of the contribution of refugees to British life in *the past*. Such smug references almost always continue by attacking those who are rejected as bogus (or 'abusive', as the official government line would now have it) asylum seekers *today*.[50] Yet the damage caused on the idealised refugees of history, especially Jews, by the pressure used to make them abandon their language(s) and culture(s), is often forgotten. For all immigrants, the pressure to assimilate (and assimilate to what?) is extremely problematic leading especially to intergenerational conflict. This is not a new problem: as early as the 1780s a pastor in the Huguenot community of East London complained of the 'growing aversion of the young for the language of their fathers from whom they seem almost ashamed to be descended'.[51] But for refugees the stakes are even higher than those who leave out of choice. For those forced to leave their homeland often having suffered themselves or having witnessed atrocities committed against those closest to them, and realising deep down that they will never return, language becomes an even more crucial part of their identities. As the former Yugoslav refugee poet Miroslav Jancic states in his London exile: 'Language is my homeland.'[52]

To summarise: the power of an often racialised discourse has been used by state and society to assimilate refugees in twentieth century Britain. Undoubtedly learning to speak and write in English has aided refugee integration, especially at an economic level and in making use of the health, housing and other services. Those refugees without fluent English have undoubtedly found life in Britain doubly difficult.[53] The pressure to assimilate has, however, often been at the expense of maintaining a dynamic link with the past. In the 1970s the journal of the Association of Jewish Refugees reflected on its sister paper in the United States, the *Aufbau*, which in contrast was published in German from the start:

> It could only have happened in America, a country of immigrants where it was considered natural that new citizens should continue to speak their native language, at least amongst themselves, and retain many of their social and cultural peculiarities. It certainly could not have happened over here. This country has a long tradition of granting asylum to the persecuted, but it has always expected them either to conform or *to go back where they came from* when persecution ended. (Refugees over here have all heard this phrase at one time or another, most of the time prompted by a total lack of understanding rather than by unkindness or antagonism.) We all knew from the start that we should have to come to terms with the English language, and it would not have occurred to anyone to publish an independent German-language newspaper or to hold public meetings where German was the main language.[54]

Such pressures have led many refugees and their descendants, who have been unable to practise or who have been forced to look down upon their mother tongue, to feel that in exile there is no longer a 'place like home'.[55]

Notes

1   Kate Engles and Nicholas Cheeseman, *Square Fish: an introduction to the UK for young refugees and asylum seekers*, London, Children of the Storm, 1997.
2   Annetta Hoffnung, *Gerald Hoffnung, His Biography*, London, Gordon Fraser, 1988.
3   *While you are in England: Helpful Information and Guidance for Every Refugee*, London, German Jewish Aid Committee, 1939, pp. 10, 12, 14.
4   Ibid., p. 16.
5   At the Evian conference on refugees in July 1938, Lord Winterton, representing the British government, stressed that asylum could only 'be applied within narrow limits' and stated categorically that 'the United Kingdom is not a country of immigration', in Norbert Kampe (ed.), *Jewish Immigrants of the Nazi Period in the USA*, Vol. 4, Part 2, *Jewish Emigration from Germany 1933–1942*, Munich, K.G. Saur, 1992, p. 338. On British Jewry see Louise London, 'Jewish Refugees, Anglo-Jewry and British Government Policy, 1930–1940', in David Cesarani (ed.), *The Making of Modern Anglo-Jewry*, Oxford, Blackwell, 1990, pp. 163–90. See also A.Gottlieb, *Men of Vision: Anglo-Jewry's Aid to Victims of the Nazi Regime 1933–1945*, London, Weidenfeld, 1998.
6   Mayerlene Frow, *Roots of the Future: Ethnic Diversity in the Making of Britain*, London, Commission for Racial Equality, 1996. In the Foreword to this book, the Chairman of the CRE, Herman Ouseley, states (p. vii) that 'A better understanding of the people of Britain

will help us to appreciate and value the historic and contemporary contributions of all our citizens and residents, and recognize that they are an integral and invaluable part of the British nation'.

7   See Muhammad Anwar, *The Myth of Return: Pakistanis in Britain*, London, Heinemann, 1979, but also Mike and Trevor Phillips, *Windrush: The Irresistible Rise of Multi-Racial Britain*, London, HarperCollins, 1999, pp. 138–40, 395–400 on Afro-Caribbeans in this respect.

8   Tony Kushner and Katharine Knox, *Refugees in an Age of Genocide: Global, National and Local Perspectives During the Twentieth Century*, London, Frank Cass, 1999, pp. 12–16, 411–17.

9   Roger Zetter, 'Refugees and Refugee Studies – A Label and an Agenda', *Journal of Refugee Studies* Vol. 1, No. 1, 1988, p. 2.

10   Hinzo Skorupan, 'Neither Here Nor There' [from 'Diary of an Exile, London Notes'] in Jennifer Langer (ed.), *The Bend in the Road: Refugees Writing*, Nottingham, Five Leaves Publications, 1997, p. 12.

11   Brochure material advertising the 'Silk Quarter', 1998. The word quality is stressed throughout but the words immigrant and refugee totally lacking in this property development. On the pressures caused by the gentrification of Spitalfields, see Charlie Forman, *Spitalfields: a battle for land*, London, Hilary Shipman, 1989; Robin Gwynne, *Huguenot Heritage: The History and Contribution of Huguenots in Britain*, London, Routledge, 1988.

12   Home Office, *Fairer, Faster, and Firmer: A Modern Approach to Immigration & Asylum*, London, HMSO, 1998, p. 35.

13   Tariq Modood et al., *Ethnic Minorities in Britain: Diversity and Disadvantage*, London, Policy Studies Institute, 1997.

14   John Simpson (ed.), *The Oxford Book of Exile*, Oxford, Oxford University Press, 1995, p. 2. Simpson adds that he includes 'not merely the more obvious political and religious exiles, but adventurers who threw everything up and headed out; misfits and ne'er-do-wells and those who were simply too intelligent or too restless or too awkward to stay at home like everyone else ...'. In fact, his anthology contains only a small amount of writing from refugees. On the tendency, especially amongst some postmodernist writers, to universalise and romanticise the concept of exile without experience of it, see Phil Cohen, 'Rethinking the Diasporama', *Patterns of Prejudice*, Vol. 33, No. 1, 1999, pp. 17–18 referring particularly to the work of Juan Goytisolo.

15   'Accepting asylum', *Observer*, 20 September 1998.

16   Lloyd Gartner, 'Notes on the Statistics of Jewish Immigration to England, 1870–1914', *Jewish Social Studies*, Vol. 22, No. 2, pp. 97–102.

17   David Cesarani, 'The Myth of Origins: Ethnic Memory and the Experience of Migration' in Aubrey Newman and Stephen Massil (eds), *Patterns of Migration 1850–1914*, London, Jewish Historical Society of England and Institute of Jewish Studies, 1996, pp. 247–54. On local 'cultural' objections to the Jews in the East End, see *Report of the Royal Commission on Alien Immigration*, British Parliamentary Papers, Vol. IX, 1903. See also Bernard Gainer, *The Alien Invasion*, London, Heinemann, 1972.

18   Bill Williams, '"East and West": Class and Community in Manchester Jewry, 1850–1914', in Cesarani, *The Making of Modern Anglo-Jewry*, pp. 15–33; Sharman Kadish, *'A Good Jew and a Good Englishman': The Jewish Lads' and Girls' Brigade 1895–1995*, London, Vallentine Mitchell, 1995.

19   David Feldman, *Englishmen and Jews: Social Relations and Political Culture 1840–1914*, New Haven, Yale University Press, 1994; Anne Kershen, this volume and 'Yiddish as a Vehicle for Anglicization' in Newman and Massil, op. cit., pp. 59–67.

20   Sander Gilman, *The Jew's Body*, London, Routledge, 1991, chapter 1: 'The Jewish Voice: Chicken Soup or the Penalties of Sounding Too Jewish'; Colin Holmes, *Anti-Semitism in British Society 1876–1939*, London, Arnold, 1979, pp. 112–14.

21   Oral testimony, J100, in Manchester Jewish Museum collection.

22   Zangwill poem quoted in Paul Morrison and Howard Cooper, *A Sense of Belonging: Dilemmas of British Jewish Identity*, London, Weidenfeld & Nicolson, 1991, pp. 76–7. On Zangwill see the introduction by Meri-Jane Rochelson to his *Children of the Ghetto*, Detroit, Wayne State University Press, 1998.

23   Paul Greenhalgh, *Ephemeral Vistas: The Expositions Universelles, Great Exhibitions and World's Fairs, 1851–1939*, Manchester, Manchester University Press, 1988, p. 93. On Lee, who changed his name from Solomon Lazarus, see, Linda Rozmovits, *Shakespeare and the Politics of Culture in Late Victorian England*, Baltimore, Johns Hopkins Press, 1998, pp. 91–5.

24   For a more positive assessment of the survival of Yiddish in the interwar period see Henry Srebrnik, *London Jews and British Communism 1935–1945*, London, Vallentine Mitchell, 1995, pp. 24–7. See also David Mazower, *Yiddish Theatre in London*, London, Museum of the Jewish East End, 1987. For a remarkable story of the quest for East End Yiddishkeit roots, see Rachel Lichtenstein and Iain Sinclair, *Rodinsky's Room*, London, Granta Books, 1999.

25   *Di Tsait* was founded by Morris Myer in 1913 and finally ceased publication in November 1950.

26   Thus the Jewish Memorial Council was set up in 1919 to counter the impact of the war itself and prewar anglicisation as well as a memorial to those who had died in the conflict. Its records are located at London Metropolitan Archives, ACC/2999 and University of Southampton archives, MS 175/66/2.

27   Tony Kushner, 'Local Heroes: Belgian Refugees in Britain during the First World War', *Immigrants and Minorities*, Vol. 18, No. 1, March 1999, pp. 1–28.

28   On Birtley see A.J.P. Taylor, *English History 1914–1945*, Oxford, Clarendon Press, 1965, pp. 19–20; *First Report of the Departmental Committee Appointed by the President of the Local Government Board to Consider and Report on Questions Arising in Connection with the Reception and Employment of the Belgian Refugees in this Country, London*, HMSO, 1914, Cmd. 7750, p. 36 and Ministry of Health, *Report on the Work Undertaken by the British Government in the Reception and Care of the Belgian Refugees*, London, HMSO, 1920, p. 8 (for the Earl's Court Camp) and p. 9 for the number of local committees.

29   Official Committee of Belgians' handbook quoted in *First Report of the Departmental Committee*, op. cit., pp. 43–4.

30   Rozina Visram, *Ayahs, Lascars and Princes: The story of Indians in Britain 1700–1947*, London, Pluto Press, 1986, pp. 122–35.

31   *First Report of the Departmental Committee*, op. cit., pp. 43–4.

32   For the removal of the Belgians after the war see Kushner, 'Local Heroes', op. cit., pp. 23–5.

33   For an example of hostility to a Flemish speaking refugee, mistaken for a German, see C.W. Hawkins, *The Story of Alton*, Alton, Alston District Council, 1973, p. 65.

34 As illustrated through the diaries of schoolgirl Ruth Dent who looked after a group of French speaking refugees in the New Forest. In the possession of her daughter, Dionis McNair.

35 Kushner and Knox, op. cit., chapter 3.

36 For the library at Atlantic Park see the minutes of the Executive Committee of the Union of Jewish Women, May–September 1925 in University of Southampton archives, MS 129/B/6 and school notebook of Liza Schlomovitz, 1924, in possession of her son, Cyril Orolowitz. Liza was briefly educated at Atlantic Park and her notebooks include copies of Wordsworth's poetry.

37 On the local impact see Allen Robinson, 'Refugees at Atlantic Park, 1920 and North Stoneham, 1937', *Eastleigh and District Local History Society Special Paper* No. 20, 1991, and letter to Katharine Knox, 1 May 1995.

38 George Mikes, *How to be an Alien* reproduced in *How to be a Brit: A George Mikes Minibus*, Harmondsworth, Penguin Books, 1986 (originally 1946 published by Andre Deutsch), p. 18.

39 John Grenville, interview with Zoe Josephs, Birmingham Jewish History Group collection. Extracts of this interview are reproduced in Zoe Josephs, *Survivors: Jewish Refugees in Birmingham 1933–1945*, Warley, Meridian Books, 1988, chapter 5. More generally see Barry Turner, *... And the Policeman Smiled: 10,000 Children Escape from Nazi Europe*, London, Bloomsbury, 1990.

40 Mikes, *How to be a Brit*, op. cit., p. 41 from the chapter 'The Language' in *How to be an Alien*.

41 Robert Miles, reviewing Keith Sword et al., *The Formation of the Polish Community in Britain 1939–50* in *Journal of Refugee Studies*, Vol. 2, No. 4, 1989.

42 Kushner and Knox, op. cit., chapter 7. See also J. Tannahill, *European Volunteer Workers in Britain*, Manchester, Manchester University Press, 1958; Jerzy Zubrzycki, *Polish Immigrants in Britain: A Study of Adjustment*, The Hague, Martinus Nijhoff, 1956; Sword et al., op. cit. and Diana Kay and Robert Miles, *Refugees or Migrant Workers? European Volunteer Workers in Britain, 1946–51*, London, Routledge, 1992; Krisha B., interviewed by Katharine Knox, 6 March 1995.

43 *The Hungarian in Britain*, records of the Refugee Council, ref. RH/QU 59.2. More generally on this neglected movement see Kushner and Knox, op. cit., chapter 8.

44 Speech by Truc Long Pham at a seminar in Southampton on Vietnamese settlers in the south of England, 5 June 1986, Southampton City Record Office, uncatalogued.

45 Refugee Action, *Last Refuge: Elderly People from Vietnam in the UK*, London, Refugee Action, 1987, p. 11.

46 Ibid., p. 1.

47 Barry Cole, 'View from the refugee frontline', *The Guardian*, 24 May 1999.

48 Home Office, *Firmer, Faster and Fairer*, passim.

49 A former university teacher in Santiago quoted in *Haven of Refuge*, Radio 4, 28 September 1982, transcript available in Refugee Council records, ref. WC/QU 56.

50 Mike O'Brien, the Under Secretary of State for Immigration, referred to the change from 'bogus' to 'abusive' asylum seeker. See the interview with O'Brien, 'In Exile', *The Refugee Council Magazine*, November 1998, p. 6.

51 Quoted in Michael Banton, *The Coloured Quarter: Negro Immigrants in an English City*, London, Jonathan Cape, 1955, p. 20.

52 Jancic quoted from a poetry reading in 1996 in the introduction to Langer, op. cit., p. 3.

53   See Alice Bloch's contribution to this volume and also Alice Bloch and Carl Levy (eds), *Refugees, Citizenship and Social Policy in Europe*, Basingstoke, Macmillan, 1999.
54   Margot Pottlitzer, 'Civilisation in Exile: The Story of the "Aufbau"', *AJR Information*, Vol. 27, No. 10, October 1972.
55   Yasmin Alibhai-Brown, *No Place Like Home: An Autobiography*, London, Virago, 1997.

4 'Shamrocks Growing out of their Mouths': Language and the Racialisation of the Irish in Britain

BRONWEN WALTER

This above remark was overheard by one of the respondents to the survey made for the report *Discrimination and the Irish Community in Britain* carried out for the Commission for Racial Equality.[1] It was made in a dismissive tone by a civil servant at a social security benefits office and encapsulates a myriad of stereotypes and shared understandings about the place of the Irish in Britain and ways in which they can be identified. When viewed alongside reports from many interviewees that they were subjected to greater scrutiny than indigenous English people[2] when claiming benefits to which they have an equal right, it also suggests that these ingrained assumptions can limit access to resources, thus having significant material effects on the lives of Irish people.

Voices and language are the clearest ways in which Irish people in Britain are identified to strangers. This identification may then trigger negative stereotypes. As Phil Cohen[3] argues, racist discourses have never confined themselves to body images, every kind of social and cultural practice has been pressed into service: 'racist discourses choose signs which do the most ideological work in linking and naturalising difference within a certain set of historical conditions of representation.' In this chapter I consider ways in which voices help to structure the place of the Irish in Britain. As the opening incident suggested, in certain situations the Irish are excluded as fundamentally different. The hostile reaction of the benefits officer was on a different scale from that directed against people from white British marginalised national, or regional, identities or non-Irish white people of a similar social class.

However, Irish 'accents' are also seen as part of the regional variation of voices within the 'British' Isles, and are not the least liked amongst them. More recently Irish accents have moved higher up the preference scale,

57

paralleling the commodification of Irishness in pubs, beers, restaurants, dance and music. Whereas accents of 'Celtic minorities' had always been minimally represented, it is 'interesting to note the gradual elevation of both Northern English (e.g. Yorkshire) and Southern Irish accents to the relatively prestigious position of chat show host and interviewer'.[4] In the late 1990s the number of Irish television presenters, for example in travel and gardening magazine programmes, multiplied out of all proportion to the 1.5 per cent of the British population born in Ireland.

Irish voices therefore convey a complex set of messages to English people and are ambiguously positioned both inside and outside the hegemonic centre. I want to pursue a number of strands of this intersection of racialisation and representation. Firstly, I attempt to conceptualise the issue of racialisation by voice. How do voices fit with notions which associate subordinated groups with marked bodies? Secondly, I consider contexts in which Irish voices are heard and the material consequences for Irish people of identification through speech and voice. In what circumstances are Irish people discriminated against when their voices identify them? Thirdly, I explore strategies of avoidance and resistance adopted by Irish people to protect themselves against these negative experiences. Fourthly, I examine implications of the 'loss' of Irish voices by people who identify themselves as Irish through the culture of the families in which they were raised in Britain. Finally, I turn to positive evaluations of Irish voices which complicate notions of discrimination and negative stereotyping. How do we explain the high ratings given to the Irish accents of media presenters?

Racialisation by Voice

A powerful reason for the denial of Irish racialisation in Britain arises out of their lack of 'visibility'. It has now become popular in the race relations literature to describe non-white groups as 'visible minorities', this automatically excludes 'white' people who may also be disadvantaged 'minorities' defined on grounds of race/ethnicity.[5] Visibility is prioritised in modernist thought, where the 'gaze' of the powerful acts as a form of control over those under surveillance.[6] Other senses, including audibility are accorded a much lower contribution to the construction of identities.

Irish people in Britain therefore have low visibility, but high audibility. The prime identifier of Irish people to the British is therefore their voices, labelled as having a distinctive 'accent'. Irish people may recognise each other through a more varied repertoire of signs, including facial features and ways of walking. British people may make other connections, for example between Catholic beliefs and Irish origins and also readily identify specific groups such as Irish Travellers by appearance and context. But in the oversimplified rhetoric of 'race', Irish identities are overwhelmingly signalled to strangers by speech alone. The substitution of Irish 'audibility' for black 'visibility' was illustrated in a comment made to the anthropologist Mary Kells: 'The thing about being Irish in England, Martin told me, reporting a joke he had enjoyed, is that they don't realise you are black until you open your mouth.'[7]

The 'Irish accent' is distinguished by structure of language as well as simply pronunciation. This sign of difference is a reminder of colonial 'mastery', a key aspect of which was the forcible imposition of the English language: 'the nation-language of master-discourse.'[8] It is the native Irish language which continues to intrude audibly in syntax and pronunciation as 'accent'. Sentence constructions which are dismissed as ungrammatical in Britain, and therefore evidence of poor educational standards, derive from the Irish language which was banned from use in Irish schools in the nineteenth century.[9] A deeply-embedded aspect of the downgrading of Irish accents as inferior to British ones is therefore the association with their origins in a colonised area.

Voices thus label Irish people as 'outsiders' in Britain. However voices are also a particularly important part of the process by which Irish people in Britain are constructed simultaneously as 'insiders'. Deviations from Standard English are used to label social classes as inferior within the British nation. Unquestioned acceptance of 'accent' as a measure of class positioning for the population as a whole makes it hard to disentangle racist responses to Irish voices from those much more widely related to social class and facilitates the denial of anti-Irish racism in Britain. It also restricts recognition of Irish cultural difference, which is reduced to class alone. Thus widespread resistance to recognition of the Irish as an ethnic group for monitoring purposes is a consequence of the insistence on 'sameness' which stems from this elision of Irish difference.

Accent has received very little academic attention as a sign of difference. In part this results from the taken-for-grantedness of accent as a social marker, but it may also reflect theoretical borrowing from the United States experience, where skin colour rather than voice is the dominant mode of differentiation. Although English-speaking was a distinguishing marker of the dominant group in the United States in the nineteenth century, it did not have the same resonance as an imperial 'master' language as it did in Britain. The centrality of immigrants to nation-building meant that variants of English were usual. Indeed, adoption of the English language itself, with whatever linguistic inflection, was sufficient evidence of 'Americanization' in the early years of the twentieth century.[10]

As a result Irish people are caught unawares by racist responses when they arrive in Britain. The homogenisation by part of Ireland and social class is particularly unexpected. Those from Northern Ireland may find themselves classed as foreign alongside those from the Republic and middle class Irish people are subjected to the working class stereotype when their voices are heard. For example, Alan, an accountant from Dublin who spoke to anthropologist Mary Kells,[11] was frequently assumed to be a builder because a number of Irish builders were working locally. Another of her middle class respondents, Caroline, a young woman from Northern Ireland, said: 'They don't like people with Irish accents; you get that feeling, you know – you're automatically excluded by quite a few people, which is … devastating really.'

The labelling of ways of speaking as inferior undermines the dualism of body/reason, since voices cross the boundary between bodies and minds. Voices are physically attached to bodies, often heard at the same time that the body is seen. However they express the thoughts in minds and are thus also intimately linked to rationality. When Iris Marion Young[12] describes oppressed groups as imprisoned in their bodies, she refers specifically to the 'epidermalizing of their world'. But her ideas could also apply to those linked to particular kinds of voices and, although voices can be changed by deliberate adoption of another 'accent', this is a difficult and often painful process.

In fact the presence of black Irish people, which links racialisation by both visibility and audibility is particularly confusing in Britain. Whiteness is assumed to be inseparable from Irishness. Thus the categories proposed for the 'ethnic question' in the 2001 Census automatically include the newly-accepted 'Irish' self-identified grouping under an initial label of 'White'.[13] Encounters with black Irish people are thus confusing and the notion that black people have Irish accents highly destabilising. One respondent to the Commission for Racial Equality (CRE) survey reported his experience in a London court:

> I was stopped by the police, no MOT, no insurance, an Irish licence. The judge was totally baffled by my accent. I was trying to explain and he couldn't get out of his mind asking me where I was from. He looked at me and said 'Irish, are you sure? With that accent you ought to be West Indian'. He was totally taken

away from the idea of the case. All the court laughed. So did the police – they were amazed. It's like I have to explain myself every time (man in his 30s, born in the Irish Republic, living in Islington).[14]

In the view of the court officials Irish people could only be labelled by their 'Irish' voices and should be 'white'. Black Irish identities were too bizarre to be taken seriously.

Contexts and Consequences of Racialisation by Voices

Voices and language are also used in specific ways to express British hostility towards Irish people. The most frequent and open form of racial abuse reported by Irish people is verbal harassment. Physical attacks triggered by hearing Irish accents also take place, including attacks by neighbours and violent reactions by police officers. The complication for Irish people is precisely that racialised voices may be attached to apparently unmarked bodies. The importance of voice alone as an identifier is vividly illustrated in a case reported in the *Irish Post* in 1998.[15] It underlines the inventedness of accent as a signifier of difference, showing how it can float free of the identification of the speaker and have a life of its own.

A North of England council has been ordered to pay compensation to a family who endured years of anti-Irish abuse from neighbours.

Easington District Council in Durham was slammed by the housing ombudsman for refusing to move a family who complained constantly of racial harassment.

The family, called the Mitchells though their true identity was kept secret, are actually English. The three children, however, aged between four and 11, developed Irish accents after the family spent five years in the Irish Republic before moving to a housing estate in Easington in late 1994.

Within six months of their rehousing the family applied to be relocated after the children were subjected to constant abuse about their accents from other children on the estate.

Bricks and stones were thrown into their garden and, in October 1996, their walls were sprayed with the letters 'IRA'. Within two years, walls around the whole estate had the same graffiti.

On three occasions in just over a month, the Mitchells recorded anti-Irish abuse against them, while a teenager on the estate threw a brick at them, narrowly missing Mrs Mitchell's head. Mr Mitchell suffered badly from depression as a result of the harassment.

> Despite their constant complaints, the council refused to regard the nature of their problem as racial harassment, saying it was in fact a dispute between a number of families on the estate …
>
> The council's stance was criticised by the housing ombudsman Patricia Thomas, who said it failed to give the family the support it needed in confronting racism.
>
> She said: 'I regard "anti-Irish" abuse as racism. The council failed to recognise this and support the Mitchell family as victims. The failure to recognise the harassment as racially motivated did cause an injustice. An earlier move away from their address could have saved them two years of harassment and consequent poverty of life.'

The council was ordered to pay compensation of £1,250 to improve its mechanisms for investigating claims of racial harassment. This lengthy extract has been reproduced because it illustrates many themes discussed in the chapter so far. Labelling this family as Irish was based solely on accent. Undoubtedly their English origins became known to the perpetrators of violence after their initial entry to the estate as strangers, but the hostile behaviour continued. Harassment did not remain at a verbal level but escalated into damage to property and later personal attacks. Because these attacks were against a white family, the council refused to accept that they were racially-motivated and it required the intervention of a national housing regulator to insist on a more inclusive definition of racism. Different interpretations of racism are therefore being applied at local and national levels, and presumably between different localities. The consequences for individuals are severe. For two years the physical safety of the Mitchell family was threatened, the father suffered mental ill-health, children's schooling was disrupted and the family's property was damaged. Harassment of this kind has frequently been reported to Irish welfare organisations, but is rarely mentioned in the mainstream British media.[16]

More commonplace, across all social classes, are anti-Irish comments which draw on a fund of negative stereotypes which are learned from an early age. Moreover, language lies at the heart of one of the most powerful stereotypes associated with the Irish, that of low intelligence and stupidity. The content of anti-Irish 'jokes' frequently relies on misunderstanding through a different construction of language to achieve its humorous impact.[17] The climate of acceptance deters Irish people from challenging this treatment, since they are likely to be further ridiculed. The voices in which they must respond trap them in the stereotype.

In the CRE research 80 per cent of respondents reported hearing anti-Irish comments at work, of which the largest proportion was 'jokes'.[18] Two-thirds of the sample always found these 'jokes' offensive, but only one-third always challenged the speaker and made their views known. Many of this latter group, which had equal numbers of women and men, were in white-collar occupations, suggesting that this group of Irish people felt more confident in asserting their rights, or perhaps that they could successfully argue their case. Other respondents had learned that the safest strategy was to keep a low profile, or select their reaction according to the circumstances. Most of the remaining 20 per cent who said they had not heard anti-Irish comments at work were women. This is perhaps surprising since women tend to be part of more mixed labour forces and to interact with non-Irish people face-to-face. It may reflect a decision to ignore such comments and refuse to acknowledge them.

Nevertheless most respondents could identify specific situations in which they experienced hostility towards Irish people in Britain. Representations in the media were frequently mentioned. Both women and men pointed out entertainment programmes where derogatory images and comments were freely expressed. One woman in her 50s from the Irish Republic, now living in London, mentioned: 'Remarks in the paper. A few remarks on TV and in the papers that I don't like. In the *Express* John Junor said that the Irish were pigs and rolling in muck. I can't think of their names. It's very degrading and I don't agree with it.'[19]

Abusive remarks were also addressed directly at Irish people or made in their hearing. These occurred in a variety of situations, including work, shopping and at leisure, usually unrelated to the context. They had become so commonplace that individual instances could no longer be recalled. Most anti-Irish comments drew on long-established stereotypes, including stupidity, drunkenness, scrounging and membership of an alien religion. These attitudes are so widespread that they are rarely commented on. Significantly many Irish people responding to the CRE (1997) survey replied 'Oh just the usual' when asked about their experiences of anti-Irish attitudes in Britain.

The situations in which hostile attitudes are expressed have important implications for the social positioning of Irish people. Experiences in the workplace, in neighbourhoods and in contacts with service providers affect the resources available to them and the extent to which they occupy shared space with the indigenous or other diasporic groups or enclose themselves within an 'Irish' environment. Discrimination in the housing market was particularly marked amongst the 1950s and 1960s migrants, when overt racism preceded the 1967 Race Relations Act:

> And of course in them days, in them days if you lived in London, and there used to be adverts in the paper shops – rooms to let, no Irish and no coloureds – at that time. You know? I mean it was like that – no Irish and no coloureds.[20]

Even when housing had been found, discrimination could continue in the form of neighbour harassment. Most frequent reports in the CRE (1997) survey were from neighbourhoods with few Irish people, where families were isolated and reminded about their difference.

At times of IRA activity in Britain, the hostility has been greatly intensified. Such a 'backlash' is clear evidence of the racialisation of the Irish community in Britain. A common ethnic identity is sufficient for all members of the collectivity to shared 'guilt by association'. Thus the stereotype of violence and irrationality is applied to all Irish people and 'naturalises' their support, or at least their presumed culpability, for the actions of an extreme few. One consequence of the backlash has been the absence of discussion about the Northern Ireland conflict in public amongst people who have the closest knowledge and concern about it, the Irish in Britain. Sarah Morgan[21] describes this as part of a 'double silence'. Not only do people avoid letting their Irish voices be heard, but they censor themselves by not speaking about Irish issues outside safe, Irish environments.

The mass media in Britain play a powerful role in the reproduction, communication and manipulation of stereotypes of Irish people. These stereotypes, which are both symbolic ('Irish = IRA') and trait-laden, become naturalised as 'commonsense' through media portrayal: 'The incorporation of racialised stereotypes of "Irishness" into the cultural fabric of the everyday places them firmly within normative, pedestrian reality.'[22] Morgan found a wealth of evidence in newspaper reports and television programmes to demonstrate that Irish people in Britain were constructed as a subversive and 'suspect community',[23] echoing back to nineteenth-century representations of the politically dangerous Irish population.[24] Trait-laden stereotypes include madness, excessive drinking, aggressiveness and stupidity which again demonstrate remarkably continuity over time. Irish people are aware of these representations, and frequently mentioned them when questioned for the CRE (1997) survey, but they lack the resources to confront and challenge them. Apart from these negative images there are very few representations of Irish people in Britain in the media to provide alternative images.

Widespread awareness of these trait-laden stereotypes in the British population may play an important part in keeping Irish people 'in their place' economically as well as socially. Construction of Irish men and women as stupid and in need of close supervision suggests that they are more suited to unskilled than skilled work. Irish people are substantially over-represented in the Registrar General's Social Class V, 'unskilled manual work' although the majority have lived in Britain well over 20 years, long enough to have availed themselves of social mobility.[25] Part of this clustering may result from a decision to remain in areas of work where other Irish people are found in order to avoid the harassment described earlier.

The original CRE brief for the discrimination research had suggested that telephone testing might be an appropriate way of measuring discrimination against Irish people at the point of job enquiries. This explicitly acknowledged the likelihood that accents are the main way in which exclusionary actions against Irish people are triggered. However the researchers argued that this might be an imprecise and indeed seriously flawed method, since Irish people may well be considered appropriate candidates for particular kinds of jobs, such as unskilled manual labour. Irish voices enquiring about construction or domestic work may be welcomed. Indeed the continuing movement of people from Ireland to Britain is a result of ongoing shortages in these employment categories. It would be much harder to measure the extent to which internal promotions are subsequently denied to Irish candidates, this could be one explanation for low social mobility rates amongst the Irish-born population, which strongly suggests that discrimination may be a cause.

Coping Strategies

A variety of strategies for limiting the damaging consequences of being identified by their voices is employed by Irish people. These include staying silent, remaining within an Irish environment, and modifying pronunciation. These actions make Irish people less noticeable and are often mistaken for signs of 'assimilation'. Combined with assumptions about whiteness and sameness, restrictions on the audibility of people identifying themselves as Irish reinforces their invisibility in the discourse of 'race' in Britain during the postwar period, despite ongoing evidence of undisguised anti-Irish hostility.[26]

One of the most common responses by Irish people to negative reactions to their voices is silence in public places. This has been particularly true of 1950s migrants, the majority of whom were working class people from rural areas of Ireland. Many lacked the confidence to challenge their treatment. Maude Casey, in her autobiographical novel *Over the Water*, described her mother's crippling fear in London in the 1950s, which she attempted to pass on to her children: 'Mammy knows no one in our road. She is so afraid of scornful glances at her Irish voice that she opens her mouth to no one. She says that we should do the same.'[27] However, middle class people are not immune from being ridiculed or patronised when they speak. A lecturer who responded to the CRE survey felt that her style of speaking was unacceptably different when she contributed to discussions in her professional capacity: 'At meetings, for example, it's not just the accent that's the problem. It's more usual in Ireland to play with language, many more registers. Here it is seen as stepping out of line.'[28]

The IRA bombings in Britain from the 1970s reinforced this fear of recognition, especially after police warnings to 'watch your Irish neighbours'. As a result Irish people have monitored themselves. The commonly-used phrase by Irish people is 'keeping their heads down' so that they would not catch the eyes of English people and be expected to speak. If they had to open their mouths, their voices would be hard to hear. Jenneba Sie Jalloh, a young woman living in London whose father was born in Sierra Leone, described her Irish mother's behaviour in the wake of bombings: 'Whenever there was a bomb scare, she used to say that she'd ask for her fare in a really low voice 'cause she didn't want them to know that she was Irish.'[29]

A Northern Irish-born woman in Erdington, now in her 70s, recalled the aftermath of the 1974 bomb: 'We didn't get a good reaction from the neighbours. If there is trouble you are all tarred with the one brush. Mr H asked if I would like a brick through my window. We kept our head down and carried on.'[30] Silence represents a complex mixture of accommodation and resistance. On the one hand it is complicit with the British ideology of enforcing sameness and therefore part of a 'double consciousness' which appears to accept that there is no place for Irishness in Britain.[31] On the other hand silence denies opportunities for expressions of anti-Irish attitudes by refusing to provide contexts for them.

In the CRE (1997) survey respondents were also asked a broader question about whether they had ever seen or heard anything directed against the Irish in Britain to which they had objected. The impersonal phrasing of the question was intentional, since people often have greater difficulty in talking about their own lives. Only one third claimed that they had not heard anti-Irish comments in Britain. However they also made it clear that they organised their lives to avoid painful situations, and chose to ignore them. The majority of these were women:

I keep away from trouble (Woman in her 60s from Northern Ireland, Birmingham). [32]

Well, I've heard 'Irish Paddy' and 'Get back to where you came from'. Things like that. It's upsetting. It is hurtful. I never say anything back. What's the point? (Woman in her 60s, London).[33]

The corollary of silence in public places is thus a retreat to the comparative safety of Irish environments, reinforcing the silencing of Irish voices in Britain. For women who emigrated in the 1950s and 1960s, the Catholic church has provided such a location, outside the home, for Anne Higgins' family in Manchester: 'We mixed mainly with other Irish people. I suppose it was our accents, but mainly our religion which set us apart from the rest.'[34] Self-segregation may also be practised by recent migrants, in this case using the secular space of Irish pubs. Many respondents to the CRE (1997) survey gave the same reasons for avoiding contact with Irish cultural groups in London.[35]

A more drastic strategy, available only at considerable personal cost, is concealing the difference of their voices. This can take a number of forms, depending on social and personal characteristics of individuals and context. The most extreme response is for Irish people to 'pass' as British by changing their speech patterns, sometimes going as far as taking elocution lessons to make a permanent change. Even middle class Irish people recognised that this option might be necessary in order to avoid negative reactions. Caroline, a statistician and lecturer in London, felt that: 'you probably have to change your accent and everything [to] be accepted by a lot of English people.'[36] Although it is sometimes suggested that 'passing' gives Irish people a ready escape from racist identification,[37] attempts to 'pass' takes considerable effort and exact a psychic cost.[38]

In the CRE (1997) survey respondents were asked: 'Have you ever felt the need to play down your Irish identity?' A substantial minority (19 per cent) said that they had, most frequently mentioning changing their accents. One woman in her 20s, living in Islington, London, reported: 'At the beginning [I did] because of people's reaction to my accent, taking the mickey out of the way you say words and you don't want to be seen as stupid. So I changed the way I spoke, but not now.'[39] This respondent's use of 'taking the mickey' illustrates the impossibility of Irish people's detachment of themselves from a language which includes anti-Irish expressions.

The variety of reactions recorded here illustrate a range of the responses and strategies identified by Brah,[40] who suggested that these included 'accommodation, complicity, resistance, struggle, transgression'. Accommodation was an important strategy adopted at particular time periods, for example the 1950s when anti-Irish racism was more overt and during periods of IRA bombing activity in Britain between the 1970s and 1990s. It might also be necessary for acceptance over the longer term in particular social contexts, such as English middle class lifestyles. Newly-arrived migrants, confronted for the first time with negative stereotyping, also felt stronger pressures to conform, but later gained the confidence to assert their difference. Others resisted by refusing to put themselves in situations where they would be exposed to ridicule. Interestingly strong resistance was expressed by the second-generation children, whose own voices classified them as 'English' and who blamed their parents for complicity when they attempted, unsuccessfully, to adopt 'posh' accents.[41]

Second-generation Identities

Another absence of voice, which increases the invisibility of the Irish in Britain, is the 'lack' of an Irish accent amongst their English-born children and grandchildren. This is an important reason why the identities of second-generation Irish people are rarely acknowledged in Britain. It contrasts with the situation faced by the children and grandchildren of West Indian and Asian-born parents in Britain who are assumed to continue to identify themselves within these ethnic groups. 'Culture' is thought to play a significant role in the continuing construction of ethnic boundaries surrounding 'black' groups, but it inexplicably disappears for those who are 'white'. This process may be actively encouraged. Meg Maguire describes the role of Catholic schools in detaching second-generation children from their Irish home backgrounds, which included 'correcting' their accents.[42]

English accents reinforce the in-betweenness of the second-generation. When they return to Ireland children can be mistaken for English people, or at least have their Irish identities challenged by strangers. Irish-born people thus collude with the denial of Irish identities to second-generation people. When Mary Kells discussed with her respondents the ideal constructs of Irish ethnicity, birth in Ireland was 'the bottom line' and 'second generation, known derisively by some as "plastic Paddies", were often considered counterfeit'.[43] But an English accent may also empower second-generation Irish people. The increasing recognition of Irish ethnic difference during the 1980s and 1990s was given a strong boost by the generation of children of 1950s migrants who had gone through the British education system, often taking part in the expansion of higher education.[44]

Positive Responses to Irish Voices

Although the evidence produced so far suggests that Irish accents trigger strongly negative stereotypes, paradoxically they can also be received more positively. Irishness is constructed as 'other' to Britishness in varied ways. On the one hand Irish stereotypes of stupidity, fecklessness and being prone to drunkenness point up the unspoken opposites in the British view of themselves as wise, controlled and sober.[45] But representations of Ireland as backward and uncivilised can be easily transformed into the 'rural idyll' which lies close to the heart of definitions of Englishness, now mourned as having been lost in the course of 'progress'.[46] This is recreated in tourist advertisements for Ireland which emphasise the slower, non-industrial way of life where there is time to linger and socialise at leisure. The 'craic' symbolises freedom from the pressure of contemporary urban post-industrial society. Indeed this polar opposite of urban Britain was intentionally adopted as the archetypical Irish landscape and way of life in the newly independent Free State in 1921.[47] It is more openly celebrated in mythopoetic representations of Irishness in European countries other than Britain where the positive characteristics of 'hospitality, beauty, artistry, naturalness and Celtic mystique' are associated with the Irish Republic.[48]

Association with a rural past may explain the paradox that Irish accents may be liked at the same time that they are despised. Peter Trudgill examined the order of preference given by respondents from the United States of America, Canada, Scottish and the Irish Republic to accents from ten different parts of the United Kingdom.[49] The results for the English listeners on the aesthetic parameter, measured on a scale from 'very pleasant' to 'very unpleasant', were as follows (with 'informal impressionistic' characterisations of the accents and readings given in parentheses):

1 Received Pronunciation (not advanced or conservative, measured delivery);
2 South Wales (mild, distinctive intonation);
3 Bradford (fairly broad, lively reading);
4 Northern Ireland (mild, soft and slow – not Belfast, very like Southern Irish);
5 Tyneside (fairly broad, confident reading);
6 Gloucestershire (fairly broad, plain delivery);
7 Glasgow (mixed – mild but a few glottal stops);
8 Liverpool (quite broad, rather hesitant);
9 West Midlands (broad, lively delivery);

10 London (quite broad, slow reading).

The positioning of the Northern Irish accent, described as very similar to 'Southern Irish', above most English accents seems at first sight very surprising, especially in the light of Trudgill's 'social connotations' thesis. However the explanation he offers is that the major underlying variable is rural-urban difference. This a fundamental axis in constructions of Englishness, whereby the rural is highly valued as a repository of national virtues.[50] The lowest-rated accents are those of large urban and industrial centres. The high status of Received Pronunciation sets it apart as the first preference, but the next popular accents are the rural ones, including the Irish. This interpretation is supported by the finding that only the Scottish listeners gave a similar ranking to the voices, with the significant exception of their demotion of Received Pronunciation to second place, behind the Welsh accent. Shared beliefs about the value of the rural are thus presumed to relate to Britain as a whole.

Amongst the remaining groups there were similarities between the US and Canadian respondents and an interestingly high correlation between the US and Irish Republic listeners, for which Trudgill could not offer a specific explanation. Could this be an example of the influence of Irish heritage in US culture? Perhaps the most important finding was the absence of overall agreement between the groups which strongly supported the hypothesis that 'social conditioning' rather than 'aesthetic merit' influenced responses to variations in the pronunciation of English.

Conclusion

Language lies at the heart of the social positioning of Irish people in Britain. It is a signifier of their different 'race' and triggers a specific stereotype which overrides other types of difference such as class and gender. Racialisation accords groups inherited characteristics, which may be biological and cultural.[51] It provides a way of naturalising processes of othering by which dominant groups define their own position as legitimate occupants of the centre. But differences established by othering are not only hierarchical. In constructing other groups as 'not us', powerful centres are also acknowledging what they lack. As Robert Young points out 'culture is always a dialectical process, inscribing and expelling its own alterity'.[52] Thus the hostility which accompanies racialisation and leads to discrimination and violence, coexists with a fascination for what is being denied, so that 'racism inhabits spaces of deep ambivalence, envy and desire'.[53] Irish accents remind British people of what they lack as well as what they are not.

The coexistence of rejection and admiration makes it possible to deny the discriminatory consequences of racist attitudes towards Irish people in Britain. One of the most striking findings in the CRE report was the 'battle to be heard' by Irish welfare and community groups.[54] Although they presented well-researched evidence of disadvantage on ethnic grounds and discrimination in access to resources, they were ignored by the 'gatekeepers' of British institutions. The CRE report itself was finally funded because of their persistence in demanding an investigation into their exclusion.

One reason for the specific resonance of language as a marker of Irish difference is the intimate relationship between language and nation. This imposition of the 'master language' is easily forgotten by the dominant society. Yet the very naming of the language as 'English' is an important reminder about the power relationships within Britain: '"British" is the name imposed by the English on the non-English.'[55] The admiration for Irish literary figures, often still claimed as 'English' because of the language in which they write, powerfully connects the processes of Irish subversion of language on the one hand and English envy of, and desire for, Irish otherness on the other.

The different meanings attached to the English language by differently positioned users remain an area of contradiction and confusion. This was richly illustrated in discussions at the time of nominations for the post of Poet Laureate in Britain in 1999 when the Irish poet Seamus Heaney was one of the four nominees, but refused to stand because of his Irish national identification.[56] That such misunderstandings continue to occur in Britain is a measure of the taken-for-grantedness of language which appears to confer sameness, whilst deeply imbued with cultural difference.

Notes

1   M. Hickman and B.Walter, *Discrimination and the Irish Community in Britain*, London, Commission for Racial Equality, 1997, p. 178.

2   Ibid., p. 174.

3   H. Bains and P. Cohen (eds), *Multi-racist Britain*, Basingstoke, Macmillan, 1988, p. 14 .

4   M. Montgomery, *An Introduction to Language and Society*, London, Routledge, 1986, p. 74.

5   See for example R. Ballard, 'Negotiating race and ethnicity: exploring the implications of the 1991 Census', *Patterns of Prejudice*, 1996, 30, (3), pp. 3–33.

6   H. Lidchi, 'The poetics and the politics of exhibiting other cultures', in S. Hall (ed.), *Representation: Cultural Representations and Signifying Practices*, London, Sage, 1997, pp. 195–8.

7   M. Kells, *Ethnic Identity Among Young Irish Middle Class Migrants in London*, London, University of North London Press, 1995, p. 33.

8   K. Mercer, 'Diaspora culture and the dialogic imagination', in M. Cham and C. Watkins, (eds), *Blackframes: Critical perspectives on black independent cinema*, London, MIT Press, 1988, p. 57.

9   J. Edwards, 'Irish and English in Ireland', in P. Trudgill (ed.), *Language in the British Isles*, Cambridge, Cambridge University Press, 1984, pp. 480–98.

10   J. Bodnar, *The Transplanted*, Bloomington Indiana, Indiana University Press, 1985, p. 190.

11   Kells, op. cit., p. 31.

12   I.M. Young, *Justice and the Politics of Difference*, Princeton NJ, Princeton University Press, 1990 p. 123.

13   Office of National Statistics, White Paper, 1999.

14   Hickman and Walter, op. cit., pp. 182–3.

15   *Irish Post*, 24 October, 1998.

16   Hickman and Walter, op. cit., pp. 116–17.

17   E. Leach, 'The official Irish jokesters', *New Society*, 20/27 December, 1979, p. viii.

18   Hickman and Walter, op. cit., pp. 191–4.

19   Ibid., p. 216.

20   Woman interviewed by the author in Bolton 1994, ESRC Research Project R000234790.

21   S. Morgan, unpublished PhD thesis, 'The contemporary racialization of the Irish in Britain', University of North London, 1997, p. 203.

22   Ibid., p. 211.

23   P. Hillyard, *Suspect community: people's experience of the prevention of Terrorism Acts in Britain*, London, Pluto, 1993.

24   M. Hickman, *Religion, Class and Identity: The state, the Catholic Church and the education of the Irish in Britain*, Aldershot, Avebury, 1995.

25   Hickman and Walter, op. cit., pp. 250–2.

26   M. Hickman and B. Walter, 'Deconstructing whiteness: Irish women in Britain', *Feminist Review*, 50, 1995, pp. 5–19.

27   M. Casey, *Over the Water*, Livewire, London, 1987, p. 2.

28   Hickman and Walter, 1997, op. cit., p. 215.

29   M. Lennon, M. Mcadam and J. O'Brien, *Across the Water: Irish women's lives in Britain*, Virago, London, p. 215.

30   Ibid., p. 213.

31   Morgan, op. cit., p. 3.

32   Hickman and Walter, 1997, op. cit., p. 213.

33   Ibid., p. 220.

34   Lennon, Mcadam and O'Brien, op. cit., p. 146.

35   Hickman and Walter, 1997, p. 209.

36   M. Kells, '"I'm myself and nobody else": gender and ethnicity among young middle-class Irish women in London', in P. O'Sullivan, (ed.), *The Irish World Wide*, Vol. 4, *Irish Women and Irish Migration*, Leicester, Leicester University Press, 1995, p. 213.

37   Ballard, op. cit., pp. 6–7.

38   M. Ang-Lydgate 'Charting the space of (un)location: on theorizing diaspora', in H. Mirza (ed.), *Black British Feminisms*, London, Routledge, 1999, p. 181.
39   Hickman and Walter, 1997, op. cit., p. 211.
40   A. Brah, *Cartographies of Diaspora*, London, Routledge, 1996, p. 138.
41   P. Ullah, 'Second generation Irish youth: identity and ethncity', *New Community*, 12, 1985, p. 314.
42   M. Maguire, 'Missing links: working –class women of Irish descent', in P. Mahony and C. Zmroczek (eds), *Class Matters: 'Working-class' women's perspectives on social class*, London, Taylor and Francis, 1997, p. 92.
43   M. Kells, 1995a, op. cit., p. 39.
44   B. Walter, 'Contemporary Irish settlement in London: women's lives, men's lives', in J. Mac Laughlin, *Location and Dislocation in Contemporary Irish Society*, Cork, Cork University Press, 1997, p. 87.
45   B. Walter, 'Irishness, gender and place, Environment and Planning D', *Society and Space*, 13, 1995, pp. 35–50.
46   R. Williams, *The Country and the City*, London, Chatto and Windus, 1973.
47   C. Nash, '"Embodying the nation" – the west of Ireland and Irish identity', in B. O'Connor and M. Cronin (eds), *Tourism in Ireland: A critical analysis*, Cork, Cork University Press, 1993.
48   M. Buckley, 'Sitting on your politics: the Irish amongst the British and the women amongst the Irish', in J. Mac Laughlin, op. cit., p. 97.
49   P. Trudgill, *On Dialect: Social and geographical perspectives*, Oxford, Blackwell, 1983, pp. 221–4.
50   J. Short, *Imagined Country: Society, culture, environment*, London, Routledge, 1991, chapter 4.
51   R. Miles, *Racism after 'Race Relations'*, London, Routledge, 1993, p. 14.
52   R. Young, *Colonial Desire*, London, Routledge, 1995, p. 30.
53   Brah, op. cit., p. 15.
54   Hickman and Walter, 1997, op. cit, pp. 99–106.
55   Young, op. cit., p. 51.
56   'Heaney leads the race for Poet Laureate', *The Guardian*, 4 February, 1999, p. 3.

5 Health Advocacy in Medicine

VERONICA L.C. WHITE

For many people from ethnic minority backgrounds living in the UK, English is not their first language. When they require medical treatment, either in emergency or routine situations, they are frequently seen by medical staff who do not speak their mother tongue. Both patients and staff have the frustrating task of trying to explain medical complaints and symptoms and, in turn, convey treatment regimes between each other.[1] Doctors can often appear uncaring and brusque in their attempts to understand a patient's problems. Patients can leave consultations feeling that they have not been adequately assessed and confused about their continuing medical care. Many hospitals and health authorities are now trying to provide interpreters, translators, Linkworkers or Health Advocates to bridge this language gap.[2] At the main hospital in East London, a Health Advocacy service was set up at the beginning of the decade. It was designed not just to provide a 'translating service', but for its advocates to feel able to span the cultural, as well as the language divide, between patients from their own ethnic group and medical staff.

In the English dictionary, the word advocate is given a number of meanings including 'intercessor', 'defender', or 'someone who pleads the cause of another'. For the purposes of this study, I looked at the role of the health advocate in our health system through the eyes of patients, doctors and the health advocates themselves, in order to discover what their job involved and what were current attitudes toward them. Patients that were interviewed all felt that the Advocacy Service was an essential feature of the hospital; some denied that they always needed to use it, but felt it was important for their non-English speaking friends and family. It was found that patients who were illiterate and least likely to know any English were also the least likely to know about the advocacy scheme. Doctors, at all grades, echoed the enthusiasm for the service and wished that it could be more widely and readily available. The advocates themselves eloquently expressed their belief that they were not simply translators of the spoken word, but that they also crossed the cultural divide and stressed their importance as the patient's defender and intercessor.

Introduction

Since the end of the Second World War, the number of people migrating from South-East Asia, Africa and the Caribbean has increased dramatically. Initially invited to come and help rebuild Britain during the postwar boom, immigration continued into the 1960s and 1970s until strict laws on residence in the UK were introduced in 1980s.[3] For many people living in developing countries, work permits enabling them to secure employment in the UK were seen as a golden opportunity to improve their family's social and economic standing. Some men came just to work, send money back to their dependants and then returned home to retire, reaping the rewards of their labour in relative prosperity compared to the neighbours they left behind. However, many others remained in the UK, either through choice or because they had insufficient means to make the return home financially worthwhile. They then either brought their families over to live with them or married the offspring of fellow migrants. For those who stayed, transition into Western society has not always been easy. There have been problems of racism, social isolation, poor housing and difficulties in accessing social and health care facilities.

This chapter considers the latter problem, specifically the difficulty of bridging the language and cultural gap between patients from ethnic minorities and UK health professionals who rarely speak their language. It examines the role of the Health Advocate in helping to guide the patients through the maze of bureaucracy and the often intimidating facade of white coats. For the basis of the study, I have focused on the advocates, patients and health care professionals at the Royal London Hospital in the East End of London. For over two hundred years, this part of London has been home to diverse groups of migrants from all around the world. At present the largest ethnic minority group is the Bangladeshis, the majority of whom come from the region of Sylhet; they now make up 30 per cent of the population of Tower Hamlets. Locally, other large groups include Somalians, Turks, Vietnamese and Chinese.

Background

There are now a sizeable number of ethnic groups living in the UK. They are mainly clustered around the inner cities, although some are now moving into suburban areas. For many, English is not their first language and, when seeking health care, there can be enormous problems of understanding between patient and health care workers, neither of whom can make themselves clearly understood.[4] Medical students are taught early on in their careers that 90 per cent of clinical diagnosis can be secured from the patients' history; that is their verbal account of their symptoms. Lack of this important tool often weakens the practitioner's ability to recognise their client's illness and communicate the necessary modes of treatment and investigation. There tends to be an assumption that the Western biomedical model of the human body and its functions are easily translated cross-culturally when, in reality, there are widespread ethnic differences in medical concepts and health care beliefs.[5] However, doctor-patient, hospital-patient communication has long been recognised as a major problem. These problems are present in the English language, even before we add the difficulties associated with patients for whom it is not their native tongue. The 1993 Audit Commission Report, *What seems to be the Matter: Communication between Hospitals and Patients*, considered a whole range of communication problems; disabled patients in wheelchairs, visual or hearing impairments, learning disabilities and patients who do not speak English.[6] In its introduction, it points out that good communication can improve not only clinical outcome, but also increase efficiency and, from an economic point of view, strengthen a hospital's market position. On the latter point, they say, 'the reputation of the hospital with patients and purchasers ... will almost certainly depend in part on how well it communicates with the patient'.

Doctors and administrators alike get frustrated by missed appointments or investigations, but much of the problem may be down to poor communication on the part of the hospital rather than the patient. Busy doctors in outpatients often hand patients a stack of papers consisting of blood tests, X-ray forms and specialist scans that need to be delivered and booked in a variety of departments, often spread throughout the hospital. If the relevance of these tests and careful explanation of where they need to be undertaken is not forthcoming, or if the doctor and clinic staff are unable to clearly explain in a language that the patient can understand, it is hardly surprising that patients return to their next appointment bemused at the disgruntled doctor who has no results for them. Conversely, there is nothing more irritating to a junior doctor, unable to organise investigations when lists are apparently full, to find out too late that booked patients did not arrive for their appointments.

From personal experience, many of the formal complaints made to the hospital about patient care, once analysed, tend to be caused by a lack of interaction between doctors, nurses and their clients. There are too many assumptions made by both parties, especially the professionals. Medical staff have long forgotten what it is like to be a layman and often fail to explain medical problems in simple terms. The use of medical jargon often heightens anxiety, even leading to frank depression in the chronically ill, when repeated use of medical terminology can be perceived as inferring that their illness is complicated and thus critical. Cultural health care beliefs may also misinterpret non-verbal as well as verbal actions. Many patients arrive at appointments with preconceived ideas which they may be unable to express; some who are needing only routine investigations will always 'fear the worst', but be unable to voice their fear of cancer or infection. Poor explanation for investigation and, worse, inadequate presentation of results only intensifies their fears.[7]

In areas where a given ethnic minority, or minorities, predominate, many health authorities are developing translating services to try to bridge communication barriers.[8] Individuals engaged in these roles are variably known as Translators, or Interpreters, or more progressively, Linkworkers or Health Advocates, and are normally from the same cultural background as the ethnic group they hope to serve. Linkworkers and advocates are generally employed not only to provide a word for word interpreting service, but also to help bridge the cultural gap between patient and doctor and to act as cultural attaché and gatekeeper.[9] This is especially important in interpreting non-verbal signs, cultural understanding and beliefs about illness and respecting and appreciating religious customs. They can often guide both the patient and doctor by adding an understanding of ethnic, social, gender and spiritual issues. Many female patients prefer to be seen by female medical staff and, not unreasonably, refuse to be examined by male members of staff. Religious beliefs may radically alter a patient's perception or reaction to their illness and the family and social support that they receive; for many Moslems, their strong religious beliefs and the 'Will of Allah' may bring a sense of peace and acceptance when told that they are seriously ill. It can be invaluable for a health advocate to be on hand to explain the situation to the patient, but also to enlighten medical staff about the attitudes and wishes of the patient and their loved ones. A patient's perspective towards ethical problems such as consent, confidentiality and terminal illness may all vary according to their cultural philosophy and customs.[10]

Not all non-English speaking patients are so fortunate. Some hospitals may have no formal translating service. Health professionals often rely on relatives, sometimes young children to interpret.[11] School children may be taken out of their classes to translate for their parents; many are quite young and find it difficult to interpret medical problems.[12] Older offspring or a spouse may take time off work, often losing pay. At other times, NHS staff, such as kitchen auxiliaries or porters are called upon when no other source is available.

These examples draw us into the tricky and contentious problems of confidentiality and the reliability of the interpretation; there are numerous anecdotal stories of hospital domestic staff being asked to break bad news such as cancer or HIV tests. Some hospitals may use commercial translating services. However, personnel may lack the necessary medical language skills to convey a complicated medical problem between doctor and patient accurately. Some institutions use telephone translation services such as 'Language Line'. However, these services are expensive and many Health Authorities restrict their use, confining their availability to ward and clinic staff, and charging individual departments.[13] Often nursing staff frantically ring around the hospital looking for some one who speaks a certain language to help translate for a patient on their ward; some hospital switchboards carry a list of potential volunteers for such duties, but inevitably, particularly at weekends, no one seems to be available. Medical staff have been known to drag other patients or bystanders from waiting rooms to interpret; on wards, neighbouring patients or visiting relatives are often coerced into helping. Again, both the accuracy of information and confidentiality are abandoned in attempts to secure information.

The current literature on health advocacy/interpreters is minimal. However, the problem is not unique to this country. The USA, South Africa and Australia have diverse ethnic groups with special translating requirements and health problems.[14] The USA alone has more than 30 million residents who do not speak English.[15] These countries have similar problems to ours; they are all exploring effective methods of improving services, including recruiting bilingual 'paraprofessionals' and training health care workers in effective use of interpreting services. One recent American paper compared the use of 'remote-simultaneous interpretation' with 'proximate-consecutive interpretation'.[16] In plain English, translating via a telephone or ear piece compared with translation when the interpreter is present in the room. The cultural and language divide becomes even more apparent in sociomedical problems such as alcoholism, drug abuse and mental illness. Here, more than with other medical problems, racial understanding and acceptance of the issues surrounding a patient's illness become much more clouded. This may be secondary to cultural and religious understanding of symptoms or the social and cultural stigma attached to the problems. Western health care professionals need to call on the services of trained health advocates to scrape even the surface when trying to take a reliable medical history, interpret symptoms and initiate treatment.

Talking To The People Involved

A health advocacy service was set up at the Royal London (teaching) Hospital eight years ago. Before its evolution, a number of interpreters were employed. The new job of an advocate, however, was designed to be different, with an emphasis on representing the patient, rather than just translating for medical staff. The service originally employed two Bengali/Sylheti[17] advocates, but has expanded to include four Bengalis, two part-time Turkish speaking, two part-time Somalis and one Chinese.

The author set out to discover the way in which the advocates regarded their role as intermediary between patients and medical staff, subsequently to learn how patients themselves valued the service and finally how doctors coped with treating patients who did not speak English.

Patients

Bengali or Sylheti speaking patients were targeted, as they make up the largest ethnic group seen in the hospital. I employed the services of an independent interpreter, who had previously been a research student in the hospital and was therefore familiar with medical terms. We selected three different outpatient clinics, and with the aid of my interpreter, we explained the purpose of the study to the patients and, using a semi-structured interview technique, invited them to answer a few questions about the advocacy service at the hospital. All of the patients readily agreed to talk to us. No one appeared to be afraid that their comments would affect their future care and we were pleased at their openness and willingness to share their thoughts with us. The patients seemed to fall into several groups. Firstly, those who spoke fluent English, but recognised the need for interpreters for their family and friends and were very supportive of the services provided. Secondly, patients who spoke basic English with whom there were difficulties in explaining complex issues. They denied that they needed the help of an advocate and felt that they understood all the treatment issues. This group of patients was predominantly male and it is possible that they were too proud to admit that they might benefit from some form of advice in their mother tongue. They may well have been living in the UK for some years and valued their independence and thus wanted to appear to be self-sufficient. One gentleman said that he used the leaflets written in Bengali that he found in the waiting room to help him understand his illness and discussion with his doctor.

The last group of patients were those whose English was quite poor. They readily agreed that they required help in making themselves understood. In one specialist clinic, where advocates were more readily available, and a specialist linkworker was based, patients were very familiar with using an advocate. Some even commented that advocates were requested by medical staff before they needed to ask, which they found very reassuring. However, in other clinics, patients with poor English skills were not always aware that a proper health advocacy service was available and that they could ask for this to be arranged by nursing staff or receptionists. Some patients knew that some kind of service existed but did not know how to, or were too frightened, to ask for help. This latter finding was quite worrying. Further discussions revealed that the Bangladeshis least likely to learn English were those who speak Sylheti only. Those who also spoke Bengali and had learnt to read and write in this language were more likely to have a good command of English. Unfortunately, Sylheti does not have a written form[18] and those who only use this one language tend to be illiterate. From the point of view of advertising any services in the hospital, there are difficulties, since posters and leaflets will not reach those who most need the services. They rely on the awareness, good will and efficiency of the clinic staff and this varies from department to department. One patient relied exclusively on his General Practitioner, who spoke his mother tongue, to translate hand written notes handed to him in clinic.

Many of the patients brought members of their families to clinics with them. Particularly for women, this was as much for a companion as an interpreter. Bengali women still rarely leave their homes without an escort, partly because it is socially unacceptable for them to travel very far from home by themselves and partly, especially for older women, for fear of racial or sexual harassment. In the clinics themselves, the company of a family member provided welcome reassurance, as well as someone else to help explain their health problems and understand their subsequent treatment and investigations. Family members often take an active role in helping with medication at home and make sure that it is taken correctly. A number of patients admitted that family members took time off work to accompany them to clinics or to visit the hospital. On further questioning it was revealed that when inpatients on the ward, relatives would regularly make sure they were present for doctors' ward rounds so that symptoms could be explained and treatments understood. Children occasionally skipped school to attend clinics with their parents. Some parents who needed help would try to arrange appointments in the school holidays. Despite the presence of family members, many patients recognised that health advocates often helped explain their problems more eloquently, having experience in using medical terms and explaining complicated investigations and treatment regimes. Some felt that confidentiality was an issue when family members were present and 'secrets' may not be revealed as easily. Certainly some female patients found it embarrassing to talk about more personal problems, particularly gynaecological issues, in front of male relatives, although generally the presence of husbands was felt to be acceptable.

There were mixed views on the gender of an advocate. Some women certainly voiced a preference for a female interpreter who would be more culturally and religiously acceptable. Male patients with problems such as impotence, which tends to occur commonly among diabetics, generally valued the presence of a male interpreter. Conversely, one male patient actually said that he preferred all female staff as they were 'more soft-hearted and understanding' and had 'more time for him'; other patients felt that advocates were professionals and, male or female, had a job to do and either would suffice.

Interviews with the patients not only provided details of communication via the advocate, but other useful anecdotal information. One patient, who was very fluent in English, commented that the signs around the hospital, which are written in both Bengali and English, used a very formal type of written Bengali. He explained that, as in many languages, some English words may have a number of different translations into his language. Having the formal and less familiar version used on the signs, was difficult for those with an incomplete knowledge of Bengali. A female patient recalled that, in common with other women of her generation, she had attended school in Britain for three to four years and had learnt English. However, now that she was married, her husband did most of the tasks outside the home, such as going to the bank or post office. Therefore she had 'lost' her use of the English language and had become 'lazy', and therefore continued to rely on others to interpret more complex issues.

Health Advocates

The advocates seemed very willing to be interviewed. A semi-structured interview technique was used with a basic list of relevant points, allowing the advocates to cover other issues as they came up. It was originally planned to tape-record the interviews, but on the whole the advocates felt uncomfortable with this suggestion. Conversations were therefore recorded on paper at the end of the interview.[19]

The most striking aspect of all the interviews was that all the advocates were resolute in that they were employed as their job title described, there to defend the rights of the patient, rather than merely as interpreters. All of them came from similar cultural backgrounds as their clients and they all recognised the importance of their role as a cultural attaché. They felt that they were able to express the rights of the patients and represent them, that they gave the patients 'confidence' in approaching the doctors; that they 'bridged the gap' and 'helped to direct the patient'. One advocate stated that their job satisfaction was being able to explain problems to patients and put their minds at rest. In turn, the advocates also recognised their role in helping medical staff express what they felt were important, yet often complicated and frightening, investigations and treatment. Many patients initially refused investigations, which appeared invasive and unnecessary, but often advocates were able to explain their relevance, thus allowing the patients to make a more informed decision as to their care. Many patients then went on to complete their care, although this was not universal and some still made the decision not to continue with Western medical treatment. As far as training was concerned, most of the advocates had worked in the community before being employed at the hospital, either in a paid or voluntary capacity. For most this was as a translator or linkworker. Formal training has now been given to some, particularly in medical matters, others have 'picked it up as they went along', making sure that they understood and could describe complicated procedures and treatments.

Having worked and lived in the East End for many years, I have been particularly impressed by the Bangladeshi community's religious faith and commitment to Islam. From an outsider's point of view, they often seem comforted by these beliefs and more relaxed in the face of illness and grief. I remember one particular traumatic cardiac arrest, I expected that the patient's family would have a barrage of questions for me the next day when I went to sign the death certificate. Instead I was met with a peaceful acceptance of events: 'It is the will of Allah ... her time had come.' I was therefore particularly interested in asking the advocates how Islam featured in the life and illnesses of the patients and indeed in their work in advocacy for them. Both Bengali and Somali advocates readily agreed that faith had an important part to play. Reassurance in religious terms was, on occasions, an appropriate part of their role. They felt that, in relation to their Western neighbours, Islam enabled patients to cope better with their illness after the initial shock of a serious diagnosis, 'they were more relaxed' and better supported by friends and family as well as being more accepting of the prognosis. Patients believed their predicament was 'God's will', 'they had been given a life and that it was not theirs to take but God's'. They believed in life after death and rarely saw illness as a punishment, rather that it was suffering they needed to go through. They would rather go through it now than in the next life.

Another cultural phenomenon examined was the patients' use of alternative practitioners. I was told that, particularly within the Chinese community, patients tend to consult their local doctors and try traditional medicines. They would then wait until their illness got worse before consulting their GP or presenting themselves to the hospital. Conversely some patients, particularly those suffering from cancer, would cut short an unpleasant course of treatment and return to their traditional practitioners, occasionally feeling much better. The Bengali and Somali patients however tended to present to Western doctors first. They would often consult their local Mullah or Imam if they were unsure about the 'correctness' of treatment. Only after treatment appeared unsuccessful did they seek alternative therapies. These therapies were particularly important among the Bengali community in cases of mental illness and overlapped with beliefs in ghosts, spirits and black magic. These spirits are strongly felt to be the cause of psychiatric problems and the afflicted are regarded as possessed. Advocates are able to help translate these beliefs between doctor and patient. Equally problematic is depression, a condition for which there is no direct translation in Bengali or Sylheti. Patients often become alarmed when they are referred to a psychiatrist who they feel is for 'mad people'. One advocate interpreted this by explaining to the patient that there were 'different levels of madness' and that 'they were being referred because their mental state had been suppressed' or that 'they had become low because of sadness or problems in their life'. 'Treatment would hopefully bring their feelings up again.' Somalians, similarly believe in other beings or angels, some good, some bad (*jin* or *shatan* – 'harmful beings'). The Somalians believe that though the spirits cannot be seen they can bump into human beings who they then possess and make unwell. There were not 'alternative practitioners' amongst the Somali community in this country although some people will return to Somalia to consult them and traditional or homeopathic medicines are often used in the villages there.

The advocates recounted several problems with their job: there were mixed feelings as to how well the medical staff used their services. Often advocates were called in 'too late', by which time the patient had already been seen in several clinics. Their main complaint was that they now work across five different hospital sites in the area and are spread rather thin; time was often wasted travelling between these sites or waiting for doctors to see the relevant patient. They share with their patients the difficulties of managing professional-client interaction with the opposite sex. Most of the advocates at our hospital are female and, particularly for urological problems, find translating personal problems for male patients a little difficult and embarrassing. One female advocate refused to attend the male sexually transmitted disease clinic after a particularly traumatic attempt at explaining a patient's symptoms. In general the advocates feel that as professionals they can tackle most situations. The reassurance that confidentiality was to be maintained and that they were experienced in translating personal matters was often enough to put patients at ease. Occasionally patients would rebook appointments when a same sex advocate was available. Calls to the obstetric and gynaecology departments are universally covered by female advocates.

As far as appearance and demeanour were concerned, most of the advocates felt that they could be themselves, although as expected in their community they would be respectful towards patients, particularly elderly ones. Many patients were quite familiar with them in the Bengali community and it was not unusual for them to be called 'sister' or 'daughter' according to age and status, and young advocates might call patients 'auntie' or 'uncle'. This familiarity sometimes went as far as asking for the advocate's home telephone number, which was politely declined. Advocates were occasionally asked medical questions outside work, but this was not seen to be a habitual problem. Occasionally meetings in the mosque or in the street would lead to advocates repeating instructions recounted in clinic or simply reassuring the individual.

Doctors

In order to seek the opinions of a range of doctors a six-point questionnaire was designed (Figure 5.1); it was sent to doctors in a variety of specialities and grades from consultant to junior house officer. Doctors are notoriously bad at returning any kind of survey, and therefore the format of the questionnaire was made necessarily simple and easy to answer. The questions fitted onto one side of A4 paper and were sent with an addressed return envelope that could be placed in the hospital's internal post.

Over half of the 150 questionnaires sent out were returned and 75 of those were subsequently analysed. In the outpatients' clinics, 80 per cent of doctors reported using advocates or interpreters either occasionally, once a month or once a week. Only 10 per cent said that they never used translating services in outpatients, the majority of whom were in junior grades. Consultants used the services most frequently, 35 per cent of them utilising advocates on at least a weekly basis. Over 50 per cent of those questioned used advocates on the

Please answer the following questions:

How often do you use health advocates/interpreters in outpatients (not patient's family members) – please circle answer:

NEVER   OCCASIONAL   ONCE A MONTH   ONCE A WEEK   EVERY CLINIC

How often do you use health advocates/interpreters on the wards (not patient's family members) – please circle answer:

NEVER   OCCASIONAL   ONCE A MONTH   ONCE A WEEK   EVERY CLINIC

Questions 3 and 4 are answers using a visual analogue scale; please mark the line at the point which most corresponds to your opinion:

Do you feel that the presence of health advocates helps your consultation with patients whose first language is not English?

NOT HELPFUL   VERY HELPFUL

_____

Do you find it difficult to arrange assistance from an advocate when you request it?

NOT DIFFICULT   ALWAYS DIFFICULT

_____

Do you think it is important to have an independent interpreter i.e. a health advocate when talking to patients or do family members provide an equal or better source of translating? - please circle answer:

FAMILY MEMBER   FAMILY MEMBER   HEALTH ADVOCATE   HEALTH ADVOCATE
BEST   ADEQUATE   PREFERABLE   ALWAYS
                                                     NECESSARY

Can you suggest any changes to the current service? Please comment:

Figure 5.1   Six-point questionnaire

wards occasionally; 22 per cent once a month and just under 15 per cent once a week or more. These lower figures compared with outpatient use may well reflect the presence of more English-speaking family members visiting inpatients and the fact that medical staff are available to talk to them at a wider range of times than in outpatients.

In the visual analogue scales, where Question 3, 'Not Helpful' represents 0 mm (millimetres) and 'Very Helpful' 100 mm, the overall average was 80 mm. Question 4, 'Not Difficult' was represented by 0 mm and 'Always Difficult' 100 mm. There, the mean score was 47 mm, suggesting a range of experiences in arranging assistance from advocates. Finally, nearly 80 per cent of all the doctors questioned agreed that Health Advocates were preferable or always necessary. Only 5 per cent felt that family members were best at translating for patients. Overall the response to the doctors' questionnaire was quite impressive. The high rate was partly due to the simple design of the questionnaire and this has been confirmed by personal comment to the author. Secondly, the good response reflected the doctors' very real feeling of dissatisfaction at frequently being unable to communicate fully with patients. A large part of the medical ethos and satisfaction is based on the doctor's expertise in securing sufficient information to work out a patient's underlying complaint. Nearly half of the questionnaires received back were from consultant staff, who work on a more permanent basis within the system and therefore encounter language barriers as an ongoing part of their career coupled with the shadow of increasing complaints and litigation from all sections of society.

Over half of the responders passed commented on the advocacy service. Most felt that the service was 'very good', and 'works well'. One or two junior staff criticised some advocates for being too chatty towards patients and possibly wasting time, but this may reflect a certain lack of awareness that the advocate is not just an interpreter. They need to greet patients in a manner appropriate to their culture, build up a rapport with someone they have probably never met before and then start to translate tricky, often personal, medical problems. Other doctors recognised that family members frequently did not provide appropriate translations and tended to 'answer for [the patient] rather than interpret'. Interestingly one or two doctors picked up on a point highlighted in the patient interviews: 'Patients, particularly men, tend to want to imply they understand what has been said even when they haven't got a clue.'

Many doctors felt that the service needed expanding, 'more advocates', 'increased numbers', 'we need more of them', 'more please'. It was felt that the service had obviously become busier and busier and it was increasingly difficult to find an advocate when one was needed, especially in an emergency. This was reflected in the range of responses to Question 5. 'A more proactive than reactive service', 'major problem is access'; 'more availability and accessibility'. The fact that the Barts and The London NHS Trust operates over five sites, with the main advocacy service stationed on one site also caused comment. There was a call for a dedicated Bengali advocate to be present throughout the day on each of the two busiest sites. This would avoid one having to rush backwards and forwards between them. A 9 am to 5 pm service Monday to Friday was also felt to be inadequate. The issue of 24 hour availability was particularity pertinent to those working in the Accident and

Emergency department and those with on-call commitments in acute specialties. Patients don't just get sick during 'normal' working hours. It is often 'out of hours' when friends and family are less likely to be in attendance, that a translating service is most needed. 'Advocates are most needed in acute settings' was one comment, at a time when communication about vital treatment may be crucial. It was suggested that an 'on-call' service for out of hours needed to be arranged, 'access to out of hours help'.

During this study, it also became clear that there was an inequality across the medical and surgical specialties throughout the Trust. The main advocacy service is available on a hospital-wide basis and funded centrally by the Trust. However, various departments and directorates also employ other 'advocates,' 'interpreters' or 'Linkworkers', mostly paid for by their own funds. In at least one case, an interpreter from the community accompanied a community nurse to an outpatient clinic, thus providing the doctors there with a translating service. Another department has a dedicated Linkworker in their specialty. She had been trained for six months in the subject, and although not nursing or medically trained, fulfilled an invaluable role within the department. She ran her own clinics and advised patients on their continued care and monitored their progress and treatment regimes. Although she was not in a position to change their prescriptions, she was often seen as a first port of call when they had problems because she was fluent in their language, and understood their cultural beliefs in relation to the disease and Western methods of treatment.

Inequalities in provision are often born from financial inconsistencies and priorities, but lead to a lack of consistency of patient care. Less regulation of those who are employed as interpreters or advocates and less clarity in their role for those employed outside the main hospital service may also result in uneven training. Some consultants reflected on their good fortune at having a dedicated advocate in their department and the benefits it produced. Others felt that 'larger directorates should have dedicated advocates', this being especially true of both general medicine and surgery which both have a large throughput of patients, particularly on the acute side. A further problem for medical staff was the difficulty with uncommon languages. Some doctors requested an increase in the range of language skills. It would not be feasible or financially viable to employ advocates in every language, but it was felt that there needed to be more availability and access to other services such as Language Line. However this is an expensive service and, not surprisingly, is not obtainable unchecked. One solution is that the current advocacy manager could monitor calls for telephone services during office hours and the duty nursing sister out of hours.

A few final points that doctors made are worth mentioning. Many hospital staff expressed the wish to take language training in Sylheti. No one would really expect to become fluent enough to take a medical history or take the place of an advocate, but it could certainly help with seemingly mundane tasks on the ward or simple instructions or directions in outpatients. Most important of all it would help to put patients at ease, knowing that staff are at least making the effort and trying to provide a more acceptable service.

Conclusion

Communication between patients and health care professionals is the corner stone of quality medical care. Interpretation services are essential in hospitals which serve large populations of non-English speaking patients. As Woloshin et al. pointed out in their paper on language barriers in medicine, 'It is a prerequisite to ensure that persons with limited English proficiency get the services they need and only the services they need'.[20] In other words, it can be argued that it is false economy not to finance adequate translating services when a vast amount of time and resources may be wasted on missed or unnecessary investigations and appointments which result from poor communication. The Health Advocacy service that is described here certainly begins to fulfil this requirement, and is well supported by the advocates themselves, patients and medical staff. Like many services in the NHS of the 1990s, it has limited funding with its personnel stretching themselves to provide an effective service, often unable to cover all the requests that it receives for assistance. The advocates are highly motivated. They not only aim to translate the verbal needs of both patient and doctor, but frequently cross the cultural divide between their own ethnic backgrounds and western medicine. It is not an easy task; having acquired a good grounding of the range of Western medical services available through their work in the hospital and the community, they often experience the frustration of trying to convince patients, frightened by the unfamiliar, to undergo complex technological investigations and treatment. Kaufert and Putsch, in a recent paper on the ethical dilemmas confronting interpreters in health care settings, argued that it can often be impossible for interpreters to take a neutral role in health care proceedings.[21] This extends the ethical and moral difficulties for advocates employed to aid the patients, but familiar with the risks and benefits of the British health care system. After all, they are not medically trained, but attend to negotiate optimal care for the patient. Conversely, medical staff are often ignorant of different cultural health care beliefs and customs and appear unwilling to negotiate a common ground in complex situations. Doctors can project a 'take it or leave it' approach or 'the doctor is always right' attitude. This must be enormously frustrating for the well-informed health advocate who is well placed to help rectify the situation.

Patients undoubtedly perceive the need for adequate translating services. Unfortunately, those most at need may not always be aware of its availability. This could be helped by making medical and clerical staff more appreciative of the necessity for advocates. Simple schemes could certainly improve matters. One would be to make sure that all patients new to the hospital were assessed for their language needs. This would not only set up a data base of actual linguistic requirements within the whole institution, but patients' appointment cards could be marked with special stickers to alert staff at subsequent hospital visits to the patient's needs. It has also been suggested that the advocacy service should be advertised in local ethnic newspapers and on Asian and other cultural radio shows, such as Spectrum and Sunrise Radio.

Doctors, conscious of the importance of communication skills, are very supportive of health advocates and wish to see the service expanded. However, some, particularly junior staff, may initially lack insight into obtaining the best from the cultural as well as linguistic skills of health advocates. Certainly, such information should be part of hospital staff induction programmes. Medical student teaching now includes modules on cultural health care beliefs and these will hopefully include information on cross-cultural communication skills.

An American physician commented some years ago, 'What the scalpel is to the surgeon, words are to the clinician ... the conversation between doctor and patient is the heart of the practice of medicine'.[22] In circumstances where there is not a common language between health carer and patient, one could contest that a skilled interpreter is the doctor's guiding arm. The place of Health Advocates in our health care system is crucial for as long as there are patients to serve. We must support and encourage their training and development, and promote their appropriate utilisation within our hospitals, working as a team to promote patient care. Only then can we provide an equitable and efficient service to all.

Notes

Acknowledgement: my personal thanks to all the Health Advocates, patients and doctors for their time and patience in answering my questions; to Nasima for her translating and cultural education; and special thanks to Professor Sheila Hillier, Dr John Moore-Gillon and Dr M. Geraint Morris for their advice and encouragement in the writing of this paper.

1   L. Haffner, 'Translating is not enough – interpreting in a medical setting', *Western Journal of Medicine*, 1992, 157, pp. 255–9.
2   L. Chiu, *Advocacy; the Leeds experience*, Community Dental Health, 8, 1991, pp. 253–6 and M. Phelan and S. Parkman, 'Work with an Interpreter', *British Medical Journal*, 311, 1995, pp. 555–7.
3   See for example K. Gardner, *Global Migrants, Local Lives*, Oxford, OUP, 1995.
4   H. Rehman, and E. Walker, 'Researching Black And Minority Ethnic Groups', *Health Education Journal*, 54, 1995, pp. 489–500 and S. Woloshin, N.A. Bickell, L.M. Schwartz et al., 'Language Barriers In Medicine In The United States', *Journal of the American Medican Association (JAMA)*, 273 (9), 1995, pp. 724–8 and comments in *JAMA*, 274 (9), pp. 683–4.
5   Rehman and Walker, op. cit.
6   Audit Commission, *What Seems To Be The Matter: Communication Between Hospitals And Patients*, London, HMSO, 1993.
7   Woloshin, Bickell, Schwartz et al., op. cit. and S.A. Williams, J.H. Godson and I.A. Ahmed, 'Dentists Perceptions of Difficulties Encountered in Providing Dental Care for British Asians', *Community Dental Health*, 12, 1995, pp. 30–4.
8   J. Hennings, J. Williams and B.N. Haque, 'Exploring the Health Needs of Bangladeshi Women: A Case Study in Using Qualitative Research Methods', *Health Education Journal*, 55, 1996, pp. 11–23.
9   Hennings, Williams and Haque, op. cit. and J.M. Kaufert and R.W. Putsch, 'Communication through Interpreters in Healthcare: Ethical Dilemmas Arising from Differences in Class, Culture, Language and Power', *Journal of Clincal Ethics*, 8 (1), 1997, pp. 71–87.
10   Woloshin, Bickell, Schwartz et al., op. cit. and Kaufert and Putsch, op. cit.
11   P. Leman, ' Interpreter Use in an Inner City Accident and Emergency Depart', *Journal of Accident and Emergency Medicine*, 14, 1997, pp. 98–100.
12   Woloshin, Bickell, Schwartz et al., op. cit. and B. Jacobs, L. Kroll, T. Green and J. David, 'the Hazards of Using a Child as an Interpreter', *Journal of the Royal Society of Medicine*, 88, 1996, p. 474.
13   P. Leman, op. cit.
14   J. Shaw, M.P. Hemming, J.D. Hobos et al., 'Comprehension of therapy by non-English Speaking Hospital Patients', *Medical Journal of Australia*, 2, 1977, pp. 423–7.
15   J.C. Hornberger, C.D. Gibson, W. Wood et al., 'Eliminating Language Barriers for non-English Speaking Patients, *Medical Care*, 34 (8), 1996, pp. 845–56.
16   Ibid.
17   The dialect for the majority of Bangladeshis living in Tower Hamlets is Sylheti, the written and official language of Bangladesh is Bengali. For more on the language issues surrounding Bangladeshis in London see A.J. Kershen, this volume.
18   See Kershen, below.

19 The interviews with the health advocates took place during July, August and September 1998 at the Royal London Hospital.
20 Woloshin, Bickell, Schwartz et al., op. cit.
21 Kuufert and Putsch, op. cit.
22 Woloshin, Bickell, Schwartz et al., op. cit.

6 Becoming a Diaspora: the Welsh Experience from Beulah Land to Cyber-Cymru

WAYNE PARSONS

Introduction

The issue of what kinds and types of migrations may be said to actually constitute a 'diaspora', is deeply problematic. Some groups, such as the Jewish people, are viewed in diasporic terms, others, such as British migrants, are not. Only time will tell if a migratory experience is to be understood as a diaspora. As Chaliand and Rageau point out:

> The history of the last few centuries is full of examples of groups which, having partly emigrated, have blended into a different set of people. Thus Poles and Italians have assimilated into the population of France, the leading host nation on the European continent. In the United States, the white minorities (over 35 million immigrants between 1850 and 1914) have almost blended into the American nation. The future will determine whether such groups that are today dispersed will be able or want to form diasporas. The desire to endure as an exiled or transplanted and dispersed group is achieved through a Network of associations and communications. These Networks ensure dynamism and fluidity; they are local but at the same time cross the boundaries of states.[1]

This desire to endure, it would seem, is absolutely central to the notion of diaspora. Diasporas involve the notion that a group is dispersed, but not dissolved. They may, as in the case of many white migrants to the USA, have 'blended' into the fluidity of Americanness, but they still retain a sense of being distinct and connected. This is achieved through the creation of modes of communication which can serve to facilitate and give expression to their identity. Diasporas in this sense involve the idea that migratory groups develop ways of aggregating and connecting to compensate for the centrifugal forces of dispersion and assimilation. Diasporas are about a two-way traffic in people, images, and myths. There is the movement of people with their hopes and dreams to the new land, and the idea of the old country which is constructed by the settlers and their descendants. The artist M.C. Escher gives us a visual metaphor for this process in his famous picture ('Drawing Hands', 1948) of one hand drawing another.[2] Diasporas similarly are about a kind of self-referencing. Diasporas are the outcome of a mutual authoring. The production of the diasporic experience is, therefore, an ongoing process: the end is always in the beginning. By countless Babylonian rivers many Zions have been remembered. Those who have migrated enact and re-enact who they are by reference to where they have come from: and for those who remain, the nation in distant lands form an integral part of their history and their attempt to make sense of who they are. Diasporas are never straight lines, as many maps show them to be, so much as continuous loops of meaning. A diaspora consequently is not an event so much as a process: diasporas are always becoming. The sense of being a diaspora, therefore, is not about charting the movement of a group in the past, so much as how a group continuously seeks to invent itself. Diasporas are the stories migrant groups construct in order to endure and cohere. When defining a diaspora size matters. There are obvious reasons for this: the larger the migrant group in a given country the more likely it is that they will build the kind of network of relationships and institutions necessary for it to retain a sense of identity. A relatively small number of white migrants to the USA, therefore, such as the Welsh, are not generally perceived to form a diaspora, whereas the Irish, by virtue of their numbers and history of long-term migration to America, are so classified.[3] However, if we see the issue of diasporas in terms of the process whereby a group seeks to endure, then the experience of the Welsh is an important case. If a highly assimilated people such as the Welsh have, despite all the odds, retained and renewed a sense of group identity, then it may be that the diasporic experience is more far universal than has been generally accepted.

The Welsh were amongst the earliest settlers in America and helped in no small way in the founding of the republic. Thomas Jefferson and a good many other signatories of the Declaration of Independence were of Welsh decent. Five of six first presidents of the USA were of Welsh origins. The descendants of the Edwards family from Pontypridd still maintain a legal claim on the Island of Manhattan. A string of American universities have Welshmen as their founding fathers: including Yale, Brown, Johns Hopkins, Brynmawr and William and Mary. The list of Welsh-Americans covers just about every aspect of American life, from Harriet Beecher Stowe to D.W. Griffith, and from Daniel Boone to Frank Lloyd-Wright and Mrs Hillary Clinton. Indeed the list of prominent Welsh-Americans is as impressive as any other migrant groups, if not all the more remarkable because of the relatively small size of the Welsh-American population. In turn, the Welsh experience of America was a vital part of the construction of Wales itself. Indeed, Wales, it might be said, is imagined by the Missouri rivers a long time before it is invented on the banks of the Taff. Welsh Nationalism first came out of Cincinnatti, rather than Cardiff. The Welsh, as we shall see, actually travelled to the Americas, to the New World, to find the 'old land' of their fathers. The story of Wales in America (North and South) is a story of failed experiments in trying to build a new Wales as far away from England as possible. On the face of it the integration of the Welsh into American culture and society is a case study in the experience of the great melting pot. The Welsh simply faded into America. However, as Chaliand and Rageau argue, diasporas are about communications and how they facilitate the endurance of a collective identity. As we shall see, with the development of computer aided communications, Welsh-Americans have been making growing use of the Internet to renew their sense of becoming a diasporic community. The Net is evidently facilitating the development of 'a Network of associations and communications' which 'are local but at the same time cross the boundaries of states'. Welsh-Americans are not on their own in this regard. The briefest of Net searches on the World Wide Web reveals a rapidly growing use of the new communications technology amongst diasporic groups in the USA and elsewhere.[4] However, given the nature of the Welsh experience in America, the use of the Net to strengthen and renew networks of relationships both with Wales and within the Welsh-American community itself is of immense significance for our understanding of how a diasporic identity will be 'reimagined' in the twenty-first century.

The Americas and the Quest for Wales

The Welsh experience of migration is, as with many other peoples, closely tied up with the construction of their identity. Four kinds of migration were to play a part in the process of making Welsh identity.

The first was internal. Wales, unlike Ireland and Scotland was not to experience outward migration on the scale of the other Celtic countries. On the contrary, during the industrial revolution Wales was a focus of considerable immigration from England and Ireland in particular. During the greater part of the nineteenth century Wales was more of an importer of people, than an exporter. This is not to say that the Welsh did not migrate to England and overseas, but that the scale of this migration was far less significant than the impact of inward immigration from other parts of Britain and Ireland and the drift of the population from the North to the South. This produced cleavages as between agrarian and industrial ways of life but also as between the anglicised South and the Welsh speaking North. These cleavages have remained a central part of the debate about what being Welsh means to this day. The second kind of migration was what we might term intellectual. With no major centres of population and with no universities or 'national institutions' the Welsh were (from 1536) inevitably forced to seek advancement in the cities and universities of England. Hence Welsh intellectual life was to take place outside Wales, and some of the most influential people and organisations that contributed to defining Wales as a nation lived, worked and/or were educated in London or Oxford rather than Cardiff or Caernarfon. The third kind of migration was economic: Welsh people emigrated to England, America and other parts of the British Empire. The numbers of Welsh people who migrated for economic reasons remained relatively small, however, until the interwar depression and the decline of the major extractive industries. Finally, Welsh migration also took the form of what might be termed utopian or nation-alistic migration. A number of attempts were made to find a place (as far away from England as possible) that would be more conducive to being Welsh.

America has an important part to play in all four of these forms of migration. Immigration and internal migration produced a Wales which was divided in terms of language and ways of life. South Wales became industrial and largely English speaking, whilst the North remained agricultural and Welsh speaking. Indeed, by 1921 Sir Alfred Zimmern could discern a distinctive 'American Wales' in contrast to 'Welsh' or 'English Wales'.[5] Later, in the 1960s, many were, like Saunders Lewis, to be critical of the all pervasive influence of American 'anti-culture' on Welsh identity.[6] However, the position of America in Welsh culture had not always been seen as a problem, so much as an opportunity. The Welsh, especially the London Welsh, had long had great sympathy with the cause of America. The American revolution met with considerable support from Welsh radicals and the experience of the republic served as a model and inspiration to those campaigning for political and religious freedom in Wales. The historian Gwyn Alf Williams has shown the vitally important place of American democracy in the development of the Welsh radical tradition.[7] Numerous Welsh intellectuals enthusiastically supported the American Revolution. One of the most important of these, for example, was Dr Richard Price, (1723–91) a friend of Benjamin Franklin. Price's *Observations on Civil Liberty* (1776) was an important theoretical statement in defence of the American revolution and was one of the earliest transatlantic best sellers. Indeed, such was his high regard that in 1778 he was invited by the US Congress to advise it on finances. He was awarded (along with George Washington) an LL.D. by Yale College in 1781. For Price and other radicals and religious dissenters America was indeed the land of democratic opportunity and religious freedom. America was also a land of economic opportunity. Like other migrants the Welsh were attracted to America for economic reasons. However, the numbers of economic migrants from Wales was significantly much lower than for other parts of Britain and Ireland (Table 6.1). Welsh migration was not very important numerically speaking (until 1875 they were grouped with the English) and was not continuous.

Table 6.1   British and Irish immigration to the USA[8]

	1890s	1900s	1910s	1920s	1930s	Total
Wales	10,557	17,464	13,107	13,012	735	54,875
England	216,726	388,017	249,944	157,420	21,756	1,033,863
Ireland	388,416	339,065	146,181	220,591	13,167	1,107,420
Scotland	44,188	120,469	78,357	159,781	6,887	409,682

Between 1890s and 1930s fewer than 55,000 Welsh immigrants settled in the USA, as compared with over a million Irish, around half a million Scots and over a million English. Where Welsh communities did exist, such as in Pennsylvania, and Ohio, there was little possibility of expansion and renewal. A good proportion of their number settled in the coal fields of Pennsylvania: towns such as Scranton and Wilkes-Barre and were quickly absorbed into the American way of life.[9] Not the least of the reasons for this was, of course, the fact that Welsh emigration to the USA was insignificant when compared to that of England, Ireland or Scotland. Ireland, for example 'exported' around 13 per cent of her population, in the 1880s Wales 'exported' less that 1 per cent (0.8) and this pattern was to persist through the nineteenth and early twentieth centuries. So, there were to be no big clusters of Welsh settlement: if Welsh migration had been on the kind of scale which took place in Ireland, it may well have been a different story.

Finally, America figures prominently in the story of Wales for utopian reasons: America was seen as the place where Welsh people could be free to build the kind of society which was impossible in Wales. This migration began in the seventeenth century with the departure of Quakers and Baptists for

Pennsylvania and Philadelphia following the restoration of the Crown in 1660. William Penn, the founder of the 'Holy experiment' originally promised the Welsh settlers that they could have their own separate colony, but this was not to be fulfilled. Later, in the eighteenth century, the idea of emigrating to America as a way of founding a new Wales was first suggested by William Jones (1726–95) who called upon his fellow 'Cambro-Britons' to seek freedom for their homeland by moving it to America. This was not a call to a diasporic exile, so much an exodus akin to the Israelites leaving Egypt. For Jones America was the new promised land where a Welsh democratic community could be built free from English oppression.[10]

Of course, some were to argue that the Welsh had discovered America in the first place, so it was the natural place to lead the tribe of Cymru – the Welsh for Wales. The tale of how Prince Madoc had found his way to America had been popularised since Elizabethan times, thanks in great part to the efforts of the notorious Dr John Dee. The myth has hung around ever since. In 1953 the Daughters of the American Revolution were to commemorate the Welsh achievement with a sign: 'In Memory of Prince Madoc who landed on the shores of Mobile Bay in 1170 and left behind, with the Indians, the Welsh language.' In the late eighteenth century the story of how the Welsh had discovered the New World long before the Spanish, gave rise to the claim that a long lost tribe of Welsh Indians had been discovered in Missouri. Thus began a strange episode in Welsh history as Welsh patriots set out to discover the lost Welsh tribe and search for a land where Wales could be rebuilt free from English domination. One explorer, John Evans, went in search of the legendary 'Mandan' Indians, the supposed descendants of Prince Madoc, whilst another, Morgan John Rhys, founded a Welsh settlement in Pennsylvania at a place called Beulah. In the period between 1796 and 1801, economic hardship drove many to seek out this new Kingdom of Wales. The inevitable failure of the project to create another Wales out of an old myth in the new world meant that, as Gwyn A. Williams argues in his fascinating account of *The Search for Beulah Land*:

> From the 1800s onwards, the settlements in Ohio, Pennsylvania and New York acted as foci for movements which soon transcended them. After the farmers and the artisans went the miners, steelworkers, tinplaters. Wilkes-Barre, Scranton, Youngstown, Pittsburgh, Edmonton, Calgary became household names in Wales ... But never again did this migration carry that powerful millenarian, national charge of the 1790s. Later movements were less ambitious, more careful and practical. They grew as Oneida county and Utica in New York grew, by gradual, piecemeal assimilation.[11]

Even so, the idea that Cymru/Wales had to relocate itself in America continued to inspire, despite the failures. Samuel Roberts (1800–85) campaigned for establishing a Welsh colony in America. Together with William Bebb he bought land in Tennessee and managed to get a few families to join them. However, by the late 1850s it became apparent that the scheme would not succeed, and like the other attempts, the dream of getting the Welsh to sail across the Atlantic to found a new Wales came to nought.

It was South America which was to become the focus of the next (and concluding) chapter in the story of Welsh utopian migration. A founding father of Welsh nationalism, Michael D. Jones (1822–98) came up with a scheme of establishing a new homeland (*gwladfa*) in Patagonia, Argentina, having concluded that the prospects for such a community would be unlikely to succeed in the USA. Eventually, in 1865, (he had originally put forward his plan in 1857) 163 emigrants sailed on the good ship *Mimosa* from Liverpool with their hopes of building a new Wales. What awaited them was a poor infertile land: as Michael D. Jones had never actually visited the place he could hardly have prepared them for the terrible hardships that were to come. But, survive they did and the numbers who joined Gwladfa slowly grew, but in the end, the Argentinian government, suspicious of British intentions (especially with regard to the Falkland Islands) put paid to the growth of the colony. And that was that. The plan to create a Welsh-speaking, God-fearing, democratic homeland failed. Gwladfa was a brave, if not downright foolhardy, attempt to create a diaspora: a Wales in exile. The dream of creating a place far away from England where Wales could become, was yet another failure to create a diaspora, even though the descendants of the would-be-disapora still retain ties to Wales, and Welsh is still spoken by a small, and declining band of Welsh-Argentinians. However, their failure was to serve the cause of Welsh nationalism in the twentieth century. Patagonia became a symbol of the struggle for Welsh identity, and in particular the Welsh language. In his BBC lecture given in 1962, *Tynged Yr Iaith/The Fate of The Language*, Saunders Lewis, called upon the Welsh to emulate the courage and heroism of those who sailed out on the *Mimosa*, in order to save the language for future generations. As Anne Knowles contends:

> Saunders Lewis's portrayal of emigration to Patagonia as a political act echoed the view of earlier Welsh leaders who had tried to cast emigration as an effort to preserve Welsh cultural identity. Their vision, however, did not reflect the opinions or motivations of most Welsh people, who saw emigration as one choice among many for improving their economic status. Thus, Welsh efforts to

politicize emigration repeatedly failed, and Welsh emigration neither became a source of inspiration for Welsh nationalism nor fostered a strong attachment to the Welsh homeland. This stands in marked contrast to the success of Irish nationalist leaders in promulgating a highly political and national interpretation of Irish emigration, encapsulated by the metaphor of exile.[12]

Thus whereas the Irish diaspora – *qua* forced exile – was central to defining Ireland and Irishness, Welsh emigration was seen as more the outcome of economic choices. In simple terms the Irish left because they had to, the Welsh left because they wanted to leave to find a better life. And, even when migration was utopian, the Welsh left Wales because they believed they could be more Welsh in America, than in Wales itself! In either case, economic or utopian, the net result was that migration did not result in the kind of ties and connections to the land of their fathers amongst the Welsh that the Irish were to feel towards exploited 'Mother Ireland'. 'What became of them?' asks Jan Morris in her book *The Matter of Wales*:

> We shall never know. They were doubtless assimilated in the end, for once they had got over their homesickness, abandoned their language, and perhaps blurred the edges of their idealism, Welsh immigrants generally became altogether American. They were seldom so assiduous as the Scots or the Irish in cherishing their ethnic image, and the several Welsh colonies soon faded into the American background, leaving only exotic place-names ... Many eminent Americans, all the same have liked to talk about their Welsh origins ... Governors, senators, generals, bankers, actors, musicians. All look back, if only from a comfortable distance, from Pentagon or Capital Hill, from Hollywood or Wall Street, to the distant hills and swart terrace towns that fostered them far away, in those 8,000 bumpy miles that hardly one of their fellow-countrymen in a thousand could place upon the *Reader's Digest Atlas*.[13]

The Welsh diaspora, it seemed, simply dissolved into America like sugar into a cup of coffee, or like butter in a melting bowl. The Welsh became apple pie Americans.

The Digital Diaspora: Towards Cyber-Cymru?

For those who advocated a utopian diaspora Wales always seemed to be an impossible proposition in Wales. Communications were all against it. The proximity of England meant that Wales, if it were to endure, had to find some remote place. This sense of the vulnerability of Wales to the forces of communications is reflected in E.G. Bowen's observation (in 1964):

> In the end it is the culture of Inner Wales that has given Wales its personality, its language, its religion and song. These survive into the modern epoch and represent the real Wales ... the continuation of Welsh life and culture in the inner zone depends to a very large extent on the ability of the mountains to defend the culture of the valleys facing west and north. We are, however, living in an age that can override geographical obstacles with ease. What was begun by the railways and carried forward by the trunk roads and the motor car, is completed with the coming of the radio and television. Geographical factors are losing their potency, for at the present time mountains, as such provide neither shelter nor protection.[14]

What William Jones, Morgan John Rhys and Michael D. Jones have in common with Bowen's twentieth century viewpoint is that they all articulate a view of 'real' Wales as an 'inner' zone' which has to be defended and almost hidden. Once it was the mountains, which served as the bastion against the erosion of the 'real' nation, but as Wales became subject to the shrinkage of space and time, so a diaspora seemed even by the late eighteenth century the only alternative. The progress of communications has meant that the issue of a small nation maintaining its identity has remained ever more problematic. However, the development of the Internet is suggestive of a new phase in the relationship between communications and the question of identity. What Bowen termed the demise in geographical potency was for so long seen as serving to erode the idea of Wales and Welsh identity, but the Net offers the prospect of the development of a new kind of 'imagined community'. This community may not be 'real' in the sense which Bowen talked about in the 1960s, so much as 'virtual': a Wales which may be built not in the frontiers of the new world, but the frontiers of cyberspace.

The idea of cyberspace was first coined in 1984 by the writer William Gibson in his novel *Neuromancer*. He describes cyberspace as:

> a consensual hallucination experienced daily by billions of legitimate operators, in every nation, by children being taught mathematical concepts ... A graphic representation of data abstracted from the banks of every computer in the human system. Unthinkable complexity. Lines of light ranged in the non space of the mind, clusters and constellations of data.[15]

Since the development of the Internet and the World Wide Web, other definitions have built upon Gibson's imagination. One of the more comprehensive is that advanced by David Whittle:

> n.1 A fictional, psychic space where minds fuse in a trance like 'consensual hallucination'. [Gibson, 1984] 2 The conceptual world of interactions between individuals and their intellectual creations and everything associated with such Networks and interactions. 3 The state of mind shared by people communicating using digital representations of language and sensory experience who are separated by time and space but connected by Networks of physical access devices.[16]

For a community as 'integrated' as the Welsh in North America, the Internet has provided a way of creating new kinds of Networks to maintain a sense of identity and attachment to Wales. The Welsh in America are making increasing use of the Internet to promote existing organisations and institutions and to develop a Welsh-American community in 'cyberspace'. To what extent can we describe the Welsh-American diasporic experience in digital terms? How real is Cyber-Cymru? What are the implications of the emergence of what we might term WASs – Welsh-American Surfers – for the future of the Welsh diaspora?

To begin with, the idea of a 'consensual hallucination' is not without some resonance in Welsh history. Indeed, one of the makers of modern Wales, Iolo Morganwg (Edward Williams, 1747–1826) contributed much to the renaissance of Welsh identity whilst frequently as high as a kite on opium: his particular hallucinations on Welsh traditions did as much as anyone to help invent Wales! As a nation Wales has long been more virtual than real. It is only in recent decades, for example, that Wales has begun to build an institutional capacity which can serve to define a structure of Welsh government. The idea of Wales as a kind of 'consensual illusion' is not entirely inappropriate: it has long existed less as a distinct nation state, or place so much as a state of mind. As we have seen earlier, those who sought to remake Wales in America saw the spatial location of Wales as an insuperable obstacle to Welshness. Utopian migrants left Wales in order to become more Welsh. The Welsh diasporic experience was not, therefore, interpreted as an exile, but as a quest. The latest chapter in the story of this quest is, perhaps, taking place in cyberspace: the ultimate domain where the disassociation between the territory of Wales and being Welsh can be seen. A brief search through the Internet reveals a fascinating array of sites set up by Welsh-Americans. At the local, regional and national level these sites reveal a diaspora that is searching to find an identify itself and secure for Welsh-Americans a place on the wide spectrum of ethnic groups and communities. At the time of writing there are Internet sites for Welsh societies in, for example:

Arizona;
Baltimore;
Colorado;
Gulf Coast;
Iowa;
New York;
Nebraska;
Central Ohio;
Connecticut;
Greater Kansas City;
Bangor, Pennsylvania;
Victoria;
Northern California;
Delaware, Maryland and Virginia;
Philadelphia;
Puget Sound;
Poultney Area;
Albany NY;
Western New York (Rochester, Buffalo, etc.);
St Petersburg and Suncoast;
Wyoming Valley;
Georgia;
Carolinas;
Fredricksburg.

The New York Welsh Homepage,[17] for example, is 'dedicated to providing comprehensive coverage of the activities and organisations of the Welsh community in New York and its environs' aimed at those from Wales, of Welsh background or interested in 'all things Welsh'. It gives access to the newsletter of the Welsh Church of New York, Llais y Llan. Details of the social activities, such as the St David's Society Party, Noson Lawen, the Welsh Women's Club. In addition to traditional activities based around religious activities it also seeks to promote Wales in general.

The Welsh American Society of Northern California[18] aims to 'preserve' and 'nourish' the 'national heritage and culture of the Welsh people'. It provides information on events, electronic mailing lists, and local Welsh history in the Bay area. The Welsh Society of the Carolinas[19] sees itself as a 'resource' to 'explore, celebrate and share the many facets of Welsh and Celtic culture'. In common with many such societies the Carolinas site shows a commitment to organising events, 'representing Welsh culture and heritage at regional community festivals and international events' and 'researching and maintaining an archive of materials' relating to local Welsh history. 'Nowadays', the site notes 'the Welsh like their other Celtic brethren ... gather to preserve their culture' so as to 'pass on the best of the old world and the new to our descendants'. The quality of the different sites vary, but all demonstrate an enthusiasm with publicising the contribution which their Welsh ancestors played in the histories of their localities and regions. At the same time, the sites also show an awareness of how their local experience is connected to other parts of America, and are keen to provide links to sites in Wales and the USA.

At the national level, for example, there are sites for :

Cymdeithas Madog (Welsh Studies Institute of North America);
Madoc Center for Welsh Studies, University of Rio Grande;
Welsh Heritage Program – Green Mountain College;
North American Association for the Study of Welsh Culture and History (NAASWCH);
North American Welsh History Links;
The National Welsh-American Foundation;
Twm Sion Cati – Welsh- American Legal Defence, Education and Development Fund;
Welsh-American Genealogical Society (WAGS);
Welsh Associated Youth of US and Canada (WAY);
Welsh National Gymanfa Ganu Association;
Welsh North American Chamber of Commerce;
Women's Welsh Clubs of America.

The Welsh National Gymanfa Ganu Association[20] aims 'to preserve, develop and promote our Welsh religious and cultural heritage, including, but not limited to the Gymanfa Ganu, and our religious and cultural traditions and to do all things necessary and proper to accomplish and enhance the same'. (A *Gymanfa Ganu* is a festival of Welsh hymn singing.) The first national meeting took place in a field on Goat Island in the middle of the Niagara river in 1929. From this event an organisation grew: by 2000 there will have been some 69 such festivals. The Board of the WNGGA is described as the 'unifying force that provides the institutional memory, selects sites for the annual gymanfaoedd, provides general guidance and supervision and assures that desired cultural and religious standards are maintained'. The Board arranges for the publication of music to be used at national, regional and local festivals. The WNGGA sees itself as the 'pre-eminent expression of Welsh culture, heritage, and the Welsh language in the United States and Canada'. The website provides membership information, an account of the historical background, information on publications, organisational structure and events. All importantly it provides links to other relevant sites and affiliated organisations.

National Welsh-American Foundation,[21] was founded in 1980 to 'provide a link between Welsh-Americans in the USA and the Welsh in the homeland who share a common interest in their culture, heritage and the promotion of the Welsh language'. Amongst their goals are: 'promoting and sharing the history of Welsh-Americans'; and 'assuring a unified and effective voice for Welsh-Americans in all aspects of American society.' To this end it recognises and sponsors a range of projects in Wales and America, including Welsh language education and 'the installation of historical markers to honour Welsh-Americans or men and women of Welsh descent or events of historical significance to the Welsh-American community'. It publishes a quarterly journal, *The Eagle and the Dragon*, and supports the publication /reprinting of books on the Welsh American experience.

The North American Association for the Study of Welsh Culture and History[22] was founded in 1995 and represents a major step forward in the development of Welsh studies in America. NAASWCH describes itself as

> a multidisciplinary association of scholars, teachers, and individuals based in North America and dedicated to advancing scholarship on Welsh studies, supporting the study of Welsh-American culture and fostering international bonds between scholars and the Welsh-American community.

It has held biennial conferences covering a wide range of topics exploring Welsh history, culture and society as well as the issue of Welsh-American identity. The website does an important job in providing a Network for scholars in North America, and many other countries interested in Wales. As John Davies noted in his inaugural address (in 1995), the establishment of NASSWCH suggests 'a confidence and a coming-of-age which is encouraging and invigorating', and starts to redress the imbalance in Celtic studies in the US which has (inevitably) been dominated by concern with Ireland and the Irish.[23] Such websites play an important role in the development of global academic contacts and promotes a wider awareness of the growing interest in the study of Wales and the Welsh migratory experience. Cymdeithas Madog,[24] is the Welsh Studies Institute of North America dedicated to 'helping North Americans learn, use and enjoy the Welsh language'. As they point out, it takes its name from Madog ab Owain Gwynedd: a 'fitting symbol of the links which Cymdeithas Madog maintains between Wales and the New World'. The site enables visitors to access Internet links for Welsh learners, find out about the range of different language courses which they run, as well as information on books, tapes and video. The institute also publishes (in pdf format) a newsletter, *Cyfeillion Madog*, aimed at language learners.

The provision of Welsh language education on the Web is impressive. In addition to the work of Cymdeithas Madog,[25] Brown University runs an on-line interactive course on the Welsh language.[26] There is Cymraeg-L,[27] an email discussion list for students of the language whose aim is to 'provide a place for Welsh language students to learn, encourage each other, ask questions, share knowledge, practice and have fun'. There is also Acean,[28] set up in 1989 by S4C in Wales (and now a limited company in its own right) which runs Web services for language learners. The Internet, through local and national sites, also provides links to Welsh language groups all over North America, from Arizona, British Columbia, to Washington and Wisconsin. There is a magazine for Welsh learners, *Lingo*, and for the most advanced, the University of Wales dictionary of the Welsh language. The way in which Welsh is being used on the Net is significant. Pamela Petro, in her book *Travels in an Old Tongue*, for example, concludes her journey around the Welsh-speaking world with the observation that:

> Languages are not territorial creatures, but the people who speak them are, and we're the ones who try to bind speech and place together. In my own country there's a battle brewing over the pre-eminence of English. Many American's believe that their national identity is inseparable from the English language, and have begun an 'English Only' campaign to combat the rise of other tongues ... By this argument the entity called the United States is dependent on English, but English ... is surely not dependent on the United States. Cymru is something that happens whenever people speak Welsh and occasionally when they don't ... Cymru is a place waiting to be spoken into life at any moment anywhere around the globe ... [29]

Welsh on the Net in Petro's sense is a 'place' where Wales can happen. It provides a domain where speech and place are separated and Wales 'happens' by being 'spoken into life'. For the growing numbers of Welsh learners in

America the Net provides an opportunity to learn, and use the language in ways that would have been unimaginable before the development of computer mediated communications.

In addition to these local sites there are three sites for newspapers and newsletters, *Ninnau*,[30] *Y Drych*[31] and *The Dragon and the Eagle/Yr Eryr a'r Ddraig*. *Ninnau* aims to:

> maintain the North Welsh-American informed of local and general news and events of interest; publicise individual contributions to community life; provide a forum for discussion and individual expression; educate Welsh people in their traditions; serve as a link between North Welsh-American people and organisations; serve as a link between the North Welsh-American People and Wales.

Y Drych (*The Mirror*) is the oldest Welsh newspaper in America and provides a range of news from Wales, and the Welsh-American community. Their site is used to promote sales and a point of contact for its readers as well as links to other pages and sites concerned with Wales and Welsh culture.

These local, regional and national sites have extensive links to sites in Wales and elsewhere. Including in these are news services in Wales, Newyddion, S4C,[32] and Total Wales[33] and newspapers and magazines such as the *South Wales Evening Post*,[34] *LOL*[35] and *Y Cymro*.[36] Users can also access libraries in Wales, especially the National Library[37] in Aberystwyth, cultural sites such as museums, galleries and publishers. News of political life can be accessed through sites for the main political parties in Wales and the National Assembly.[38]

To facilitate contact with Wales Undeb Cymru a'r Byd/Wales International[39] (founded in 1948 as Undeb y Cymru ar Wasgar/Union of Welsh People in Dispersion) has a website which aims to

> Forge close and abiding world wide links between Wales and the people of Welsh descent and friends of the language, culture and traditions of Wales; to promote Wales and its culture outside Wales and to encourage and assist in the establishment of Welsh societies wherever possible.

The union's magazine, *Yr Enfys*, is now distributed in over 50 countries. Wales International also supports email and provides information and events. In common with other Welsh sites, it has a discussion forum (through Deja.com). And, of course, if a WAS wants to visit Wales, there are sites, such as that provided by the Wales Tourist Board[40] which can help them plan a vacation.

But, if a vacation is a problem, it is possible for take a look at Wales through the sites of CADW: Welsh Historic Monuments;[41] find out about Welsh choirs, castles, pop music, opera and theatre, sport and other activities from golf to Welsh wine. The WAS can visit a bed-and-breakfast in Betws-y-Coed, have a look around St Davids, explore Welsh history, or the Dylan Thomas Centre[42] in Swansea, and music, and with just a click of a mouse take a look around Wrexham or virtual Llanelli, Carmarthen, or roam the streets of Celtic Town: 'An info-tainment Internet arts community for the Celtic peoples of Wales, Scotland and Ireland.'[43] An important part of this virtual experience is the opportunity to participate in chat rooms and forums in English and Welsh. These enable WASs to become involved in talking about Welsh issues, or just 'listen' in to the exchange of ideas, opinions, abuse, information and gossip in the various villages of Cyber-Cymru. The WAS can get to know about the ins and outs of Welsh rugby through mailto:Gwl@d.wales.com and Gwl@d.wales.com,[44] or seek information or news through Total Wales, and get to know the Cardiff club scene at Virtual Cardiff,[45] or find out more about the Welsh language at the Welsh Language Board.[46]

Welsh-American sites also provide links to a fast growing range of other WWW resources, such as World Wide Wales,[47] Virtual Wales[48] and West and Wales Web,[49] Wales and Things Welsh, [50] Network Wales,[51] Wales Connect,[52] The Land of my Fathers,[53] Everything Celtic on the Web,[54] Cilmeri.com[55] and Welshworld.[56] Indeed, such has been the growth in Welsh websites that a site run by *Ninnau*, Cyber-Cymru[57] which, in addition to providing links to over 100 sites in 16 different categories and a bookstore, also reviews Welsh sites giving awards: Wales Best for English language sites; Gorau Cymru for those that use Welsh as one of the main languages and the Gold Dragon/ Ddraig Euraidd for those which 'are especially good and are of great service to the Welsh Internet Community'. To participate sites have to meet four conditions: they must contain Welsh material; be of service to the Welsh community; be of wide interest; and use Welsh as one of the main languages, if they are to qualify in the Gorau Cymru category. Again, indicative of the growing interest in Cyber-Cymru is Nawr.com, founded in 1998 as the 'North American Welsh Room'.[58] Nawr.com provides a host space for promoting Welsh language and culture. Nawr hopes to 'provide a congenial center for Welsh culture in North America'. For a modest fee it will host, design and create a site for Welsh-American societies and organisations.

As Wales itself becomes more and more accessible via the Net, then we can envisage a time in the not too distant future when WASs will be able to explore every aspect of life in Wales – from the smallest village to government and business organisations and forge new economic, social, artistic, political links and relationships. At the same time, of course, the opportunities afforded by e-business and e-government will also have a considerable impact on the kind of image which Wales projects to the wider world and the ability of Wales to exploit the potential of the information society. This was recognised by the Welsh Office in 1996[59] and is the major concern of the Wales Information Society (WIS),[60] whose mission is 'to build consensus to generate the determination to enable Wales to obtain real economic and social benefit from the information society'. The success of this mission will involve the creation of, quite literally, a Welsh information society: an infrastructure of computer mediated communications

Chorus: 'Home, Home on the Page ... '

In addition to the sites for local, regional and national organisations, there are countless 'personal' home pages which provide an insight into how people are choosing to use the Internet to explore their own Welshness and provide information and contacts for others similarly surfing the Net for reasons of personal development and exploration. Conservative estimates show that some 40 million people are now on-line. In America this means over six million computers are connected to the Internet and that some 600,000 Americans have their own personal home page, and the figure has continued to grow apace.[61] These personal home pages may be statements of family history, 'photos of holidays in Wales or personal experiences and thoughts on what being a Welsh-American means to them. Personal home pages are precisely the kind of sites which *Ninnau*'s Cyber-Cymru excludes from the award scheme, but in many ways, because they are so personal and yet so very public, they constitute fascinating examples of how many Americans want to use the Internet to reinvent themselves as 'Welsh-Americans' and thereby get recognition for the role their ancestors played in the creation of America. WASs are, it seems, fighting back against the WASP categorisation and are seeking to establish themselves as individuals with a distinctive Celtic ancestry. Karl Welcher's site, for example, leads a surfer through a journey along a 'path of healthy pride in who you are'.[62] He tells us that, although born and raised with the 'great melting pot' idea of America, he has 'come to reject the concept of [his] family history is only 150 years old and to replace it with an understanding that [his] family's history reaches back into the ancient Celtic peoples'. Karl Welcher's personal journey, which uses many links to other sites, is both an exploration of his own identity, but also a sharing of a collective history. 'If', he writes, 'you are truly to feel the essence of CYMRU; you must also explore and discover the culture of our people. Visit our museums and experience them'. Push this button and go to an Eisteddfod, another and 'visit' the National Museum of Wales, another to have a musical experience.

If these personal home pages with personal histories, Welsh holiday snaps, Welsh recipes, names, jokes, family history, takes on local history, songs or whatever, seem at first rather unimportant, it is well to think about why people find the need to create such home pages. The Internet gives people the opportunity to write a new self: to define, announce, celebrate and reconstruct who they think they are, where they have come from and what they want to be. Home pages are, to parody the immortal lines of Dr Brewster Higley, the new ranges where the skies are not cloudy all day, and where 'seldom is heard a discouraging word'. If the age of mass communications and transportation tended to swamp and dissolve Welshness, the Internet is helping many Americans to rediscover and reconnect with their ancestral spirits. Cyberspace is a place of affirmation: a wide open untamed domain where virtual buffaloes roam. It is a place where the American dream can play and where a young man (and most users of the Internet are young men) can put down roots and raise a barn. Hence, one of the most popular types of site are those concerned with genealogy, such as WAGS: Welsh-American Genealogical Society.[63] By setting up a home page on the Net which tells the story of their own quest for identity, WASs are weaving countless threads of personal exploration into a new kind of collective fabric. In the nineteenth century, when old Doc. Higley wrote 'Home on the Range', young men went West to build a new life: in the twenty-first they may well be encouraged by the likes of wild Bill Gates to 'Go Web'.

Personal homepages are not simply being used to publish holiday photos from Caerfilli or Llanfairpwllgwyngyllgogerychwyrndrobwllllantysiliogogogoch (the latter being the longest URL on the Web!). They are places where Welsh-Americans construct a personal and public identity. As Daniel Chandler observes:

> Websites are frequently labelled as 'under construction'. However, the construction involved is more than the construction of their makers' identities. Creating such pages offers competent web authors an unrivalled opportunity for self-presentation in relations to any dimension of social and personal identity to which one chooses to allude. Such a virtual environment offers a unique context in which one may experiment with shaping one's own identity.[64]

Personal home pages offer their authors a way of managing the problem of identity: when Welsh-Americans use the web to experiment with their Americaness they are in a sense acknowledging the 'nested' nature of who they are. The 'links' are points of reference in their journey to construct and present themselves: they are 'clues' in the conundrum of who they (we) are. The exploration of self becomes a very public process to which all are invited. Through web authoring a 'community' identity – in this case Welsh – is forged. The links are a vital dimension of this activity, as it demonstrates that the author is 'not alone': there are other Welsh-Americans 'out there' on the wide expanse of the cyber-prairie. However, the Wales that they are making on the information superhighway may have little – if anything – to do with the reality of modern Wales. Home pages oftentimes reveal a curious preoccupation with a imagined land half buried in the mists of a Celtic twilight rather than the real lives lived by people in Merthyr or Llanrumney, Wrexham or Port Talbot. But then, in real Wales, the skies are cloudy most of the day and buffaloes hardly ever roam.

Surfing the Problem of Identity

The Internet offers new possibilities for diasporas, providing as it does a mode of communication which transcends particular times, places and locations. Cyber-Cymru is being formed out of the multiplicity of links and networks, which are both local and global, crossing as they do the boundaries of nations and time-zones. Cyberspace constitutes an entirely different way in which to experience and transact an identity such as being a Welsh-American. From being a relatively small, dispersed, fragmented and highly assimilated group, Welsh-Americans are, it seems, in the process of creating a different kind of space where being Welsh or experiencing Wales virtually happens. Whereas in the past Welsh Identity was sustained in the context of local contacts and national organisations, the Internet offers the prospect of encountering and authoring Wales (and being Welsh) on an entirely different level. It allows different Welsh communities to learn about each other; it enables networks of relationships to form, information to flow, and renewed sense of belonging to a highly dispersed and dissolved group. Through the Net Americans can diasporically reinvent themselves. Tomorrow, who knows, other identities and personae can be explored. Wales becomes another kind of 'consensual hallucination' in Cyberia. The land of your fathers can be just the kind of place you want it to be. Tomorrow it might be the Polish or Greek or whatever part of you that is surfed. You make sense of your life by linking up with those with whom you have things in common: being a Welsh-American is but one part of the Network of connections which enable you to make sense of who you are. Identities are multiple, and surfing the Net is one of the ways in which we may seek to manage or create ourselves. As Sherry Turkle observes, such activity may: 'help us achieve a vision of a multiple but integrated identity whose flexibility, resilience, and capacity for joy comes from having access to our many selves.'[65] Then again, as she points out, such opportunities for multiple identity may create new kinds of identity crisis.

In the past the idea of a diaspora was located in specific spatial and temporal contexts: the experience of migratory populations in different countries and in different times. As we enter the new millennium the idea of diasporas may be transformed by the impact of electronic communications, just as in earlier centuries migratory patterns and experiences were shaped by boats, trains and planes, along seaways, railways, airways and road ways. New modes of communication, point towards different ways in which people may choose to make sense of, and construct, their identities and experiences as they travel down the 'information superhighway'. There is a growing literature concerned with 'civic networking'[66] as information technology begins to impact on forms of political and civic participation. Perhaps we should also be concerned with the issue of 'cultural networking'. In the emergence of Cyber-Cymru are we witnessing the shape of things to come, whereby diasporic communities seek to reconstruct themselves by the means of a powerful networking process which facilitates both local and global communications as well as personal construction of identity? Cultural nets such as those we find amongst the Welsh-American offer much to those small minority groups who are not big enough to enjoy the benefits of being 'really' connected, but can become more effective when virtually connected. Welsh communities which were thinning in real institutional, physical and spatial terms can thicken and become more 'enduring' as, 'social aggregations that emerge from the [Internet] when enough people carry on those public discussions long enough, with sufficient human feeling to form webs of personal relationship in cyberspace'.[67] That is, as virtual diasporic communities.

Digital diasporas may consequently provide multiple foci or sites where identity in the twenty-first century are enacted and transacted and lead to a new kind of cultural topography. In cyberspace you can pick and mix from a complex array of identities: strengthen ties and discover new contacts. The Internet can, therefore, as Schmidtke notes, facilitate the 'formation of a common sense of belonging and collective identity'.[68] Interaction in virtual space can both serve to promote face-to-face local contact, as is the case in so many Welsh-American sites, but also give rise to new forms of collective transnational networks of relationships. The potential for the Net to generate meetings and encounters in physical space is a vitally important dimension of cyberspace. The Net is often viewed as creating another kind of space which takes place on a computer screen, but it is also a powerful way for bringing people together in real time and real space. So many of the sites in Cyber-Cymru are linking people for the purposes of meeting-up at social, cultural, educational and other gatherings. A good illustration of this is the SWS site in New York. SWS (which stands for 'Social Welsh and Sexy' and means kiss in Welsh)[69] is a club based in London which opened a branch in New York in 1999. Members include many Welsh celebrities including Sian Phillips, Catherine Zeta Jones, Bryn Terfel, and Ioan Gruffydd. The club is indicative of a growing sense of confidence amongst Welsh people and those of Welsh descent. Its members, the New York site tells us, 'are people proud of their past but they are also proud of the present and passionate about the future'. The SWS website is certainly not about getting people together on the Net *per se*, but using it to get people together with a drink in their hand in a convivial place in New York. The point about conviviality comes across strongly in the Welsh North American Chamber of Commerce site.[70] Their first goal, for example is to 'promote a sense of fellowship and to create Networking opportunities within the USA and Canada among Welsh born business people and business people with an interest in Wales'. The website aims to 'promote a sense of fellowship and Networking opportunities between our members, when, for example, a member travels to another member's location'. The president of the organisation himself pledges to 'take any WNCCC who visits Miami to Joe's Stone Crabs on Miami Beach for lunch/ dinner!'

So although the Net is creating a new form of communication amongst the Welsh, it is also helping to develop old-fashioned face-to-face social interaction 'in real life' – or 'IRL' in cyber-speak. The Net is being used to disseminate real life information and publicity for various kinds of real events. As a community noticeboard, therefore, the Net is not replacing social interaction, so much as supplementing the efforts of groups to get their news and messages across to their members and the wider community. Indeed, the Net might best be viewed as the 'campfire' around which the Celtic tribes of the twenty-first century will gather to exchange stories and discuss things. As Whittle observes:

> Cyberspace represents a revolutionary advance in our means of interactive socialization. Never before has it been possible for groups to assemble, co-

operate, explore, organize, discuss, transform, synergize, and progress around such a large campfire, with so little interference from the barriers of time and space.[71]

Thus the Net, far from making for a nerdish world where we are all relating to one another through a computer, may well facilitate greater social interaction amongst groups such as the Welsh in America who are relatively small in number and rather fragmented as a community. Virtual diasporas may, perhaps, lead on to a greater sense of being a real diaspora. Virtual campfires can lead to real social heat and energy. In the past new modes of communication and technology were so often destructive of community and a sense of shared identity. Might it be that the Net presages a more re-constructive phase in the history of communications? If so, then as may be seen in the case of the Welsh-American experience, what was seen to be a one way process of inevitable decline in Welsh identity in the USA, is, through the Net, witnessing something of a renaissance. An instance of this is the way the Net has been used by the NWAF to organise its campaign to get Welsh-Americans counted on the 2000 US census: 'Census 2000–Count Us In America.'[72] In addition to using the Net as a way of bringing its campaign to the wider public the Internet site can also support campaign materials to be used by Welsh societies up and down America. This campaign is itself indicative of the revival of Welsh-American identity which has taken place since the 1980s. Launching the campaign the President of the NWAF said that:

> It is absolutely amazing how many Americans have Welsh ancestry, but do not identify as Welsh. The NWAF will attempt, working with Welsh Societies throughout America to make sure he or she is counted as Welsh in Census 2000. It is ironic that there has never been an accurate count of Welsh-Americans, even though the Welsh made an enormous, if unrecognized contribution to the very founding of America. Indeed, Thomas Jefferson, the author of the Declaration of Independence was Welsh, as were approximately half the signers of the Declaration, five of the first six presidents of the US (John Adams, James Madison James Monroe, and John Quincey Adams, and, among other presidents, perhaps America's most revered president, Abraham Lincoln.[73]

As Rhodri Owen observed of the way in which the US census has become a measure of the new sense of Welsh-American identification:

> In the USA a census of the population in 1990 revealed that 2,033,893 Americans reported their Welsh ancestry – two-thirds of the current population of Wales

itself. The figure represented just one per cent of the US total population, but marked a 22 per cent rise over the 1980 census, showing that more Americans have been recognising their Welsh ancestry.[74]

The Net cannot be said to be driving this kind of diasporic revivalism, but as the NWAF acknowledges, the 'shift in technology' is undoubtedly facilitating an 'unprecedented interest in Wales and Welshness'. Indeed the role the Net is playing in the making of the Welsh-American diaspora well illustrates Esther Dyson's general argument about the impact of the Net.

> The Net is not going to push us into some antiseptic, digital landscape. It is a medium for us to extend our intellectual and emotional selves, but it will not change our basic characteristics ... On the contrary, the Net will celebrate human nature and human diversity ... if we do it right. Precisely because there will be so much to learn to value human connections more, and they will look for it on the Net as in other places.[75]

The big question, of course, is the issue of whether the Net will serve to integrate or further fragment American society? In the case of the Welsh the desire to be identified as Welsh-Americans does not imply a weaker attachment to America, so much as a reattachment to an idea of Welshness. The reintegration of a diasporic community does not necessarily involve a disintegration of American identity per se so much as a redefinition of what being an American means. As the Census 2000 campaign well illustrates, the assertion of being a Welsh-American is about laying claim and drawing attention to the significant contribution which their ancestors made to the making of America.

In terms of understanding migration at the turn of the century, therefore, the Internet has an enormous potential to reconnect people and foster diversity and a sense of being part of a diaspora. As we have seen the Net is being used to preserve, stabilise and enhance local Welsh-American communications whilst in so doing contributing to the building of an entirely new level of global interaction: a kind of Welsh Cyber-Gwladfa! Thus in the next century, as the Internet continues to grow, there may well be far more people experiencing a 'collective hallucination' called Wales or Cymru than actually living in the 'real' nation that is wedged so very precariously between England and the Irish sea. For a people that has, for so long, struggled to find a place where Wales could be possible, and have oftentimes aspired to what Knowles terms an 'aspatial' idea of culture,[76] Cyber-Cymru or Web Wales may prove to be an ironic fulfilment of the hopes and dreams of all those in the past who sought to build a Welsh homeland in the wilds of America and Argentina. Like Wales itself, the Welsh diaspora it seems, is (in the language of the World Wide Web) still 'under construction'.

Notes

1   G. Chaliand and J.-P. Rageau, *The Penguin Atlas of Diasporas*, Harmondsworth, Penguin, 1995, p. xviii.
2   It is interesting to note that Escher's drawing is used as a cover design on the annual report, 1997 of The Institute of Migration and Ethnic Studies, based in Amsterdam.
3   For excellent accounts of the wider experience of Welsh emigration see: Gwyn A. Williams, *When WAS Wales?*, Harmondsworth, Penguin, 1991; John Davies, *A History of Wales*, Harmondsworth, Penguin, 1994; and Jan Morris, *The Matter of Wales: Epic Views of a Small Country*, Harmondsworth, Penguin, 1986.
4   See, for instance, Everything Celtic on the Web (http://og-man.net/) for an insight into how other Celtic groups as using the WWW.
5   A. Zimmern, *My Impressions of Wales*, London, 1921.
6   Saunders Lewis, 'Tynged yr Iaith', BBC Radio lecture, 13 February 1962.
7   See Williams, op. cit. and *The Search For Beulah Land, The Welsh and the Atlantic Revolution*, New York, Holmes and Meier, 1980.
8   J.S. Olson, *The Ethnic Dimension in American History*, 2nd edn, New York, St Martin's Press, 1994, p. 113.
9   See W.D. Jones, *Wales in America: Scranton and the Welsh 1860–1920*, Cardiff, University of Wales Press, 1997.
10 See G.H. Jenkins, '"A Rank Republican [and] a Leveller": William Jones, Llandgadfan', *Welsh History Review*, 17, 1995, pp. 365–86.
11 Williams, op. cit. (1980), pp. 182–3.
12 A.K. Knowles, 'Migration, Nationalism, and the Construction of Welsh Identity', in G.H. Herb and D.H. Kaplan, *Nested Identities: Nationalism, Territory and Scale*, Lanham, Rowman and Littlefield, 1999, p. 290.
13 J. Morris, *The Matter of Wales: Epic Views of a Small Country*, Harmondsworth, Penguin, 1986, p. 337.
14 E.G. Bowen, 'The Geography of Wales as a Background to its History', cited in T. Herbert and G E. Jones (eds) *Post-War Wales*, Cardiff, University of Wales Press, 1995.
15 Cited in D.B. Whittle, *Cyberspace, The Human Dimension*, New York, Freeman and Company, 1996, p. x.
16 Ibid., p. 9.
17 http://www.mindspring.com/~pcgraves/croeso.htm.
18 http://wasnc.org.
19 http://virtual-places.com/welshcar/ and http://virtual-places.com/welshcar/.
20 http://wngga.org.
21 http://www.wales-usa.org/ and http://www.wales-usa.org/.
22 http://www2.bcedu/~ellisjg/naaswch.html and http://www2.bcedu/~ellisjg/naaswch.html.
23 J. Davies, 'Wales and America', Inaugural Address of NAASWCH, 1995: http://www2.bc.edu/~ellisjg/davies.html.

24   http://www.madog.org/ and http://www.madog.org/.
25   See http://www.madog.org/hotlist.html#Welsh Language.
26   http://www.cs.brown.edu/fun/welsh/Welsh.html.
27   http://www.oseda.missouri.edu/~diana/cymraeg-l.html.
28   http://www.acen.co.uk and http://www.acen.co.uk.
29   P. Petro, *Travels in an Old Tongue: Touring the World Speaking Welsh*, London, Flamingo, 1998, pp. 324–5.
30   http://www.castles-of-britain.com/ninnau.htm.
31   http://www1.minn.net/~ydrych/ and http://www1.minn.net/~ydrych/.
32   http://news.bbc.co.uk/hi/welsh/static/default.htm and http://www.s4c.co.uk/ and http://www.s4c.co.uk/.
33   http://www.totalwales.com.
34   http://www.thisissouthwales.co.uk/.
35   http://members.tripod.com/~lolwyr/.
36   http://www.nwn.co.uk/NWNInternetpages/YCymronews.html.
37   http://www.llgc.org.uk/.
38   http://www.wales.gov.uk/index_e.html and http://www.wales.gov.uk/index_e.html.
39   http://homwpages.enterprise.net/jjones/main.html and http://homwpages.enterprise.net/jjones/main.html.
40   http://www.tourism.wales.gov.uk/ and http://www.tourism.wales.gov.uk/.
41   http://www.castlewales.com/home.html.
42   http://www.westwales.co.uk/dylanthomas/ and http://www.westwales.co.uk/dylanthomas/.
43   http://celtictown.com and http://celtictown.com.
44   mailto:Gwl@d.wales.com and Gwl@d.wales.com.
45   http://virtualcardiff.co.uk and http://virtualcardiff.co.uk.
46   http://www.bwrdd-yr-iaith.org.uk/.
47   http://snowcrash.cymru.net/~nwi/.
48   http://www.virtualwales.com/.
49   http://westwales.co.uk/index.htm and http://westwales.co.uk/index.htm.
50   http://www.connect.net/gevans/wales.html and http://www.connect.net/gevans/wales.html.
51   http://www.network.wales.org.uk/ and http://www.network.wales.org.uk/.
52   http://members.xoom.com/-xoom/walesconnect/index.htm and http://members.xoom.com/-xoom/walesconnect/index.htm.
53   http://www.cyberbeach.net/~slucas/wales-vt.html, http://www.cyberbeach.net/~slucas/wales-vt.html.
54   http://og-man.net/ and http://og-man.net/.
55   http://cilmeri.com/ and http://cilmeri.com/.
56   http://members.tripod.com/Welshworld/ and http://members.tripod.com/Welshworld/.
57   http://members.xoom.com/cyber_cymru/ and http://members.xoom.com/cyber_cymru/.
58   http://www and http://www_.nawr.com/.
59   See *Meeting the Challenge – The Competitiveness of Wales*, Cardiff, The Welsh Office, 1996. For a review of the issues see J. Osmond, *Wales Information Society*, Cardiff, Institute of Welsh Affairs, 1997.
60   http://wis.org.uk and http://wis.org.uk.
61   Sources: http://www.asc.upenn.edu/usr/sbtuten/phpi.htm and http://www.asc.upenn.edu/usr/sbtuten/phpi.htm_; http://www.wis.org.uk/english/wis_proj/report/intwww.html and http://www.wis.org.uk/english/wis_proj/report/intwww.html.

62 http://www.geocities.com/WestHollywood/3922/history.html and http://www.geocities. com/WestHollywood/3922/history.html.

63 http://www.familyhistory.com/societyhall/viewmember.asp?societyid=352 and http:// www.familyhistory.com/societyhall/viewmember.asp?societyid=352.

64 D. Chandler (1988): 'Personal Home Pages and the Construction of Identities on the Web' [WWW document]: http://www.aber.ac.uk/~dgc/webident.html and http://www.aber.ac.uk/ ~dgc/webident.html.

65 S. Turkle, *Life on the Screen: Identity in the Age of the Internet*, New York, Simon and Schuster, 1995, p. 268.

66 See C. Bryan, R. Tsagarousianou and D. Tambini, 'Electronic democracy and the civic networking movement in context', in R. Tsagarousianou, D. Tambini and D. Bryan (eds), *Cyberdemocracy:Technology, Cities and Civic Networks*, London, Routledge, 1998.

67 H. Rheingold, *The Virtual Community: Homesteading on the Electronic Frontier*, New York, Addison-Wesley, 1993, p. 5.

68 O. Schmidtke, 'Berlin in the Net: Prospects for cyberdemocracy from above and from below', in Tsagarousianou, Tambini and Bryan, op. cit., p. 71.

69 http://swsny.com and http://swsny.com.

70 http://waleschamber.org/ and http://waleschamber.org/.

71 Whittle, op. cit.

72 http://home.earthlink.net/~philipsbrown/LatestNews91599.html and http://home.earthlink. net/~philipsbrown/LatestNews91599.html.

73 http://home.earthlink.net/~philipsbrown/CensusPrRel.html and http://home.earthlink.net/ ~philipsbrown/CensusPrRel.html.

74 Rhodri Owen, 'Home from Home – with just a touch of *hiraeth*', *Western Mail Magazine*, 20 November 1999, p. 4.

75 E. Dyson, *Release 2.0: A Design for Living in the Digital Age*, London, Viking, 1997, p. 4.

76 Knowles, op. cit, p. 310.

PART TWO
LABOUR

7 'I Asked How the Vessel Could Go': the Contradictory Experiences of African and African Diaspora Mariners and Port Workers in Britain, c. 1750–1850

IAN DUFFIELD

Introduction: A Paradox

> The first object that saluted my eyes when I arrived at the coast was the sea, and a slave-ship, which was then riding at anchor and waiting for its cargo. These filled me with astonishment which was soon converted into terror ... [When aboard] I asked how the vessel could go? [my countrymen] told me they could not tell; but that there were cloths put upon the masts by the help of the ropes I saw, and then the vessel went on; and the white men had some spell or magic they put in the water when they liked in order to stop the vessel.[1]

Thus Olaudah Equiano described the trauma of his first experience of the sea and the ship about to carry him on the middle passage. As the scene is represented, neither the child Equiano nor his adult fellow slaves can comprehend the ship as a mechanism. Equiano's rhetoric here can still shock readers into empathy but also constitutes a profound paradox of which the author was necessarily aware. By the time of writing his narrative, he had acquired vast experience as a mariner: as a slave and a free man; aboard naval and merchant ships. Who, then, better understood 'how the vessel could go', or the complex social, political and cultural currents of eighteenth-century maritime life? As Peter Linebaugh has stated, using Equiano as an exemplar; 'Shipboard communication was decisive to the formulation of eighteenth-century pan-Africanism.'[2] All that communicated knowledge had to be concealed, to achieve his 'bereft childhood recovered' effect. Naïve readers would never juxtapose one part of his narrative with another, never perceive this paradoxical recreation of childlike incomprehension from adult expertise, and might conclude Equiano was a 'simple fellow'.[3] Equiano often thus masks himself in his narrative, allowing space for such goofy readings and presumably laughing up his sleeve at them.[4]

'I asked how the vessel could go?' is a trope throughout this study, in the sense that black seafarers in Britain 1750–1850 remain substantially obscured from us, as well as indicating the paradoxes and contradictions of the period's black mariners' experiences. In 1968, Jesse Lemisch justly debunked all those images of 'Jolly Jack', rough but hearty and childlike, which had long dominated maritime historians' representations of eighteenth-century North American seamen (and for that matter, of metropolitan British seamen).[5] If Britain's black seamen of 1750–1850 have largely escaped such representations, that merely indicates their ultra-marginal position (if that) in most of our corpus of maritime history.[6] They are touched on in studies in various fields but piecemeal and in passing. An often paltry knowledge is thus fragmented into artificially bounded research fields, scarcely aware of each others' existence, still less of a rich history still largely enveloped in an historical silence. Like all such silences, this one is no mere oversight but is constituted by the power relations and effects of how historical knowledge itself has been constructed.

Barely Visible over the Horizon? Black Seafarers in 'Africans in Britain' Historiography

The historical literature cited in this study notwithstanding, the absence of monographs and dearth of shorter studies on black seafarers in Britain in the century following (or before) 1750, tells its own story. Black seafarers of our period stroll briefly in and out of most general accounts of Africans in Britain published since the early 1970s, but without sustained empirical enquiry or serious analysis.[7] One such work provides thirteen consecutive pages on black students, a very small occupational category in Britain's black population then, although not without historical importance. It has 21 more (but scattered) pages concerning the large African occupational category of servants/domestics/valets; and only 5 scattered pages mentioning sailors.[8] Nevertheless, Equiano, the black author of our period who is most famous today and was the most successful in his own time,[9] although briefly beginning his formal acquisition of literacy as a child slave in London, developed and secured it at sea as a Seven Years War naval rating.[10]

Neglect of black mariners might be extenuated because they were, by definition, highly mobile and so are arguably elusive. That will hardly stand. Like other seamen, ashore they were highly concentrated in major ports, especially around moorings, docks and wharves. Furthermore, three 1990s studies produced remarkably parallel findings, strongly suggesting that seamen were an exceptionally large occupational group among black people resident in Britain between 1780 and 1852. Two of these studies by Norma Myers,[11] drawing on occupational records of Newgate Gaol inmates and trial accounts in the *Old Bailey Sessions Papers,* found that 26 per cent of identifiable black male inmates or defendants, 1785–1830, were seamen, and 14.3 per cent domestic servants. These were easily the two largest occupational categories for black males found in these sources. By contrast, among her comparative sample of white Newgate inmates in 1802, only 3.6 per cent were seamen and 0.2 per cent servants.[12]

In 1993, Duffield attempted a reconstruction of the occupations of Africans in Britain, 1812–52. This utilised transported convict records in Sydney and Hobart, whose physical descriptions of all incoming convicts allowed blacks among them to be identified, and which contained a wealth of data about occupations, place of origin and place of trial (among other social, demographic and penal data).[13] In Duffield's male sample, 34.8 per cent were seafarers; adding such related occupations as sail makers, caulkers, watermen and boatmen, the percentage rises to 39.5 per cent, an astonishing concentration in a related group of occupations. However, in Duffield's sample male domestic servants were not so far behind the seafarers in being 30.3 per cent of the total.[14] Neither Myers nor Duffield suggest that their data are more than indicative but the broad indications are striking indeed. Both reject any suggestion that what they are exhibiting is a seafaring black 'criminal class'. Indeed, both reject the very notion of a 'criminal class', whether or not ethnically labelled. In this latter point they are absolutely aligned with the very strong consensus of historians of crime and punishment in eighteenth- and nineteenth-century Britain, since the 1970s.[15]

Duffield was also influenced by arguments in a 1988 study, that the British and Irish convicts transported to New South Wales were a broadly representative cross section (including in work skills and experience) of the contemporary British and Irish working class.[16] If this is true for convicts transported from Britain and Ireland generally, by analogy it should be true for the black convicts among them. Nevertheless, this indirect method of identifying and acquiring information about black seafarers has its obvious limitations.

One as yet neglected source which promises much rich data on black sailors is the muster books regularly submitted to the Admiralty by all operational British naval ships.[17] Most of these survive in Admiralty records in the British Public Records Office. It is not good enough to plead that the sheer volume of these records is off-putting, as does Michael Lewis in his 1960 book, *A Social History of the Navy 1793–1815*. Of course, Lewis was writing long before user-friendly computer hardware and software existed. Nevertheless, he is not so easily excused. His book devotes almost 20 pages to the geographical origins of naval officers, under two to those of ratings. This quarterdeck bias is common in the older naval histories, though fortunately not rife throughout Lewis's book. While naval historians gave such cavalier treatment to (white) 'Jack Tar', 'Black Jack' was certain to remain virtually invisible in their pages.[18]

If black seamen 1750–1850 are barely visible over the horizon in all the major general historical studies of Africans in Britain published since 1972 (precious little was written earlier),[19] they were very visible on the contemporary waterfront. Indeed, Duffield found that among *all* the black males in his sample (from throughout the United Kingdom as then constituted), 69.1 per cent were tried in port towns, this indicating approximate place of residence when arraigned.[20] Of course, historians are inevitably somewhat guided by previous studies. In 1956, an American scholar, J.J. Hecht, published a solid book on domestic servants in eighteenth-century England, including blacks,[21] following up his 1954 work on continental and colonial servants in England in the same century.[22] These studies cued later scholars of Africans in Britain; as did a natural interest in legal cases concerning slavery in eighteenth-century England and Scotland.[23] Many of the most important of them, such as Strong's Case, Somerset's Case and, in Scotland, Knight *v.* Wedderburn, concerned runaway slave domestics.[24] Still, fruitful lines of enquiry can eventually become ruts. Britain's black mariner's of the slavery era are now overdue extensive scholarly attention.

Historical Processes and Contradictory Experiences

The argument here is that black mariners 1750 to 1850 were at the forefront in understanding their dire historical circumstances and in navigating the hazardous channels leading to self-liberation. Contradictorily, while there were *some* positive opportunities in seafaring, albeit they had to be made and seized to be effected; yet these were beset with grave perils *specific to black seafarers.* The most obvious was this; in the ports of those wide trans-Atlantic regions where slave owning was fundamental to local wealth and power structures, any free black crewman aboard a merchant ship was in jeopardy of being resold as a slave by an unscrupulous ship's captain, or indeed any white knave ashore.[25] As for slave seamen, they could be sold off anywhere at their owners' discretion.

An example here (as so often) is Equiano, sold by his owner Lt Michael Pascal RN to Captain Doran at the end of the Seven Years War, just when Equiano himself eagerly anticipated imminent emancipation. Pascal simultaneously pocketed his slave's accumulated naval service wages and prize money, on the principle that what 'belongs' to a slave belongs to his master.[26] Seamen, white or black, were impressed during wartime, flogged at sea for disciplinary offences (real or imagined), cheated in multiple ways of ration entitlements aboard ship, suffered the many hazards of navigation in the age of sail and the chicanery of those who emptied Jack Tar's pockets ashore. Only black seafarers faced the horrible prospect of arbitrary and illegal re-enslavement if free, or equally arbitrary if formally legal resale into unknown hazards if slaves. Under these circumstances, a black seaman could never be entirely certain how his white shipmates would react. Held aboard the *Charming Sally* in Portsmouth Harbour in 1762 as Captain Doran's newly purchased slave, Equiano offered a crewman a guinea[27] to help him escape. The money was cynically pocketed without any assistance ensuing. However, some white shipmates from his last naval ship travelled to Portsmouth and, as previously promised, attempted (if fruitlessly) to secure his release.[28] A more contradictory set of circumstances can hardly be imagined. Such experiences may well have inured black seamen into accepting white shipmates' help when it was genuinely available but well short of relying on their good faith until it was unequivocally demonstrated.

Nevertheless, Equiano eventually accumulated by seafaring the £40 to buy his freedom from his last owner, Robert King, a Philadelphia Quaker with extensive West India property and business. He was able to earn this money by petty trading on his own behalf, while serving on his master's vessels on voyages to the West Indies.[29] Thus seafaring did become Equiano's channel to freedom – but not to secure freedom. In 1767, now free although still serving King, Equiano sailed aboard King's sloop the *Nancy* on an unlucky cruise. Surviving the 'ordinary' hazard of shipwreck on the Bahama Banks, he obtained a passage from New Providence to Savannah, Georgia. There, while residing with a black friend called Mosa, both were arrested by the watch and threatened with a fine or flogging, for the offence of having a light in the house of a 'negro' after 9 pm. Soon after having talked his way with difficulty out of this sticky situation, two Savannah white men mendaciously claimed him as their runaway slave.[30] Again, Equiano talked his way out of trouble. How tenuous the 'freedom' of a free black seaman could be, with no white patron at hand to vouch for him, is well illustrated.

In June 1776, he was again threatened with illegal re-enslavement. Having amicably ended a period of employment with Dr Irving on the Mosquito Coast, he boarded a sloop on 'agreed terms' for a passage to Jamaica. The owner, a forsworn wretch called Hughes, then pressed him to engage as a crewman on another of his vessels, a short-handed schooner. When Equiano refused this offer, Hughes threatened 'he should not go out of the sloop as a free man', revealing that anyway it was bound for Cartagena (in what is now Venezuela) and swearing to sell him there. Next, Hughes had Equiano painfully strung up and suspended by the ankles and wrists. Ultimately, Equiano escaped to the shore by a ruse, in grave danger of being shot by his would-be enslaver.[31]

Most of these escapades happened far from Britain. However, such perils faced any black mariner embarking from a metropolitan British port for the Americas, as given the major routes of eighteenth-century Atlantic shipping, many certainly did. Indeed, free black seamen could be in jeopardy of re-enslavement even in Britain itself. Again, Equiano's narrative is instructive. In Spring 1774, he obtained a place as steward on the ship *Anglicania*, then fitting out in the Thames for a voyage to Turkey. Next, he successfully recommended 'a very clever black man, John Annis, as cook' to the *Anglicania's* captain. Annis, however, possessed only an equivocal freedom, as former slave to a St Kitts' master, William Kirkpatrick. The parting had been 'by consent, though [Kirkpatrick] afterwards tried many schemes to inveigle the poor man'.[32] At law, following the important 1772 judgement by Lord Mansfield in Somerset's Case, slaves could not be forcibly removed from England against their will. Nevertheless, Kirkpatrick, now in the London area, had Annis forcibly kidnapped from the *Anglicania* with the prearranged complicity of the ship's captain and mate.

At first unaided and then with the help of Granville Sharp, the hero of Somerset's Case, Equiano strove to release his friend. Annis, nevertheless, was forcibly shipped to St Kitts, staked out and mercilessly flogged on arrival and eventually died there of continuing ill usage. Evidently Mansfield's recent ruling was one thing, effectively enforcing it against a resolutely unscrupulous slave owner another. Annis himself was not some imagined white abolitionist archetype of the inarticulate and helpless slave, bleating for the kind white people to save him. He was either literate or, anyway, had the nous to resort to literate friends to write on his behalf when in dire straits. Equiano received from Annis, before he died, 'two very moving letters' from St Kitts.[33] Evidently freedom might be far from secure for black mariners in Britain itself, even after the Mansfield Judgement.[34] Equally evidently, a black mariner in dire straits might think a resourceful free black friend the best source of assistance.

It would be extraordinary if Equiano's testimony about the perils faced by Black Jack (as opposed to any Jack), were the result of atypical personal experiences and one-in-a-million observations of highly unusual tyrannies suffered by others. Evidence exists of other arbitrary attempts to re-enslave free (or *de facto* free) black mariners in Britain. N.A.M. Roger reports that in 1751, William Castillo, a black seafarer threatened with sale ashore, persuaded the master of the Boston Massachusetts merchant ship he was serving on to buy him. The understanding was that when Castillo's wages amounted to his purchase price, he would be free. After five years, presumably realising that his new master never intended to free him, Castillo ran away. He had the ill-luck to encounter this man in Portsmouth in 1758 and was promptly claimed and literally collared – with iron. By now an impressed naval seaman, Castillo appealed to the Admiralty who informed his commanding Admiral, Admiral Holbourne 'that the laws of this country admit of no badges of slavery' and insisted that Castillo himself should receive his naval wages, not his former master. Roger complacently states that 'to anyone bred on the plantation, this must have been a refreshing world of equality'.[35] It seems more plausible that their Lordships were unwilling, during a major war, to lose a prime seaman and provide a precedent for further such losses. As to the legality of slavery in England, the predominant legal rulings up to 1758 were still in its favour. Thus, Castillo's freedom in fact remained contingent and equivocal. Assuming he survived the war to be discharged from the navy, it is most unlikely that the Admiralty took any further interest in his continuing freedom.

However, by the early 1800s (and perhaps somewhat earlier), Britain had become a more secure berth for black seamen. Some years before 24 July 1820, when he was sentenced in Kent to transportation for seven years, Thomas Day, born a slave in Kingston, Jamaica, in the mid-1790s, was taken by his master from Jamaica to Bermuda to be sold. To evade this fate, Day presented himself as a free man to the captain of a ship bound for England and negotiated for a passage, probably by volunteering as a crewman. The captain was worried at the possibility of harbouring an escaped slave (indicating that escapes by sea were common enough) and demanded to see Day's nonexistent freedom certificate. Nothing daunted, Day found and bribed a literate soldier to forge a certificate, the text of which Day dictated. Although illiterate himself, Day clearly knew the formal language of manumission. Thus he was enabled to embark for England and freedom. Quite likely the black mariners' trans-Atlantic oral information network,[36] had assured him that breaches of the Mansfield Judgement were now unlikely, which was indeed the case.[37] Evidently for Day, *effective* liberty was the magnet that drew him to England. Once that was gained, he had to earn a living as a free worker, taking to seafaring among other occupations. This brief version of his story further illustrates that seafaring could offer advantages as well as perils to black men. For Day, a ship and the sea were means to achieve freedom and then to material maintenance of a free life.[38] Thus the ongoing enslaving effects of the middle passage were for some slaves reversible, *via* other facets of the same Atlantic shipping complex and knowledge of differing freedom prospects under varying jurisdictions.

Slave seamen not opting for the high risks of running, might nevertheless utilise seafaring as a liberating mechanism. As seen, Equiano earned the purchase price of his freedom while serving on trading voyages as Robert King's slave. A similar spectrum of practices was adopted by other slaves in or from the Americas, who formed practical agendas to achieve and then maintain themselves in freedom. John Annis certainly arrived in Britain by sea and happily took up the place aboard the *Anglicania* arranged for him by Equiano. Thus, the 'Black Atlantic' network provided practical mutual help among black seafarers, as well as vital long-range information about both everyday and critical circumstances around the ocean's coasts.

Seamen were the largest occupational category among those African-Americans who, having supported King George during the American Revolution (for their own pragmatic reasons at a time when their white masters were at each other's throats), came to Britain as refugees at the end of the war.[39] Had they remained in the United States, the best many of these refugees could have expected would have been a return to the tender mercies of patriot masters, whom they had deserted during the war, on the British promise of freedom and opportunities for payback under arms to buckra. The war of 1812, however, operated a different kind of leverage on African-American seamen than the American Revolution.

They, as much as white American seamen, resented impressment into King George's Navy, during the French Revolutionary and Napoleonic Wars. When this American grievance escalated into the war of 1812, many shellback and salty free blacks in the Northern States treated the war as an opportunity to display themselves as emphatically *free* Americans, through naval war service.[40] It is vital to understand that, varying with specific circumstances, service in a British King's Ship might be perceived by African-North Americans as either liberating or the reverse, because this seesaw illustrates an important point. Like all other Atlantic Diaspora Africans, black seamen were at the very rough end of the historical processes of the Atlantic Slave Trade and colonial slavery all right, but they were not mere victims of those processes. Under circumstances which required courage plus nice judgement concerning which way to jump, they made history as well as endured it. Thus, for black sailors of our period, the phrase 'the fortunes of war' has very particular implications. If white nations were at war they might change sides if the terms offered seemed sufficiently attractive; or alternatively, establish claims to a higher status where they were by steadfast patriotic zeal. Such stratagems were always a gamble but the risks could be born by people whose *status quo* was also intrinsically dangerous.

The War of 1812 was not the last swing of the pendulum concerning which way it might be best for African-American seamen to leap for freedom. Douglas Lorimer has recounted several revealing 1850s incidents, in which African-American mariners found life ashore in Britain a distinct mark-up on that in the contemporary United States. One such 'Black Jack' married a white wife in Liverpool and went to Philadelphia with her. Meeting with hostility there, they returned to Merseyside. In 1857, aggrieved black crewmen 'fought with their white officers on an American vessel anchored in the Mersey'. During the subsequent magistrate's hearings, both 'court room spectators' and the Liverpool press 'took the side of the crew against their white officers'. From the 1820s to the 1850s the Foreign Office periodically made diplomatic representations about Black British sailors imprisoned or even enslaved in the Southern United States. Knowledge of such actions by the British Government would certainly have had its effect on the sensitive 'balance of advantage' mental apparatus of African-American seamen. It might be thought that engaging aboard British merchant shipping, with its far poorer wages, historically, than United States merchantmen, would not have been an attractive option. Contrary to any such supposition, Bolster states that by the mid-nineteenth century, African-Americans 'were finding fewer opportunities at sea'. Their wages were being reduced well below those of white seamen, while black segregation into a dwindling range of posts aboard ship became the norm. As all this coincided with a sharp deterioration in even white American seamen's terms of employment, the effects on blacks were commensurately dire.[41] At least one American fugitive slave in mid nineteenth-century England, John Brown, 'claimed that a black British sailor enslaved on a Georgia plantation had inspired him with his vision of British liberty'.[42] That may have been a deliberate piece of *congosah*,[43] designed to play up to his British Abolitionist audiences' distinct tendency to preen themselves that Britain, not the upstart United States, was the true home of liberty.[44] The scattering of cases incidentally related by Lorimer, however, may indicate that alongside fugitive slaves there may also have been a seepage of free African-American seamen to Britain in the mid-nineteenth century. As, however, British merchant seamen's wages and terms of service were also then deteriorating, and many seamen might not be well qualified for landsman's work, any such seepage was probably slight.

Nevertheless, in many British ports, especially London, blacks from across the Atlantic would have found the reassuring presence of other black people. At that time, 'when Englishmen wanted to employ men of African origin, they first looked for them in the docks'. Thus, many of the 158 blacks preferentially recruited for the Niger Expedition of 1841, were found in English ports.[45] This positive employment discrimination in the biggest and most expensive single British religious-humanitarian enterprise in Africa of the mid-nineteenth century was also, however, a contradictory experience with a vengeance. The expedition was an utter disaster, with appalling mortality rates from tropical fevers. It fed the rising negrophobia intrinsic to the Mid-Victorian British swing against abolitionism and towards a reinvented racism. Charles Dickens, no less, effectively satirised the Niger Expedition through his creation, Mrs Jellaby in *Bleak House*. Instead of attending to her proper duties as a wife and mother, she devotes all her energies to fatuous meetings and correspondence concerning an expedition to uplift the irredeemable Africans of 'Borioboola Ga'. Dickens's more knowing readers could easily place this settlement as not a thousand miles from the Lower Niger. The Niger Expedition was as cruelly paradoxical and contradictory in outcomes as anything in this study.

Black Waterfront Life in London: in the Docks and in the 'Dock'

Eighteenth-century London dock workers were engaged in prolonged, large scale struggles against employers, property owners and the state.[46] What dock workers regarded as customary perquisites supplementing irregular cash wages, the state through the ever-expanding 'Bloody Code', defended as the property rights of merchant capital. Theft of such property was made punishable, according to defined criteria of its value and the spatial circumstances of its appropriation.[47] The penalties included transportation for longer or shorter periods (never less than seven years) and hanging (often commuted to transportation for life, especially late in the century). Thus the shipyard worker who continued (as many did), to take away 'chips' – often substantial balks – the waste product of processing timber into masts, futtocks, treenails, keelsons and the many other constituent components of a wooden ship, was criminalised. The same was true of lumpers who took perquisites/ stole from the cargoes of vessels they were unloading. Linebaugh nicely distinguishes two meanings of 'to lump' in this sense; 'to contract to unload ships or to pilfer around the docks.'[48] Lumpage dues mainly accrued to the master lumpers who recruited and paid lumper gangs, while job redefinition expanded the range of tasks required of lumpers themselves. Thus the lumpers acquired intensified motives for taking retaliatory compensation through pilferage while simultaneously defending customary 'rights' as they understood them. For some incoming commodities, notably slave-produced sugar, pilferage became so extensive that owners called it plundering.[49]

Further, there are striking connections between the birth of the modern prison, in the sense used by Foucault in *Discipline and Punish* and new late eighteenth-century ideas and practices concerning dock security. The Panopticon concept came not from Jeremy Bentham but his brother Samuel, who managed a chaotic, violently disorderly new dockyard in Russia for some years from 1779. Jeremy visited this shambles in 1786 and wrote approvingly of Samuel's idea of a round inspection house from which all the dock workers could be scrutinised – or at least feel so. Later on back in London, Samuel constructed model panopticons, Jeremy industriously refined their specifications.[50] Simpler technologies had long sought to protect naval dockyards from pilferage and plundering, by surrounding them high with solid walls, as at Chatham and Deptford since the seventeenth century.[51] The mother of all securitised wet docks for berthing, loading and unloading merchant ships, however, only began to take shape at the turn of the eighteenth-century. London's huge West India Docks, which required the raising of £1,750,000 of capital (vastly more in real terms today), was completed in 1802. 'Its perimeter was guarded by a gap of 100 ft between it and the nearest building; a moat 6 ft deep and 12 ft wide; and a wall 30 ft high.'[52] Such arrangements greatly facilitated the policing of all persons and goods entering or leaving. They did not, however, entirely foil the ingenuity of waterfront men of any colour. In the nature of things, though, far better information is available on those who got caught than those who eluded these defensive fortifications of capital, property and profit.

One of these less fortunate West India Dock thieves was Thomas Brett, an umbrella maker. A black man born in Lisbon, he was tried at the Old Bailey in the 30 November 1814 session, on charges of having stolen a watch, a seal, a shirt and a handkerchief, cumulatively valued at £1 7s 4d.[53] The trial is revelatory in several respects. The owner of the stolen goods, James Hodge, was a customs officer whose property had been filched whilst he slept in the course of duty aboard the *Captain Burton,* a Jamaica-bound ship. On awakening, he found his box broken into and the shirt and handkerchief removed, while the watch had been sneaked from his hammock. In his evidence, Hodge stated 'I went into the office and informed the [police] officer, and asked if he had been out of the dock with a bundle', suggesting that even dock employees in occupations of trust were in fact not entirely trusted. The first question Hodge was asked in court was 'Did ... [the prisoner] work on board the ship'. Although this was not the case, the question is again deeply revealing of how little trusted were those inside the dock's moat and wall and about their legitimate duty. Here is a sure sign that the security system was not entirely secure after all. Information of the theft soon reached Ebenezer Horton, a constable at the outhouse of the Export Dock. He stopped and searched Brett and found the shirt and handkerchief in his bundle, the watch and seal 'concealed in his trowsers'. Brett tried to convince Horton that he had some of these items from a ship's mate but he could not show a dock pass when asked for one. Another technology of dock security is revealed.[54] Brett's defence was very unconvincing:

> I had the watch of the gentleman that belonged to the clothes he gave me his hammoc [*sic*] to take away. I was to have two shillings for carrying the hammock; the officer stopped me and asked me what ship I came from. I said the Fanny, he took the watch from me and all the clothes. The man that gave them me, I do not see in Court.[55]

Nevertheless, this is informative in other respects, as it indicates the existence of unregulated casual dockside portering, which could only tend to breach the tight official security system. At a symbolic level, there is something compelling in a black man attempting to steal from a customs-house officer, aboard a Jamaica-bound ship in the West India Docks, before the 1834 emancipation of Britain's colonial slaves. The circumstantial connections with the circuit of Caribbean slave production are too obvious to gloss further. A poor black man might well feel a certain moral right to steal under such circumstances. Brett was sentenced to transportation for seven years.[56] He arrived in Sydney at a time when the volume of shipping calling there had risen to a level offering excellent pilfering and plundering opportunities around Sydney Cove and in the anchorages of Port Jackson.

By contrast, the 1815 case of Jacob Morris, a 57 year old New York-born cook and seaman,[57] who committed robbery with violence against a just discharged naval seaman, Joseph Uxbridge,[58] reveals assumptions among black seamen of mutual aid; unfortunately in this case unfounded on Uxbridge's part. The case is extremely unusual, however, in both the accused and the victim being blacks,[59] suggesting that Uxbridge's assumptions were reasonable even though he misjudged Morris. In his evidence, Uxbridge stated; 'before I came on shore, the prisoner had asked me and some of my shipmates to come and lodge with him.'[60] When Uxbridge arrived with several other fellow-ratings from HMS *L'Aigle* at St George's Parish, Blackwall, where Morris lodged, he was extraordinarily free in showing his money, placing a £20 note in Morris's hands:

> I gave … [Morris] a twenty pound note, and told him to go and get something for supper; and then I had three twenty pound notes … all wrapt up together. He went down and gave the note to the landlady, and she got change; she came and gave me a three shilling piece and told me I had better go to the cook's shop, and get some supper. I said mother, you take care of the change.[61]

The easy familiarity in address between ordinary black and white people in London is also seen here. While 'mother' was perhaps demotically honorific to a (presumably) older woman, it hardly exudes deference.

A more conventional theme illustrated by this case is the vulnerability of any naval seaman, of whatever colour, who had just come ashore at the end of a cruise and received substantial pay and prize money. In Uxbridge's case this amounted to £84 19s 6d (nominally, £84 97.5p), at a conservative estimate around £5100.00 in 1999 sterling values.[62] To put this in perspective, in 1815 the wages of the carpenter aboard a first-rate man-of-war (a warrant officer of great technical importance), were £5 16s[63] (£5.80) a month, a rate of reward well exceeding that of many clerks ashore and indeed the stipends of many inferior unbeneficed Anglican clergy. Evidently *L'Aigle* had enjoyed a profitable last cruise before Bonaparte surrendered in 1814. If life at sea on naval ships was harsher in many respects than on merchant ships, the navy was at least meticulous in payment of wages and prize money due and there is no evidence that its black ratings were excepted. Under the particular circumstances of a fortunate cruise, a man like Uxbridge could for a while forget all want and care when paid off.

The theatricality of a criminal trial at the Georgian Old Bailey has been justly remarked on. The principal actors, spatially separated from the audience as in any theatre, certainly included the defendant.[64] Of course, the show sometimes flopped. There was nothing dramatic about the trial of Thomas Brett, least of all his own performance. Jacob Morris, however, understood that, literally, the performance of his life was required. If found guilty (which he was), the sentence could only be death (in his case later commuted to transportation for life).[65] He was charged with 'assaulting Joseph Uxbridge on the King's Highway' (actually, up a Blackwall back-alley but technically as stated); of 'putting him in fear' [of his life]; and of stealing from Uxbridge three banknotes value £60 *and* a handkerchief value 6d (0.5 p).[66] Leaving out the last item, Uxbridge had been robbed with violence on the King's Highway, of enough money to hang an entire frigate's crew, if they had all individually committed similar crimes but each only for his *pro rata* fraction of £60.

Morris's performance ranged from low comedy, to pathos and melodrama. His words, like those of any gifted actor enlivening a potentially dull monologue of previous events offstage, give the illusion of vividly encountering reality;

> By the good God I am innocent of robbing this man, I had the note to take care of for him as a friend. I went down to Woolwich and went on board his ship, knowing some of the crew; and he being a stranger, and a man of my own colour, I asked him to lodge with me when he came to London, which he agreed to. He told me I had better stay on board, for there would be blankets and things which would be throwed away, and as I might as well have them as anyone else. When the crew was paid off, he sent one for half a gallon of rum, and we all got quite comfortable; and when we were coming off, they all made me commodore, and this here Jack, (pointing to the prosecutor) was drunk, and very riotous, and disobeyed my orders; when we came on shore, he would have more rum; I told him I was commodore; I was a superior officer, and would not let him, but he would have some, and went and got some. We hired a cart to bring up the chests, and my blankets and things, and we all got on board, but Jack was very drunk and quarrelsome, and would have something to drink, at every public house he came to. After we came up, he changed one note and gave me the rest to take care of; and went to a cook's shop, and got something for supper; we went into him at the cook's shop, and he wanted to go with girls; we went to a house where there were some, and another got one, and this Jack made a bargain with a lady, but something was the matter, and she went away. I fancy they did not agree. Jack made a row, because she would not stay, and blamed me for it, saying I took her away. At last we agreed to go home to our lodgings; he was

very quarrelsome and swore he would kill me in Portugue. I was obliged to knock him down to take away the knife, and when the watchman came up, he swore I had robbed him and I was taken to the watchhouse (addressing himself to the prosecutor). You Jack, you know it was all a drunken frolic; so help me God Almighty I am as innocent as the child unborn.[67]

Every element of the popular image of 'Jack Tar' ashore appears: the hard boozing; the comradeship; the uproariousness; the quick temper when 'Jack' was in his cups; the search for, negotiations and rows with, 'girls' (evidently prostitutes); the flashing and squandering of hard-earned money. The allegation that Uxbridge had sworn 'in Portugue' to kill Morris is a gem, a reminder of the poly-ethnic Atlantic seafarers' multilingual argot.[68]

The focus of the speech is on Morris himself as protagonist and Uxbridge as antagonist. The former is represented as the jovial but judicious master of the revels and befriender of a homeless fellow black; the latter as wilful, foolish, quarrelsome, unruly and worst of all, forsworn against his black brother and benefactor. The language of black brotherhood and the brotherhood of 'Jolly Jacks' is unleashed by Morris to veil its actual antithesis in his deeds; an instance of real vice paying tribute to equally real (in the sense of historically existent) virtues. By comparison, Equiano's language of black brotherhood when writing about John Annis or Mosa, though somewhat heightened, never protests too much.

Though Morris's account is constituted through a cunningly shaped language of deceit, all he says is not untrue. His tale's general architecture is significantly corroborated by Uxbridge's version, although naturally with an opposite slant. It is good evidence that although 'Black Jack' might place special reliance in his black brothers, he was not estranged from white comrades-in-arms, as shown by his presence in the carnivalesque antics of his shipmates. Indeed, it is clear that a 'Black Jack' might take the central role in such a carnival – Morris was or had been a sea cook, knew some of *L'Aigle's* crew and was evidently very familiar with sailors' customs as well as their needs and desires. Note that he was elected 'commodore' for the peripatetic revels from Woolwich to Blackwall. This reminds us that such mariners' customs were a mimicry of pirate practices in early Georgian times and those of the naval mutineers at the Nore in 1797. Such practices inverted established shipboard authority by seamen electing officers from their own ranks and even obeying them – insofar as they chose.[69] In another exceptionally dramatic naval mutiny, John Brown, a black who claimed to be an American citizen from Virginia,[70] was impressed at sea by HMS *Danae* in 1800 and shortly after was among the ringleaders of a mutiny aboard this frigate off Brittany. The event was doubly sensational for once in command, the mutineers made for the nearest French port where they were feted, rewarded and given refuge.[71]

The story of one black loyalist refugee, William Blue, a Deptford lumper in the 1790s further shows London and its docks and waterfronts as providing both opportunities and hazards for blacks. Much later in his life, Blue briefly summarised his story of active service in arms for King George during the American Revolutionary War, in petitions to the Governor of New South Wales.[72] After that war black loyalist refugees, like white ones, could claim compensation from the government's Commission for American Claims, for losses caused by their adherence to the British cause. In practice blacks' claims were usually discounted because of the bureaucratic demands of the application process and official suspicions.[73] There was, it seems, an official culture here that black loyalists were liars; or when not, should anyway be grateful enough for having had their hides saved by refuge in Britain.[74] Many black claimants, like Blue, were illiterate.[75] They could rarely substantiate their claims, a matter much easier for literate white refugees, accustomed to the practices of legally documenting ownership rights over property.[76] If Blue ever claimed compensation, it is unlikely that he received any. It appears that, like many black loyalist refugees in London, he slid into the extreme poverty that caused them to be labelled in the 1780s as 'The Black Poor'. As such, they became the object of private philanthropic and eventually state concern.

The name William Blue occurs among the Black Poor who received 'Bounty from the Government'; the only Bounty recipient of that name.[77] That this Blue was our William Blue, while not absolutely certain, seems extremely likely.[78] However, those who received the Bounty were also expected to migrate to found that new model colony, the 'Province of Freedom' in Sierra Leone. The extent to which this scheme, underneath its apparent philanthropy, was really a racist forced expulsion of black people whom the government and philanthropists alike had come to regard as an unwanted financial and social problem, is now a vexed question.[79] Whatever the truth here, Blue was among the majority of Bounty recipients who took the Government's money and then made themselves scarce. He and like-minded black veterans perhaps regarded the Bounty as belated, if officially unacknowledged, American War compensation, in return for which they felt disinclined to accept any particular obligations.

Quite some years later in September 1796, Blue was working as a lumper in Deptford, unloading sugar from the West Indiaman *Sir Richard Halliday*. In true lumper style, he twice attempted to pilfer from the cargo but was foiled by the ship's mate. When on a third occasion he was caught with 20 pounds of sugar concealed under his clothes, the machinery of the law was put in motion, although Blue was not collared on the spot but later at a Shadwell tavern across the river. While it might be thought no man would lump who could get better employment, this underestimates Blue. He was also engaged in petty entrepeneurship as a chocolate maker, a process requiring sugar.[80] One can only wonder at the source of his cocoa beans. Lumping could certainly provide opportunities for stealing them too. It is inconceivable Blue was unaware that sugar and cocoa were the products of slave labour and highly likely that he obtained a subversive kick from subjecting these imports to his personal impost. That would be entirely consistent with his later practices in and around Sydney, where long before he died in 1834 he had become proverbial for his subversively entertaining street-theatre antics; entrepreneurship as Sydney's first ferryman and also as a smuggler; and artful manipulation or facing down of official and class superiors. Significantly, in Sydney he gained the nickname of 'The Old Commodore'. Armed with this 'office', he insisted that all passing him in the street saluted him politely. Those who failed to do so received a salty bawling-out on the spot,[81] no doubt much to the glee of the Sydney crowd of convicts, ex-convicts and their children, when the recipient was a member of the colonial upper echelons. At the same time, in Sydney as in Deptford he sometimes took a risk too many, came a cropper and paid the consequences.[82] The outcome of his lumping exploits was transportation for seven years handed down by Maidstone Quarter Sessions, Kent, on 4 October 1796. At the time, the war with France imposed more urgent priorities on the deployment of shipping and seamen than transporting convicts to Botany Bay. As a result, he did not arrive in Sydney till 1801 and was free (by servitude) less than two years later.[83] His years in the London area, set in the context of his wider life history, reveal an extremely resourceful man who, through all reversals of fortune, was determined to guard and extend his own autonomy by hook or by crook. Blue epitomises the opportunistic resourcefulness of black mariners and waterfront workers in Britain during Georgian and early Victorian times. In an Atlantic world where most blacks were themselves tradeable commodities, the moral economy of Blue and his like saw no reason to respect the property rights of whites who traded in slave-produced commodities.

Black Jacks in Britain: at the Hub of the Black Atlantic and British Ultra-radical Politics

The growing maritime power of Britain in our period, both in relation to its merchant shipping and the Royal Navy, put alongside the fact that Jack Tar often enough had an African face, embeds these seamen in several historical processes of the first importance, and not only those connected to the composition of the nautical workforce essential to Britain's expanding maritime trade and power. Although detailed empirical studies, using Admiralty and merchant shipping records to define the dimensions of the black seaman's presence, have yet to be undertaken, several important works point the way forward in other respects.

Rediker notes the importance of black workers, slave and free, in the port workforces of such major Atlantic ports as London, New York and Boston in the period 1700–1750. His Atlantic seamen interact in port with a diversity of workers of other trades and ethnicities, including black slaves.[84] However, what does not quite emerge is that by the late seventeenth and early eighteenth centuries, the Atlantic seaman himself could be black, a slave and even a pirate.[85] Given that Rediker was well aware of the liberational nature of late seventeenth- and early eighteenth-century piracy, of its capacity to challenge the ever harsher terms of employment, discipline and power relations imposed on contemporary seamen, he missed an important point concerning the attractions of piracy to some slave seamen.[86]

Here, however, one must agree with Bolster that;

> Piracy shaped the lives of far fewer mariners of color than did more prosaic forms of slavery. Maritime slavery played an indispensable role in the plantation complex, notably in coastal boats, but increasingly in deep-sea work as well as the eighteenth century wore on.[87]

Furthermore, Bolster is spot-on about the importance of London, for the Atlantic African diaspora:

> More Africans from distant regions congregated in London than anywhere else, making it the hub of the black Atlantic. Among other attractions, London remained the clearinghouse for news about efforts to meliorate the hemispheric plight of black people, such as the Somerset decision in 1772 that led slaves who had once set foot in Britain to regard themselves as legally free.[88]

Duffield's sample of Africans transported to Australia from Britain and Ireland,

1812–52, fully bears out the diversity of origin of the male African population of this period (the black transported females were too few to reach any such conclusions). Thirty-three and a third per cent of the males were born in North America (including the Canadian colonies); 30.8 per cent in the West Indies plus the Bahamas and Bermuda; 19.5 per cent in England; 7.7 per cent in Africa; 1.5 per cent each in Ireland and Scotland; and 6.5 per cent elsewhere.

Within the broad overseas zones, there was a further great variety. The West Indians, for instance, included men from: Antigua; Barbados; Bermuda; Cuba; Demerara; Dominica; Guadeloupe; Jamaica; Nevis; Martinique; St Croix; St Domingo; St Lucia; St Kitts; St Thomas; St Vincent; and Tobago. As the native place of some others was recorded only as 'West Indies', the actual diversity of specific Caribbean origins was probably even greater. As for the North Americans, although many had 'America' recorded as their native place, 13 specific or relatively specific birthplaces occur: Annapolis (Virginia); Baltimore; Boston; Halifax (Nova Scotia); New Brunswick; New York; Nova Scotia; St Johns (New Brunswick); New Orleans; Maine; Maryland; Pennsylvania; Philadelphia. The maritime location of these colonies, states and towns is significant. In Britain, as well as rubbing shoulders with those born in England, Scotland, Ireland and the Isle of Man, they might also encounter others born in, for example: France; Germany; Mauritius; Peru; Portugal; and St Helena, plus of course men born in Africa itself. They, however, were the least likely to have precise or relatively precise birthplaces recorded,[89] a rather sinister record phenomenon. This reminds us that the slave trade ripped all first-generation African slaves from precise places, kinships and societies and hurled them into a social limbo if not exactly social death.[90]

To assume that most of these men had made but one great voyage in their lives, from their birthplace to Britain, would be absurd. These data therefore underplay the extent of their travels and therefore knowledge of the Atlantic world – and sometimes of remoter oceans and shores. Further, 48.2 per cent of these men were tried in London/Middlesex; additionally, 41.2 per cent of the black seamen transported from Britain and Ireland were tried in London/Middlesex.[91] Throw in those who were tried in immediately adjacent counties and over half the male sample is accounted for.

If London and its environs was the hub of the Atlantic world, it was equally the capital of Black Britain. Bolster and other scholars provide abundant qualitative evidence that this was equally true in the eighteenth century. Cutting through the airy 'guesstimates' of various eighteenth-century whites (which have been repeated by many modern scholars), after careful reconstructive demography from a variety of sources, Myers cautiously estimates that in the later eighteenth century, London's black population was 'at least 5,000', possibly twice as many, with a minimum figure for the country as a whole of 10,000.[92] The convergence between her findings, concerning the concentration of Britain's black population in and around London, and Duffield's for a somewhat later period, suggests some long-term demographic continuities.

Unsurprisingly, black seamen featured significantly in London's turbulent and often subversive plebeian social and political life. Viewing some of the great scenes of urban popular protest in Britain from the mid-eighteenth to the mid-nineteenth centuries, black seamen were there, sometimes in prominent roles. In spring and summer 1768, London was racked with street protests and other forms of popular action. Among these was striking the sails of shipping in the Thames by river workers, immobilising shipping and the port; the very word 'strike' for a collective down-tools and walk-out by workers may come from this incident. The river workers signalled their action by hoisting the red flag, till then the maritime signal for battle stations but also the future proletarian flag.[93] During a Liverpool seamen's strike in 1775, the striking seamen went so far as to bring ordinance ashore from their ships.[94] Red flags were also in evidence in a November 1792 Tyneside seamen's strike.[95] Black Jacks and watermen would certainly have witnessed and some, it is probable, been active in such events – at least in London and Liverpool, where any crowd of river workers and mariners had black faces in it. During the 1780 Gordon Riots, an African-Virginian, Benjamin Bowsey, was the 'bell wether' or *de facto* leader of the mob that forced open Newgate prison and released the inmates (including fellow blacks), while another black man, John Glover, was the first in his column of rioters to cry 'Now Newgate'! At the gate his voice was again heard, threatening if necessary to burn the gate down, which was soon done.[96] A third African prominent in these riots, Charlotte Gardiner, led the sacking of a publican's premises near Tower Hill.[97] While Bowsey and Glover were servants, not seamen (at least at the time of the riot), Bowsey's movement from Virginia to London around 1774 at least establishes a maritime connection. All three of these riot leaders were subsequently hanged.

Linebaugh and Rediker have remarked on 'the strategic position that many urban slaves or free blacks occupied in the social division of labour in the port towns' of the eighteenth-century North American colonies.[98] The same was evidently true in some British ports, above all London. From their 'strategic position' and exceptionally strong interest in turning the established order upside down, it followed that blacks in London were extremely prone to ultra-radical activism. Indeed, it has been noted that while ex-servicemen in general strongly participated in 'every insurrection plot in London from 1798 to 1820', this was especially true of black and Lascar ex-servicemen.[99]

In the early nineteenth-century period of popular turbulence in London, the most obvious examples of black ultra radicals of major consequence are Robert Wedderburn and William Davidson, both Jamaicans, both the sons of white masters by slave women and both men who underwent early in life the further brutally radicalising experience of late eighteenth-century naval service. Davidson ended up on the scaffold as one of the five Cato Street Conspirators, executed in 1820 for plotting to blow up the reactionary British Cabinet on the urgings of a police spy and *agent provocateur*.[100]

Wedderburn's childhood experiences of Jamaican slavery were direr than Davidson's and he lacked Davidson's considerable education. In London he saw (and perhaps participated in) the Gordon Riots and after a conversion experience in 1786 became an antinomian preacher on the wilder fringes of subversive popular Methodism and later an ardent Spencean revolutionary and active ultra-radical author too. By 1819, his preaching and debates in a hayloft in Hopkins Street, Soho, attracted elements of London's poorest inhabitants with rough blasphemous buffoonery and violent denunciations of the wickedness of slave owners (to be extirpated by slave revolution), the clergy, lawyers, landowners and all other tyrants. At the same time, the Hopkins Street loft was used for storing pikes and drilling his ragged followers for the envisaged violent English revolution. He was temporarily gagged by a conviction and prison sentence for blasphemy in 1819, which at least saved him from the likelihood of being swept into the Cato Street Conspiracy and onto the gallows alongside Davidson.[101]

Richard Simmonds an African-American pastry cook who was prominent in the 2 December 1816 Spa Fields Riot in London, provides an overlooked and significant addition to blacks who were prominent in ultra-radical action. He was transported for seven years for his pains. Recorded as aged 23 on arrival in Sydney in 1817, he was shipped-on to Van Diemen's Land (now Tasmania).[102] It is a reasonable speculation that he worked his passage to Britain, perhaps as a sea cook. Why should he do this? His specific motives remain unknown but the Black Atlantic[103] grapevine was quite capable of informing him that he might find a degree of everyday social equality among plebeian Londoners, without isolation from other blacks.[104] Like Bowsey, Glover and Gardiner, he was prominent in a major riot. These rioters were enflamed into arming themselves immediately to effect the English Revolution, by the fiery oratory at the Spa Fields Mass Meeting. They broke into Thomas Rea's gunsmith's shop in the Minories, after plundering the nearby premises of Randall & Company. Randall's were evidently also gunsmiths, for when the mob reached Rea's premises, it was already armed with firearms. From Rea's they took more arms worth 'upwards of £1000' and £8.50 in money.[105] John Hall, a merchant and prosecution witness, related Simmonds 'had a sabre in his hand, and seemed very active. The noise was very great, I could not hear him …; he kept brandishing his sword, and making the various cuts of the broad sword exercise.'[106]

The latter point suggests Simmonds had a familiarity with swordsmanship, perhaps gained as a naval seaman or privateer crewman. John Wilson, a private in a detachment of Life Guards sent to disperse this dangerous crowd, seems to have felt a sneaking admiration for Simmonds's pluck, although he was rather more proud of his own martial skills; 'he stood more bold than the rest, flourishing his sword; I demanded that he should lay his sword down; I struck him with the flat of my sword and he gave it up.'[107] Nevertheless, Simmonds then made his getaway and in a direction strongly suggesting familiarity with the sea and seamanship. He was arrested by a police officer on 10 December 1816, at Northfleet, aboard an outward bound East Indiaman. How would such a man pay his passage on the long voyage to India, except by working as a seaman?[108] After these various accounts of derring-do, Simmonds' defence, although effective in (relatively) minimising his sentence, was rather tame-sounding: 'I was in the Minories; there was a great crowd there; a man came up to me, and put the sword into my hand. I had drank half a pint of rum, I began to flourish it; I did not take anything, nor was I in the shop.' In other words, 'I only happened to be there Governor, I was drunk at the time and I didn't do nothing'. The court evidently at least believed he was not a shop breaker and this saved him from the very real prospect of a death sentence.

There is an apt coda to this story. On arrival in 1817 in Van Diemen's Land as a transported convict, Simmonds was anything but tamed. He appears at first to have been put to work in or near to Hobart and soon had a number of relatively minor offences and punishments clocked up.[109] However, some time after 22 June 1818, he was packed off to George Town, then a small settlement, on the Tamar Estuary at the opposite end of the island. There, he was handed down 100 lashes with the fearsome cat 'o nine tails for assaulting the Chief Constable. Such punishments were truly dreadful but in this instance flogging only fired Simmonds up. On 8 April 1819, he was given a further 50 lashes and also sentenced to labour in irons at George Town for three months, another brutal physical punishment. His new offence was amongst the most serious a Van Diemen's Land convict could then commit – bushranging, the Australian term for being an armed bandit at large in the bush. Bushranging, mainly then an activity of runaway convicts, had become a serious problem in the colony in the years since the end of the Napoleonic Wars.[110] Evidently Simmonds' outbreak was short lived but he had not finished yet in defying the Van Diemen's Land authorities to do their worst. On 7 August 1819, he was sentenced to yet another 50 lashes and to be transported for three years to the penal station at Newcastle,[111] far away on the coast of New South Wales. Evidently the Van Diemen's Land authorities had decided that it was prudent to pass the buck to their parent colony. Although its later acts were played out far away in Australia, Richard Simmonds' life exemplifies the truculent libertarian politics of the Black Atlantic.[112]

Conclusions

Enough has been said to establish that African and African Diaspora mariners and port workers in Britain, 1750–1850, were no petty footnote to the history of their times but were rather at the cutting edge of some huge and transformational historical processes. They not only knew 'how the vessel could go' but in what direction they wished to steer it – towards meaningful freedom for themselves and others like themselves. Despite the limitations on the evidence that can at present be mobilised it is clear that throughout the period addressed, they kept the pressure up while typically responding with astute opportunism to any fluid circumstances. If their victories in the struggle for liberation were typically transitory, piecemeal and rather inconclusive, the same can be said for the Atlantic maritime working class generally. There is nothing the least parochial about their lives and struggles, locked as they were into events and processes that connected and shook several continents. Indeed, because of their transoceanic mobility they were able to act as international oral transmitters of subversive news, liberational ideology and practical experience and information. On these grounds, this study has avoided labelling them as 'Black British', not for exclusionist reasons but because that seems altogether too parochial an identity to fit them. At the same time, their knowledge and experience peculiarly fitted many of them not merely to 'join in' white British plebeian ultra-radical and protest movements of the time but often enough to be prominent among those who emerged from the crowd to guide and lead the upsurges of those movements. For this reason, it might be asked in what sense these can be considered 'white' movements, in any essentialised sense.

Equally, the eventual forced relocation of some of these men as far away as Australia teaches us not to regard the 'Black Atlantic' as completely segregated from regions far beyond its wide geographical grounds. Nor was this only a matter of black mariners who were transported as prisoners to Australia. In 1768, Joseph Banks took two black servants, Thomas Richmond and George Dorlton aboard the *Endeavour,* to accompany him on James Cook's first voyage to the Pacific. Poor Richmond was to lose his life as a result, a casualty of Banks's zeal for botanising in the dire climate of the mountains of Tierra del Fuego.[113] In the light of this, perhaps we should begin to enquire how many other black men embarked from British ports aboard British ships for the South Seas, even before the late eighteenth-century upswing of southern whaling sucked many North Atlantic mariners of every hue into far southern latitudes. At the very least, Richmond and Dorlton serve somewhat to challenge white triumphalism about the exploits of the likes of Banks and perhaps other 'big name' white explorers of the Pacific. That a rich young English landed gentleman of that era would have black servants (were they slaves too?) and would require them, as a matter of course, to minister to his needs when on his travels, should not be a matter of surprise. One is tempted to say that such men often could not function without black servants; as well as their practical services, the presence of their black servants defined socially who such men were. Also, we should not essentialise the world of black seamen and port workers addressed in this study into a static homogeneity. As David Dabydeen has observed of Equiano's narrative, so with these men's lives: 'instability and non-linearity was a reflection of the complex and confused experiences of an African enslaved in a variety of … white societies.'[114] In the increasingly unstable and non-linear world we experience today, this too constitutes an aspect of their claim to our greater attention.[115]

Notes

1   Olaudah Equiano (ed. with intro. and notes by Vincent C. Carretta), *The Interesting Narrative and Other Writings*, Penguin, Harmondsworth, 1995 (1st edn published by the author as *The Interesting Narrative of the Life of Olaudah Equiano or Gustavus Vassa, the African, Written by Himself*, London, 1789), pp. 55 and 57. I have used Carretta's edition, because of its new standard of excellence in editing and footnoting. The passage quoted is embedded in a sustained passage, pp. 55–61, about Equiano's total middle passage experiences.

2   See Peter Linebaugh, *The London Hanged; Crime and Civil Society in the Eighteenth Century*, London, Allen Lane, The Penguin Press, 1991, p. 136. Linebaugh's 'pan-Africanism' indicates an important conceptual distinction originating in G.A. Shepperson, '"Pan-Africanism" and "pan-Africanism": Some Historical Notes', *Phylon*, XXIII, 4

(Winter 1962), pp. 346–58. This defines 'Pan-Africanism' as the institutionalised movements emerging in the late nineteenth century and generating, for example, the Pan-African Conference of 1900 and subsequent Pan-African Congresses, 1919–45; 'pan-Africanism' as the more fluid, informal ideologies and associated practices *avant la lettre,* that nurtured a collective identity among the African Diaspora from the eighteenth century onwards and engendered and sustained an inspiring idea of Africa among that diaspora. I add that if this idea of Africa was essentially utopian, rather than historically specific, that was salutary and necessary given the extreme dystopia experienced by the African diaspora.

3   At the close of his narrative, Equiano again disingenuously flourishes his 'naïve' guise: 'I am far from the vanity of thinking there is any merit in this Narrative; I hope censure will be suspended, when it is considered that this was written by one who was as unwilling as unable to adorn the plainness of truth with the colouring of imagination'; see Equiano, op. cit., pp. 235–6. A reviewer for *The General Magazine and Impartial Review,* July 1789, was dopey enough to take Equiano at his literal word here; see Equiano (ed. with intro. by Paul Edwards), *Equiano's Travels,* Oxford, Heinemann Educational Publishers, African Writers Series, 1996, p. xxii.

4   Nevertheless, as Paul Edwards warned posthumously, one must not see ironic laughter at whites everywhere in Equiano's narrative; see Edwards, 'Unreconciled Strivings and Ironic Strategies: Three Afro-British Authors of the Late Georgian Period', in David Killingray (ed.), *Africans in Britain,* Ilford, Frank Cass, 1994, pp. 28–48. I am unconvinced, however, that the label 'Afro-British' is apt for Equiano, who profoundly seems rather to be of the 'Black Atlantic', transcending and indeed transgressing all merely national boundaries. Several United States' scholars, on more slender grounds, have claimed Equiano as an African-American and may be mistaken for the same reason: e.g. William L. Andrews, *To Tell a Free Story; The First Century of Afro-American Autobiography, 1760–1895,* Urbana and Chicago, University of Illinois Press, 1986, ch. 2. Linebaugh, op. cit., p. 169, gives Equiano an even odder original identity; 'A Fanti blacksmith boy from Nigeria'. No *Nigerian* identity then existed and the Fanti lived (and live) in what is now Ghana. Equiano himself asserts he was an Igbo. F.O. Shyllon, 'Olaudah Equiano; Nigerian Abolitionist and First National Leader of Africans in Britain', *Journal of African Studies,* 1971, pp. 433–51, co-opts Equiano into a nationality not then conceived and promotes him to a position in Britain then nonexistent. Of course, *modern* Nigerians and African-British can reasonably feel proper pride in Equiano's achievements.

5   See Jesse Lemisch, 'Jack Tar in the Streets: Merchant Seamen in the Politics of Revolutionary America', *William & Mary Quarterly,* XXV, 1968, pp. 371–407.

6   They either appear not at all or minimally, not recognising they might have serious historical importance, in such works as Michael Lewis, *A Social History of the Navy 1793–1815,* London, George Allen and Unwin, 1960; Ralph Davis, *The Rise of the English Shipping Industry in the Seventeenth and Eighteenth Centuries,* London, George Allen and Unwin, 1962; J.A. Harris (ed.), *Liverpool and Merseyside; Essays in the Social and Economic History of the Port and its Hinterland,* London, Frank Cass, 1969; David Syrett, *Shipping and the American War, 1775–1783,* London, Athlone Press, 1970; N.A.M. Roger, *The Wooden World; An Anatomy of the Georgian Navy,* London, William Collins, 1986; K.O. Morgan, *Bristol and the Atlantic Trade in the Eighteenth Century,* Cambridge, Cambridge University Press, 1993. I was unable to lay hands on Brian Lavery, *Shipboard Life and Organisation, 1730–1815,* Aldershot, Ashgate, 1998, before completing this study. As for that venerable journal of maritime history, *The Mariner's Mirror,* its eyes are so firmly

fixed on the quarter deck, the ward room and maritime technologies, that it can hardly notice anything so lowly as black seafarers. Even Marcus Rediker, *Between the Devil and the Deep Blue Sea; Merchant Seamen, Pirates and the Anglo-American Maritime World, 1700–1750*, Cambridge, Cambridge University Press, 1987, has little to say about black *seamen*. Important exceptions to this rule of general neglect, and of great value to this study, are W. Jeffrey Bolster, *Black Jacks; African-American Seamen in the Age of Sail*, Cambridge, Mass. and London, Harvard University Press, 1997; Julius S. Scott, 'Afro-American Sailors and the International Communication Network: The Case of Newport Bowers', in Colin Howell and Richard Twomey (eds), *Jack Tar in History; Essays in the History of Maritime Life and Labour*, Fredericton, New Brunswick, Acadiensis Press, 1991, pp. 37–52; Peter Linebaugh and Marcus Rediker, 'The Many Headed Hydra: Sailors, Slaves and the Atlantic Working Class in the Eighteenth Century', in ibid., pp. 11–36; and Linebaugh, op.cit.

7   Edward Scobie, *Black Britannia; A History of Blacks in Britain*, Chicago, Johnson Publishing Co., 1972, ch. ix, is entitled 'Black Jacks, Boxers, Artists'. This is rather a job lot of occupations and on perusal the 'Black Jacks' receive thin treatment. James Walvin *Black and White; The Negro and English Society 1555–1945*, London, Allen Lane, The Penguin Press, 1973, indexes only five (separate) pages on black sailors, three of these concerning the twentieth century. Folarin O. Shyllon, *Black Slaves in Britain*, London, Oxford University Press for Institute of Race Relations, 1974, offers a revisionist interpretation of slave emancipation within Britain; black seaman are therefore outside its remit. Shyllon, *Black People in Britain 1553–1833*, London, Oxford University Press for Institute of Race Relations, 1974, has only five scattered indexed pages addressing black sailors. Peter Fryer, *Staying Power; The History of Black People in Britain*, London, Pluto Press, 1984, has significantly more indexed references than Walvin or Shyllon but no sustained treatment. Ron Ramdin, *The Making of the Black Working Class in Britain*, Aldershot, Gower Publishing Company Ltd., 1987, scoots across 1550 to 1900 in 57 pages so has little to say on black seamen of our period which had not been said before. Jagdish S. Gundara and Ian Duffield (eds), *Essays on the History of Blacks in Britain; From Roman Times to the Mid-Twentieth Century*, Aldershot, Ashgate, 1992, offers nothing on slavery and emancipation era black seamen. Gretchen Gerzina, *Black England; Life Before Emancipation*, London, John Murray, 1995, has no indexed references to seaman and certainly no sustained treatment of them. However, James Walvin's recent specialist study, *An African's Life; The Life and Times of Olaudah Equiano, 1745–1797*, Cassell, London and New York, 1998, pays substantial attention to Equiano's life at sea within the wider context of contemporary black seafaring. In the 1990s, 'mainstream' Africanists began to consider the contribution of Africans to the 'Atlantic world' in the era of the Atlantic Slave Trade, but have not (to the author's knowledge) addressed black seamen and port workers to any extent. Thus, in John Thornton's excellent study, *Africa, Africans and the Making of the Atlamtic World, 1400–1800*, Cambridge, Cambridge University Press, 1992 and 1998, while Africans are represented as historical actors on both sides of the Atlantic, African mariners are an 'absent presence', except insofar as ch. 1 presents the technological and oceanographical constraints on coastal West Africans engaging in autonomous trans-Atlantic vayages, before and during the early period of European navigation to West Africa. Thornton, op. cit, p. 16, summarises Ivan van Sertima's claim 'that Africans made frequent voyages to the Americas since about 800 B.C.' but, like most scholars outside van Sertima's school, rejects this claim. Thorton, ibid., concedes that

West Africans possibly made very occasional and inadvertent *one way* voyages to the Americas before Columbus. For Ivan van Sertima's views, see his *They Came Before Columbus; The African Presence in Ancient America*, New York, 1979, pp. 37–109.

8   Shyllon, op. cit.

9   For the print history of Equiano's narrative and his successful entrepreneurship in publishing, publicising and marketing edition after edition up to his death in 1797, see James Green, 'The Publishing History of Olaudah Equiano's Narrative', *Slavery & Abolition*, 16, 3, December 1995, pp. 362–75. Roger, op. cit., essentially a study of the Royal Navy during the Seven Years War, has a brief discussion of its black seamen on pp. 159–61.

10 Equiano, op. cit., pp. 78, 92–3, 108. Equiano's life at sea is extensively treated in Walvin, op. cit., esp. chs 2, 3, and 6–9.

11 Norma Myers, 'Servant, Sailor, Soldier, Beggarman: Black Survival in White Society 1780–1830', *Immigrants & Minorities*, 12, 1, March 1993, pp. 47–74; Myers, *Reconstructing the Black Past; Blacks in Britain 1780–1830*, London, Frank Cass, 1996, esp. ch. 4. Myers 'blacks' include South Asians, while Duffield's (see note 7 below) are all Africans/diaspora Africans (as in the present study).

12 Myers, op. cit. 1996, Table 4.1, p. 68. The same data occur in her 'Servant, Sailor, Soldier, Beggarmen'.

13 Ian Duffield, 'Skilled Workers or Marginalized Poor? The African Population of the United Kingdom 1812–1852', in David Killingray (ed.), *Africans in Britain, Immigrants & Minorities* (special issue), 12, 3, November 1993, pp. 49–87; reprinted in Killingray (ed.), *Africans in Britain*, Ilford, Frank Cass, 1994, pp. 49–87.

14 Ibid., pp. 59–60 and Table 3, p. 65.

15 This is discussed and the literature on crime in Britain extensively cited in Ian Duffield and James, 'Introduction; Representing Convicts?', in Duffield and Bradley (eds), *Representing Convicts; New Perspectives on Convict Forced Labour Migration*, London, Leicester University Press, a Cassell Imprint, 1997, pp. 1–18; and in most subsequent chapters of this book.

16 Stephen Nicholas (ed.), *Convict Workers; Reinterpreting Australia's Past*, Cambridge and Melbourne, Cambridge University Press, 1988.

17 Carretta, op. cit., has used these extensively to verify Equiano's naval career; from his footnotes it is evident that the RN muster books commonly identify blacks serving on naval ships' crews as such.

18 Lewis, op. cit., p. 81, states 'it is an overpowering surfeit of knowledge'. Ibid., ch. II, 'Homeland: Geographical Distribution', devotes pp. 60–80 to officers and 80–82 to men.

19 The chief exception is an historical sketch within a work whose gaze was mainly contemporary; see Kenneth Little, *Negroes in Britain*, London, Kegan Paul, 1948. For the late eighteenth century, Christopher Fyfe, *A History of Sierra Leone*, London, Oxford University Press, 1962, gave solid attention to the origins of the Sierra Leone Colony in the heated question of what to do with the 1780s London 'Black Poor'. The most comprehensive subsequent work on this community is Stephen J. Braidwood, *Black Poor and White Philanthropists; London's Blacks and the Foundation of the Sierra Leone Settlement*, Liverpool, Liverpool University Press, Liverpool Historical Studies No. 9, 1994.

20 Duffield, 'Skilled Workers or Marginalised Poor?', p. 64. In numerical terms, this was 47 out of 68 seafarers.

21   J.J. Hecht, *The Domestic Servant Class in Eighteenth-Century England*, Routledge and Kegan Paul, London, 1956.

22   J.J. Hecht, *Continental and Colonial Servants in Eighteenth-Century England*, Northampton, Mass., Smith College, 1954.

23   Black domestic servants and English and Scottish legal cases concerning slavery are strong themes in Walvin's pioneering *Black and White* (1973), which in turn strongly influenced the focus of later general works on Africans in Britain, even those written by Shyllon and Fryer, who were hostile to Walvin's work.

24   These three cases are especially extensively discussed in Shyllon, op. cit. and Fryer, op. cit.

25   See Jonathan Press, *The Merchant Seamen of Bristol 1747–1789*, Bristol, Bristol Branch of the Historical Association, 1976, p. 2, n. 4.

26   Equiano, op. cit., pp. 92–4.

27   A gold coin nominally worth £1.05 in 1999 sterling currency; in real terms worth many times that.

28   Walvin, op. cit, p. 52.

29   See Equiano, op. cit., chs, VI and VII.

30   Equiano, op. cit., pp. 147–59. Should the name of Equiano's friend in Savannah be glossed as 'Musa' and if so, was 'Musa' a Muslim as the name implies? It is perfectly possible. When years ago the late Paul Edwards and I co-authored a study on Equiano and Islam (see n. 34 below), we missed Equiano's putative friendship with an African-American Muslim.

31   Ibid., pp. 211–3.

32   Ibid., p. 179.

33   Ibid., pp. 179–81.

34   For the Annis incident discussed at greater length and in wider context, see Paul Edwards and Ian Duffield, 'Equiano's Turks and Christians: An Eighteenth-Century African View of Islam', *Africa, the Caribbean, and the Southern United States: Linkages*, special number of *Journal of African Studies*, 2, 4, University of California, Winter 1975–76, pp. 433–44.

35   Roger, op. cit., p. 161.

36   For a rich exploration of important aspects of this information network and its historical implications, see Scott, 'Afro-American Sailors and the International Communication Network', in Howell and Twomey, op. cit., pp. 37–52. Walvin, op. cit, p. 79, comments; 'Blacks in London learned of incidents in the colonies and even on the high seas, even before they broke cover in the British press and public discussion'.

37   For the *de facto* achievement of freedom by most slaves in Britain by the 1790s, largely through their own actions not legal rulings in the courts, see Douglas A. Lorimer, 'Black Slaves and English Liberty: A Re-Examination of Racial Slavery in England', *Immigrants & Minorities*, 3, 2, July 1984, pp. 121–50; and Lorimer, 'Black Resistance to Slavery and Racism in Eighteenth-Century England', in Gundara and Duffield, op.cit., pp. 58–80. Lorimer's views have been contested by W.R. Cotter, 'The Somerset Case and the Abolition of Slavery in England', *History*, 79, 255, February 1994, pp. 31,56 – not very convincingly, since Cotter supposes that because generations of later British and United States legal experts believed Mansfield had effectively liberated slaves in Britain in 1772, it must be so. Is Cotter innocent of 'legal fictions'? This one might be very convenient, as it presents emancipation as a privilege graciously handed down by benevolent whites, so negating freedom as fought for from below by slaves. Cotter seems innocent the power relations embedded in supposedly impartial legal texts.

38 For an extended study of Thomas Day, see Ian Duffield, 'Daylight on Convict Lived Experience; The History of a Pious Negro Servant', in the press at time of writing this study, for Hamish Maxwell-Stewart (ed.), *Exiles of Empire; Convict Experience and Penal Policy, 1788–1852*, special issue of *Tasmanian Historical Studies*.

39 See Douglas A. Lorimer, *Colour, Class and the Victorians; English Attitudes to the Negro in the Mid-Nineteenth Century*, Leicester, Leicester University Press, 1978, p. 29; Braidwood, op. cit., p. 24; Bolster, op. cit., p. 94.

40 See Bolster, op. cit., pp. 103–4. At the same time other African-Americans, in the Chesapeake slave states, flocked to the British seaborne operations in Chesapeake Bay during the War of 1812.

41 Ibid., p. 213, and thence throughout his final chapter, 'Toward Jim Crow at Sea'.

42 See Lorimer, op. cit., pp. 39–40.

43 *Congosah*; the Sierra Leone Krio term for rumour or downright invention. Why use a Krio term here? Why accept the dowdy limits authorised by the motheaten gatekeepers of the 'Queen's English'!

44 For this theme, see Fiona Spiers, 'Black Americans in Britain and the Struggle for Black Freedom in the United States, 1820-1870', in Gundara and Duffield, op. cit., pp. 81–98.

45 Lorimer, op. cit., p. 38.

46 See Linebaugh, op. cit., chs 11 and 12. What immediately follows in my main text is summarised from the complex mass of detail and argument in these chapters.

47 For example, theft from a vessel in a navigable river became a separate category of serious offence with its own tariff of punishment. It had long before been established that theft from one's legitimate workplace was the serious offence of larceny and that theft by breaking and entering (or leaving) premises was the serious offence of burglary.

48 Linebaugh, op. cit., p. 418.

49 Ibid., pp. 471–8.

50 Ibid., pp. 372–3.

51 Ibid., p. 391.

52 Ibid., p. 425.

53 Archives Office of New South Wales (hence AONSW), *Bound Indents of Convict Ships* (hence *Indents*), entry for 1817; Thomas Brett, arrived Sydney from England *per ship Fame*, 8 March 1817; *Old Bailey Sessions Papers* (hence *OBSP*), First Session 1814, pp. 33–4. Brett was 36 according to the first of these sources, 30 according to the second – both probably guesses by Brett himself. One shilling nominally equalled 5p, four pence nominally equalled one third of that.

54 See *OBSP*, First Session 1814, pp. 33–4.

55 Ibid., p. 34.

56 Ibid.

57 AONSW, *Indents*, entry for 1817.

58 *OBSP*, Seventh Session 1815, pp. 386–7 and 39; in the original, through a printer's error, there is no page 388; i.e., the text is complete but the page numbering is faulty.

59 Neither Duffield nor Myers in their publications on Africans in Britain in this period, based on criminal records, can offer any other criminal trial in which both accused and victim were blacks.

60 *OBSP*, Seventh Session 1815, pp. 386–7 and 39, evidence of Joseph Uxbridge and Jacob Morris.

61 Ibid., evidence of Joseph Uxbridge.

62 *OBSP*, Seventh Session 1815, pp. 386–7 and 39, evidence of Augustus Scott, Clerk of the Navy Office at Woolwich, who had paid this sum to Uxbridge. In his own evidence in ibid., Uxbridge could remember the £84 and the denominations of the bank notes but not the exact amount of the shillings and pence, which unfortunately supports the image of Jack Tar as feckless. In this case, there were plenty of high jinks in the record, but none of the dodgy allegations of seamen awash with prize money frying newly bought gold watches in pans or eating banknotes between slices of bread as sandwiches.

63 Lewis, *A Social History of the Navy*, Table VII, p. 294. Ibid., Table VII, p. 300, gives monthly rates for Able and Ordinary Seamen in 1815 as £1 13s 6d and £1 5s 6d respectively.

64 See Linebaugh, op. cit., pp. 75–8.

65 *OBSP*, Seventh Session 1815, pp. 389; for his commuted sentence see AONSW, *Indents*, 1816, entry for Jacob Morris, arrived Sydney from England *per* ship *Mariner*, 11 October 1816.

66 *OBSP*, Seventh Session 1815, p. 386, abbreviated indictment of Jacob Mason.

67 *OBSP*, Seventh Session 1815, pp. 386–7 and 39, prisoner's defence. Although care was taken in this source to convey the flavour of Morris's actual language, the printed version is unlikely to be verbatim. Recording orature (possibly by shorthand) and then printing it, are inescapably 'interventionist' acts with reshaping effects, regardless of intent.

68 Such polylinguality is an important point in Linebaugh and Rediker, op. cit.

69 See Rediker, op. cit., for extensive discussion of late seventeenth- and early eighteenth-century pirates and their customs. For a recent study of the Nore Mutiny, devoid of the officer-centred focus of some older works, see Joseph Price Moore III, '"The Greatest Enormity That Prevails"; Direct Democracy and Workers' Self Management in the British Naval Mutinies of 1797', in Howell and Twomey (eds), op. cit., pp. 76–104. Moore mentions no black mutineers but it is inconceivable that there were none among the 7,000 men involved. A consensus exists that *c.* 15 per cent of RN ships' personnel, 1793,1815, were 'foreigners' by birth. Confusingly this includes colonial subjects (e.g. from the Caribbean). This predicates a black presence. Americans were especially problematical at the time, as impressment officers often suspected both black and white *British* merchant seamen on American ships of carrying false 'Protections' certifying American citizenship. It is generally assumed that the 85 per cent of 'non-foreign' seamen on the muster rolls were all white. A small minority of these too, however, are likely to have been blacks. For 'foreigners' among RN crews, see Tom Malcolmson, 'Muster Tables for the Royal Navy's Establishment on Lake Ontario during the War of 1812', in *The Northern Mariner/Le Marin Du Nord*, IX, 2, April 1999, pp. 41–67, esp. p. 43. Malcolmson cites six scholars agreeing on around 15 per cent.

70 Naval impressment officers and gangs were well aware that many British seamen (of whatever colour) served on American merchant ships, because of the better pay and terms than on British ships and because in practice during wartime they could obtain 'protection' certificates issued by American consular officials, declaring them to be American citizens. Further, the British held stiffly to the position that original nationality could not be repudiated; under this doctrine genuine British emigrants to the USA and even any American born before British recognition of the United States (as were most American seamen in 1800), were held to be fair game for RN impressment. See Lewis, op. cit., pp. 434–9.

71 Dudley Pope, *The Devil Himself; The Mutiny of 1800*, London, Alison Press Book, Secker and Warburg, 1987, refers to Brown as John Brown III, following the practice of naval muster books, to distinguish men of the same name. For references to John Brown III, see

Pope, pp. 48, 77, 82–3, 85, 87, 89, 112, 128 and 131. Brown, like most of these mutineers, was never apprehended and tried.

72 See for e.g. Mitchell Library, State Library of New South Wales Sydney, manuscript Ab 31/52, Humble Petition of William Blue of Northampton near Sydney to His Excellency Sir Thomas Brisbane, … Governor … of New South Wales, 28 October 1823; AONSW, Colonial Secretary's Papers (hence CS), main series of letters received, Bundle 19, 1823, R6052, 4/1764, p. 215, Humble Petition of William Blue to His Excellency Sir Thomas Brisbane, … 17 November 1823. For the tens of thousands of African-Americans who flocked to British lines during the American Revolution, and their military service roles under the British, see Benjamin Quarles, *The Negro in the American Revolution*, Chapel Hill, University of North Carolina Press, 1960, pp. 111–34 and 160–81.

73 See Braidwood, op. cit., p. 29.

74 Braidwood argues that the Commission for American Claims did not practice 'direct racial discrimination' but also says: 'The majority of blacks who joined the British forces in America had been slaves, with few possessions of their own. They had therefore lost very little on account of the war, and had in fact gained their liberty; so that, according to the Commission's narrow terms of reference, they were not entitled to anything from the British Government'; see ibid., p. 29. This suggests what is now called institutional racism and so undermines Braidwood's position.

75 All his petitions were signed with a cross accompanied by the words, 'William Blue, His Mark'. Also see Braidwood, ibid.

76 Ibid.

77 See No. 50, William Blue, in 'An Alphabetical List of the Black People Who have Received Bounty from the Government', PRO T1/638, reproduced in Graham Russell Hodges (ed.), *The Black Loyalist Directory: African Americans in Exile After the American Revolution*, Garland Publishing Inc., in association with the New England Historic Genealogical Society, New York and London, 1996, Appendix 2, p. 227.

78 Not only is Blue the only *black* convict of that name transported to Australia, out of several hundred now known to me, he is also the *only* convict transported to Australia known to me with the surname Blue; and I have scrutinised records of well over 100,000 convicts in search of blacks and other ethnic and national minorities amongst them. Also, I have never found reference to any other black person with the surname Blue, in the now quite extensive historical literature on Africans in Britain.

79 Studies positing a thinly disguised racist expulsion include: Shyllon, op.cit., Walvin, op. cit, Fryer, op. cit. Braidwood examines the evidence more minutely than any of them. He demonstrates that: no blacks left for Sierra Leone against their will; their spokesmen secured terms important to the emigrants themselves; and far more blacks received the Bounty than emigrated. See Braidwood. op. cit., ch. 3. This has the attractive feature of allowing for black agency and provides good evidence of it.

80 See Meg Swords, *Billy Blue the Old Commodore*, North Shore Historical Society pamphlet, North Sydney, 1979, pp. 8–9. Swords is a valuable empirical source but her interpretations are challengeable.

81 For samples of Blue's artful practices from the Sydney press, see letter from 'An Observer' and editorial reply in *Sydney Gazette and New South Wales Advertiser*, 31 October 1833; and his obituaries in: *Sydney Gazette and New South Wales Advertiser*, 8 May 1834; *Sydney Morning Herald*, 8 May 1834; and *The Australian*, 9 May 1834. For an ex-convict of his firmly plebeian station and dodgy record to receive even one, let alone three press obituaries,

was extraordinarily unusual and reveals the hold he had achieved on the imaginations of Sydneysiders as an almost mythical antihero.

82 For these aspects of Blue's life, see Ian Duffield, '"Billy Blue"; Power, Popular Culture and Mimicry in Early Sydney', in *Australian Popular Culture, Journal of Popular Culture* (special issue), publication imminent at time of writing.

83 AONSW, CS, Register of Pardons & Tickets of Leave, Vol. 1, pp. 540–1; Swords, op. cit., pp. 8 and 11.

84 Rediker, op. cit., pp. 29, 62, 67–8 and 112.

85 The work which has made this point most clearly is Bolster, op. cit., ch. 1; for Bolster's black pirates, see pp. 13,16.

86 See Rediker, op. cit., chs. 5 and 6. B.R. Burg, *Sodomy and the Pirate Tradition; English Sea Rovers in the Seventeenth-Century Caribbean*, New York and London, New York University Press, 1984, explores liberational sexualities among pirates but has nothing to say on black pirates.

87 Bolster, op. cit., p. 16. Bolster demonstrates that maritime slavery was as important to the Caribbean as the North American plantation complex; see ibid., pp. 18–23. Metropolitan British experiences of African-American seaman's are also addressed in his study. There is no 'American Exceptionalism' (i.e. 'great- republic' parochialism) about this work.

88 Ibid., pp. 19–20.

89 Duffield, op. cit. 1993, p. 67, Tables 5 and 6.

90 I much admire of Orlando Patterson's, *Slavery and Social Death; A Comparative Survey*, Cambridge, Mass., Harvard University Press, 1982. Nevertheless, his thesis that slavery entails 'social death' tends to take slave owners desires as total effects. Slave owners could impose hugely on slaves but not totally control their actions, still less their memories and thoughts. Here, I own the influence of scholars who have emphasised the agency of those subjected to relations of domination: e.g. James C. Scott, *Domination and the Arts of Resistance; Hidden Transcripts*, New Haven and London, Yale University Press, 1990; Ranajit Guha, *Elementary Aspects of Peasant Insurgency in Colonial India*, New Delhi, Oxford University Press, 1992 – and more broadly the subalternist school of historians whom Guha has led. I am indebted to Tamsin O'Connor, Department of History, University of Edinburgh, for alerting me to the importance of Scott's *Domination and the Arts of Resistance*.

91 Duffield, op. cit. 1993, p. 66; see Table 4 for data on black seafarers.

92 Myers, op. cit, pp. 34–5. Her estimates are 'baseline' estimates.

93 Linebaugh, op. cit., p. 311. Also see Moore, '"The Greatest Enormity"', in Howell and Twomey, op. cit., p. 82.

94 See R. Barrie Rose, 'A Liverpool Sailor's Strike in the Eighteenth Century', *Transactions of the Lancashire and Cheshire Antiquarian Society*, 68, 1958, pp. 85–92. I thank Hamish Maxwell-Stewart of the Department of History, University of Tasmania (Hobart) for drawing my attention to this article.

95 Moore, op. cit., pp. 76–104, esp. p. 82.

96 Linebaugh, op. cit., pp. 336, 337 and 348–9.

97 Ibid., pp. 349 and 351.

98 Linebaugh and Rediker, op. cit., pp. 11–36, passage quoted p. 19.

99 Iain McCalman, *Revolutionary Underworld; Prophets, Revolutionaries and Pornographers in London, 1795–1840*, Cambridge, Cambridge University Press, 1987, p. 54.

100 For an account of Davidson's life and death, see Fryer, op. cit., pp. 214–20. Ibid., p. 215, states that he ran away to sea after three years as apprentice to a Liverpool lawyer and while at sea was twice impressed.

101 For Wedderburn, see Iain McCalman, *Revolutionary Underworld*; McCalman, 'Anti-Slavery and Ultra-Radicalism in Early Nineteenth-Century England; The Case of Robert Wedderburn', *Slavery & Abolition*, 7, 1986, pp. 99–117; Robert Wedderburn (ed. and intro. by Iain McCalman), *The Horrors of Slavery, and Other Writings*, Edinburgh, Edinburgh University Press, 1991; Fryer, op. cit., pp. 220–7.

102 Archives Office of New South Wales, Sydney (hence AONSW), Richard Simmonds, in *Bound Indents of Convict Ships*, C.O.D. 143, arrived Sydney from England *per Almorah*, 31 August 1817. Also see Archives Office of Tasmania, Hobart (hence AOT), 71 Simmonds, Richard, in Con 23/3, *per Almorah* to NSW 1817 then *per Pilot* from New South Wales to Van Diemen's Land 1817. The former describes his complexion, hair and eyes as black; the latter has the variant, eyes dark brown, and adds the remark 'Man of Colour'.

103 It seems apt, here, to borrow (as have other scholars) from the title of Paul Gilroy's *The Black Atlantic; Modernity and Double Consciousness*, London and New York, Verso, 1993.

104 Scott, 'Afro-American Sailors and the International Communication Network', in Howell and Twomey, op. cit., pp. 37–75, richly illustrates how news born by refugees from the enormous slave revolution in 1790s St Domingue (Haiti) excited African-Americans and disturbed whites along the eastern US seaboard; from there to London too, one imagines.

105 *Old Bailey Session Papers* (hence *OBSP*), Second Session 1817, case 216. Richard Simmonds, p. 91, evidence of Thomas Rea.

106 Ibid., evidence of John Hall, Esq.

107 Ibid., p. 92, evidence of Private John Wilson.

108 Ibid., p. 92, evidence of Thomas Brancombe.

109 AOT, Con 31/38, 71 Simmonds, Richard, *per Almorah & Pilot*, 1817, entries for 23 December 1817, 20 January 1818, 14 March 1818 and 22 June 1818. All these were heard by one or other, or both, of the Hobart magistrates, A.W.H. Humphrey and Rev R. Knopwood.

110 See Hamish Maxwell-Stewart, '"I could not blame the rangers"; Tasmanian Bushranging, Convicts and Convict Management', *Tasmanian Historical Research Association Journal*, 42, 3, 1995, pp. 109–27.

111 AOT, Con 31/38, 71 Simmonds, Richard, *per Almorah & Pilot*, 1817, entry for 7 August 1819. Unfortunately, his offence on this occasion is not specified in this record. Simmonds was still at Newcastle NSW in 1822; see Carol J. Baxter (ed.), *General Muster and Land and Stock Muster of New South Wales, 1822*, Sydney, Australian Biographical and Genealogical Record, in Association with the Society of Australian Genealogists, entry no. A19172, p. 434. Simmonds does not appear in Malcolm R. Sainty and Keith A. Johnson (eds), *Census of New South Wales, November 1828*, Sydney, Library of Australian History, 1980. Either he was by then dead; or had escaped; or had received a pardon and legally left the colony (which seems unlikely); or been returned to Van Diemen's Land (such shuttling to and fro of troublesome convicts did occur); or this imperfect census overlooked him. If he had received no more extensions of sentence, after arriving at Newcastle, he would have become free by servitude in 1826, through completing his original sentence plus three years' extension. Nevertheless he would in principle, if in the colony, have remained within the remit of the 1828 census takers, who were required to record all free persons as well as those undergoing sentences of transportation.

112 John Goff or Gough, a Napoleonic War era black seaman born in the Isle of Wight in the 1790s and later transported had a much more spectacular career of resistance in Australia than Simmonds, including leading two convict insurrections and the second time paying for it on the Sydney scaffold; see Ian Duffield, 'The Life and Death of "Black" John Goff: Aspects of the Black Convict Contribution to Resistance Patterns During the Transportation Era in Eastern Australia', *Australian Journal of Politics and History*, 33, 1, 1987, pp. 30–44. I am aware of no ultra-radical activities by Goff in England, however, so have excluded him from the main text.

113 See Patrick O'Brian, *Joseph Banks: A Life*, London, Collins Harvill, 1988, pp. 68 and 82. From this account, it appears that poor Richmond probably died of hypothermia, possibly aggravated by consumption of alcohol in a mistaken attempt to keep himself warm.

114 David Dabydeen, 'Olaudah Equiano Freedom's Slave', The Observer Profile, *The Observer*, 8 August 1999, p. 23.

115 This study is dedicated to Emeritus Professor G.A. (Sam) Shepperson, my first mentor and continuing inspiration in studying the rich history of the African diaspora.

8 Patterns of Resistance: Indian Seamen in Imperial Britain

SHOMPA LAHIRI

Introduction

By utilising the private/public dichotomy found in feminist theory,[1] this chapter demonstrates that while the working lives of Indian seamen in late nineteenth and early twentieth-century Britain were subject to imperial imperatives, their private lives offered a sphere in which they were able to exercise greater agency. The first half of the chapter examines the size of the lascar population in Britain during the period, recruitment practices and how the stereotype of the docile and controllable lascar developed. The remainder explores patterns of resistance in relation to missionary activity focusing on the language of conversion; overt and covert opposition to conversion; responses to ill treatment by the host society and lascar politicisation.

Most secondary literature on the subject of Indian seamen in Britain reinforces perceptions of lascar subordination and weakness by representing lascars as passive victims of Indian *serangs* (superiors), shipping companies, trade unions, legislation, poverty and racism. More recently however, Norma Myers has attempted to move away from this traditional stance by investing late eighteenth and early nineteenth century lascars in Britain with a limited degree of initiative.[2]

This study is partly based on reports garnered from missionary society records.[3] While researchers in the field have touched upon these sources, they have not been fully utilised. Clearly these accounts must be treated with caution, exhibiting as they do many of the race and class prejudices of the imperial period. But given the paucity of primary evidence, it would be foolish to dismiss missionary reports altogether, as they provide one of the few opportunities to delve into the lives of South Asians in Britain prior to the Second World War. Unlike their middle class co-nationals, who left accounts of their encounters with metropolitan British society,[4] high levels of illiteracy among lascars have effectively silenced personal testimony, a problem common to all subaltern[5] history. However, by reading between the lines, it is possible to give a voice to the often faceless, mute masses incorporated in the term 'ethnic labour'. While this voice has been partially submerged and subverted by the fact that it emanates from missionaries, nevertheless it is still audible if one listens hard enough.

From the middle of the nineteenth century lascars – a collective term applied to South Asian, Chinese, Arab, Malay and African seamen[6] – became an increasingly visible component of Britain's maritime labour force, forming approximately 10 per cent in 1891 and, by the First World War rising to 18 per cent. Britain was a major force in world shipping, owning over half of the world's steam tonnage by the turn of the century.[7] This served to further amplify the importance of colonial seamen to maritime trade as, although lascars were employed exclusively in steam ships, they outnumbered all other foreign seamen. By 1937 over a quarter, 27 per cent, of crews employed in British registered ships were classified as lascars.[8]

Several factors led to the steep rise in Indian seamen after 1850. The repeal of the Navigation Act in 1859 to meet the demands of Free Trade put an end to discriminatory legislation which had prevented Indian seamen being classified as 'British' for navigation purposes during peacetime, thereby allowing lascars to meet increased demand during periods of war; the replacement of sailing ships by steam navigation resulted in the de-skilling of seamen and alteration in conditions of marine employment, whilst the building of the Suez Canal opened up shipping routes which fed rapidly expanding international trade. Demand for cheaper labour allowed 'Shipowners more freedom … to replace unionised high-waged crews of one country with relatively unorganised, lower-paid crews of another'.[9] At the outbreak of the First World War, lascar wages were only between a third and a quarter of British wages. Indian wages had not increased since the beginning of the nineteenth century, making Indian seamen the lowest paid of all ethnic sailors, costing less than Chinese or Arab crews. Wages remained depressed by the oversupply of labour and overmanning. But despite extremely low wages, lascar pay still compared favourably with rural wages in India.

Recruitment Practices

The twin features of overmanning and the relentless supply of cheap labour were inextricably connected to lascar recruitment practices. Up until the 1850s most lascars came from the coastal areas of the Indian subcontinent, but they were not hereditary sailors as suggested by the 1903 Parliamentary Committee on the subject. Most were agriculturists who supplemented their income by going to sea. Consequently lascar work patterns were irregular and based on maritime demand for labour and agricultural conditions. A sea captain who had worked with lascar crews, Captain Hood, claimed that originally lascars came principally from the western seaboard of the Indian peninsular, from the townships and villages lying north and south of Bombay, along the whole length of the coastline. Hindus from Surat formed the principle component of sailors registering in the port of Bombay. But, by the turn of the century, the Shipping Master of Bombay informed Captain Hood that 'sailors came from all over India ... from the Himalayas to the Cape of Comarin'.[10] Captain Hood, who was more familiar with Western India, neglected to include traditional maritime communities from Eastern India, mainly from East Bengal recruited from the port of Calcutta.

The nineteenth century expansion of railways across India allowed new sources of labour from further inland to be delivered to the major ports. New areas of recruitment included the Maldives, Punjab and North India. These newcomers were mostly Muslim, although recruitment patterns varied between regions. For example, in the province of Bengal, deckhands came from Noakhali and engine room staff were mainly Sylhetis. Religious demarcation lines were evident for other provinces. The historian, Conrad Dixon, noted that Muslim Punjabis and Pathans were to be found below deck, in the engine room, Surati Hindus on deck and Christians from Goa and Cochin in the saloon.[11] The reason for this intriguing division of labour is not known. However 'Divide and Rule', an important feature of British rule in India, appears to have operated successfully on board ship. Religious groups, either through accident or design, were segregated, undertaking various occupations in different parts of the ship.

The supply and recruitment of lascars was controlled indirectly by Indian intermediaries, known as *ghat serangs* at the ports of Bombay and Calcutta. The *ghat serang* was a combination of 'moneylender, labour recruiter and lodging-house keeper'.[12] Another *serang* was employed on board ship to supervise and pay the men. This system was vulnerable to abuse and corruption. In the port of Calcutta, young inexperienced men replaced experienced and capable seamen, who had signed articles. This was possible, as seamen were not required to show proof of identification. The substitute seamen were cheaper than experienced sailors, making them more attractive to *serangs*.[13] Although the burdens of indebtedness and crimping were common to sailors worldwide, they were not institutionalised in the form of a *serang* as in India.

Limited knowledge of the English language caused lascars to be heavily dependent on *serangs*. Also chronic indebtedness was a feature of rural Indian society. This was exacerbated by the temporary nature of a sailor's job contract, which only lasted six to 12 months at a time. Lascars had to find temporary accommodation on shore, while waiting to be recruited, a practice which left them in debt to lodging housekeepers. The system of recruitment was effectively a 'closed shop', based on informal family networks and contacts. The 1903 Parliamentary Committee, which investigated the employment of lascars, provided evidence of the way *serangs* blocked attempts at reform and claimed to represent lascar interests. A *ghat serang* at Bombay, Khan Bahadur Ruttonjee Chichgar, claimed to be a spokesman for lascars. He told the Committee in London that lascars had informed him that they did not want improved conditions.[14]

Both official British discourse and secondary literature has emphasised the power of the *serang*. However an article by G. Balachandran has cast doubt on the alleged power of these intermediaries, by arguing that any profit made by the *serang*, through bribery and corruption, eventually ended up in the pockets of *ghat serangs* and European shipping brokers.[15] Ultimately British shipping companies were prepared to turn a blind eye to corruption, representing it as a traditional Indian cultural practice, although the involvement of European shipping brokers would seem to refute this assumption. *Serangs* were seen as indispensable to exercising control and discipline over Indian crews. Language and race barriers meant that a direct relationship between British officers and Indian crews was not regarded as possible or desirable.

As the evidence above shows, not only did shipping companies perceive Indian seamen as a cheap, renewable source of labour; this opinion was reinforced by the belief that as a group lascars provided an exceptionally controllable workforce. Not just by virtue of their relationship with the *serang*, but as part of a wider spectrum of stereotypes surrounding lascars.

Images of Lascars in Britain

The impression given by contemporary accounts of lascars was one of super-exploitability. Although they were complemented for their sobriety,[16] industriousness, patience and discipline, these all served a larger purpose – control. Some captains claimed to prefer lascar crews. One wrote: 'Taken altogether a much more efficient state of discipline prevails on lascar-manned steamers than can ever be hoped for on similar vessels manned by ordinary types of European crews.'[17] Another captain with experience of lascar crews, Captain J. Walsh, believed that this obedience made the lascar more trustworthy than his British counterpart.[18] At first sight this preference for lascars, based on greater efficiency, seems to imply that Indian seamen were superior to British sailors. In fact, in a perverse piece of logic, it was argued that the reverse was true. Captain Hood stated that it was the lascar's low level of skills, greatly inferior to the highly skilled British sailor, which were sought after in the era of steam. He wrote: 'There is very little sailorising, as seamen call it, to do nowadays.'[19] A reference to the de-skilling of the seaman's occupation. Similarly a journalist commented that 'with steam the lascar became more a labourer than a sailor'.[20]

Thus the lascar's alleged inferiority, in particular, his ability to do mundane, repetitive, unskilled work, regarded as lowly and degrading by British sailors, enabled him to compete successfully. Hood opined 'in distinct contrast to his European brother, he will sit patiently, day after day ... until the task is completed. Not so content at this harassing work is the European'.[21] This statement is revealing, as it shows how racial ideology, based on the innate superiority and inferiority of the races worked in such a way that even apparent attributes assigned to lascars by the British were based on congenital subordination. According to this argument the British sailor's superior skills, brain-power, initiative and self-reliance had priced him out of the market. He could lead but he could not follow. Lascars, on the other hand, could follow, but were in need of strict leadership to keep them in line, without which they would become 'cowardly' and 'incompetent'. In keeping with the perception of lascars as a low-grade, under-skilled reservoir of workers, they were denied any measure of responsibility and were even regarded as too unreliable to stir the wheel of the ship.[22]

Although lascar supporters in Britain denied allegations of cowardice, physical weakness and susceptibility to cold climates, these myths continued to perpetuate throughout the nineteenth century. The historian, F.J.A. Broeze, made a crucial point, when he wrote: 'the larger crew size easily convinced the British that Indians were physically inferior to their European colleagues.'[23] But it was lack of warm clothing and inadequate healthcare, rather than genetic make-up, which led to higher incidences of mortality among Indian crews in higher altitudes. In recognition of this fact the Board of Trade modified regulations which prohibited employment of lascars in vessels going to Boston by providing suitable heating and warm clothing.[24] The impression of vulnerability, which characterised Indian sailors by the end of the nineteenth century, was strengthened by their recent history in Britain. The high death rates and appallingly squalid living conditions endured by lascars in early nineteenth century London, led to the establishment of a Parliamentary Committee of Enquiry, which revealed the misery of dock life for Indian seamen in the capital city of the empire. As a result the East India Company became responsible for the repatriation, feeding, clothing and welfare of lascars, while in British ports.[25]

Undeniably there is ample evidence of the exploited position of lascars, completely at the mercy of agricultural, trade and labour conditions. As Indian seamen did not enjoy the protection of British trade unions, shipping companies were able to use them as 'blackleg' labour when dock labourers took industrial action. Thus the image persisted of an inherently biddable workforce. 'Easily satisfied'[26] and 'contented with their lot'[27] – just a few of the phrases commonly used to describe lascars. However, while the British essentialised the Indian sailors' character and abilities in their own interests, the stereotype of the docile, loyal lascar did not always match with reality. Evidence suggests lascars were not as contented as their employers liked to believe. Indeed they were extremely unwilling to take over the duties of striking dockers in London, but felt unable to defy their employers' wishes.[28] While they could exercise little control over forces impinging on their working lives, in contrast, their inner lives provided a terrain in which they were better equipped to withstand external pressures, particularly from missionaries.[29]

Development of Missionary Activity Among Lascars

The development of missionary concern for non-Europeans in Britain was part of the wider growth in missionary activities during the nineteenth century. These included societies such as the London Mission Society, Church Mission Society and Wesleyan Methodist Society, concerned primarily with evangelising in Britain's overseas territories. Brian Stanley in his book *The Bible and the Flag* captures the arrogance and self-confidence of missionaries in the following phrase: 'It was assumed that the poor, benighted 'heathen' was in a condition of massive cultural deprivation, which the gospel alone could remedy.'[30] Prior to the last quarter of the nineteenth century the spread of Christianity was associated with Western culture and commerce, but after 1885 the purely religious message became detached from Britain's cultural baggage. Theological thinking had changed, emphasising worldwide evangelisation, rather than conversion linked to social transformation.

Missionary societies were alerted to the plight of lascars sojourning in British ports, particularly London, by the establishment of a 'Committee of Gentlemen' in 1786, followed by the formation of the Society for the Protection of Asiatic Sailors in 1814 and the setting up of a parliamentary inquiry to look into the treatment of lascars in 1820. Nevertheless, they were comparatively slow to act, only taking the initiative in the 1850s, when the secretaries of various missionary societies set up an appeal to establish a Home for Lascars in London. This remarkable, if somewhat belated, display of unity by the various Protestant denominations demonstrates how seriously they had come to regard the issue. A golden opportunity for conversion had presented itself in the shape of the 'heathen at the gate'. Missionaries had hitherto been wedded to the belief that only by travelling to the colonies was it possible to proselytise colonial subjects. The movement of the colonies to Britain, in the person of lascars, created a new sphere of missionary endeavour. The inconsistency of 'spending tens of thousands of pounds ... annually, preaching the gospel to the heathen in foreign lands' while neglecting to attend to the spiritual needs of natives much closer to home, informed the decision taken by missionaries to extend their field of activities to non-Europeans in Britain. Henry Venn, Secretary to the Church Missionary Society, expressed this view when he spoke at the meeting for the establishment of the Strangers Home for Asiatics, Africans and South Sea Islanders: 'It seemed incumbent on those especially who take part in sending Missionaries to all the world, to take measures for evangelising those who, in the providence of God, are brought home to our own doors.'[31]

Several organisations and individuals became interested in the salvation of the lascar's soul. The Strangers Home for Asiatics opened in 1857 (the year of the Indian Mutiny) in the West India Dock Road, London. Although this was the first organised overture towards lascars, there is evidence of missionary interest in Indian seamen prior to this date. In 1814 a missionary tract calling on Christians in Britain to meet the challenges posed by a lascar population in their midst suggests that two Indians had been engaged to translate the gospel and a sermon had been given in Islington, London.[32] Also an organisation called the Lascar Benevolent Institution appointed a missionary to lascars in 1843, known simply as Mr Thompson.[33] The London City Mission placed one of its missionaries, Joseph Salter, at the disposal of the Strangers Home. He continued his work among lascars even after the Home replaced him in 1876, not retiring from active work until 1898. Salter wrote two books about his experiences, *The Asiatic in England: Sketches of Sixteen Years Work among Orientals* and *The East in the West or Work Among the Asiactics and Africans in London,*[34] Abraham Challis, Salter's assistant, later replaced him, devoting most of his time to the Lascar Institute in Tilbury, founded in 1906. In 1887 several missionary societies – the Bishop's Fund, the additional Curates Society and St Andrew's Waterside Church Mission – appointed Rev. Ebenezer Bholonath Bhose, a Bengali, as curate of St Luke's and missionary to lascars. Bhose had been educated at Bishop's College, Calcutta, which trained many Indian clergymen. He became missionary to Indian indentured labourers in British Guyana and official government 'Translator of East Indian Languages'. After retirement he left Guyana and moved to Britain, where he became associated with the Society for the Propagation of the Gospel. Prior to taking up his post at St Luke's he had been curate of St Andrews, Bethnal Green, in the East End of London.[35] Bhose's reports are particularly interesting, as he appeared to have internalised many of the Christian prejudices against lascars harboured by his white colleagues.

Conversion Strategies and the Language of Conversion

Missionary reports reveal the methods adopted to spread the gospel to Indian seafarers. In the nineteenth century, one of the earliest missionaries took advantage of the economic hardships experienced by the lascar population to, effectively, bribe lascars in order to gain their attention. Thompson wrote: 'To many of them I give a little pecuniary assistance, this makes them, for the first time at least, willing to listen to what I have to say about their spiritual welfare.'[36] The relative improvement in lascar living conditions during the late nineteenth and early twentieth century prevented both Joseph Salter and Ebenezer Bhose from resorting to financial inducements to secure the interest of Indian seamen. However, both were alive to the tremendous possibilities of attending to lascars when they at their most vulnerable and, in theory, least able to resist. Consequently they sought out lascars, not just on ships, but in the Dreadnought Seamen's Hospital in Greenwich and in prisons. In 1875 Salter even visited opium dens. He wrote of how prison life disposed Asian inmates to think on spiritual matters and made them particularly susceptible to the gospel.[37] Similarly Bhose, writing 20 years later described how he actively sought out sick lascars in hospital believing, like Salter, that 'hearts softened by pain and sickness'[38] would be more responsive to the Christian message. Not only were Europeans missionaries employed to preach to lascars, full use was made also of lay Indians who acted as interpreters, such as converted Brahmin, Maharaj Tarry.[39] In addition, Bhose was aware that it was crucial to harness the enormous authority wielded by the *serang*. He wrote: 'A person in his position can, if so inclined, place obstacles in our way and it is therefore of the utmost importance that we should cultivate his friendship and be on good terms with him. Once his goodwill has been gained, he will, if requested send his men to the mission and occasionally come himself with them.'[40] The decision to cultivate the *serang* reinforced his power over lascars and further served to limit lascar agency.

Nevertheless, despite the unrelenting advocacy of the gospel, success proved elusive and the number of conversions was negligible. Lascar ability to repel missionary onslaughts on their beliefs should not be reduced to a simple rejection of Christianity. The rest of the study will explore the subtle and complex strategies adopted by lascars to outmanoeuvre missionaries. Crucial to the 'cat and mouse game' played out between lascar and missionary was the control of language. Linguistic skills offered huge rewards for its beneficiaries. On the one hand, ability to speak Indian languages was the key qualification for missionaries working with lascars. Equally, on the other hand, lascar dependence on *serang*s stemmed from their inability to understand orders in English, which had resulted in the need for intermediaries. Missionaries viewed language in its functional capacity, 'a pragmatic vehicle of communication'[41] through which they could make the gospel known. Its utility was limited to a fixed purpose: understanding lascars and thereby gaining access to their souls.

Joseph Salter stressed that his ability as a linguist was essential to his work. He had started to learn Hindustani in 1857, when he was a missionary in West London. He befriended an Indian living in a refuge and members of the Nawab of Surat's party who had taken up residence in Paddington. He gave English language lessons, while improving his knowledge of Hindustani. Salter was tenacious in achieving his goal. Despite his aversion to the smell of Indian food he mastered 'the oriental gutturals and other strange sounds',[42] committing the main parts of the scriptures to memory. At the beginning of the nineteenth century a pamphlet was published which exhorted young Christians to come forward and work with Indian seamen in Britain. The pamphlet emphasised the ease with which Indian languages could be assimilated. Hindustani was described as the easiest Indian language to learn, taking a mere three months to translate the gospel. Even Bengali, which was viewed as the most difficult Indian language, as it originated from Sanskrit – one of the Indo-Aryan group of languages – could be mastered in four months.[43] Bhose's previous post as translator of Indian languages in British

Guyana, made him particularly well suited to the position he occupied. Joseph Salter and Abraham Challis, however, were confronted with additional problems. The heterogeneous nature of the lascar population in London required missionaries to be conversant with a variety of vernaculars. Salter spent many nights cramming to learn new dialects, but, as he stated, the chief difficulty was in acquiring colloquial language.[44] A corrupted form of Hindustani known as *Laskari Bat* was spoken on board ships manned by lascar crews. A ship-surgeon, Dr Parry, compiled a manual for ship surgeons containing useful phrases and vocabulary for surgeons working with Indian crews. The manual affords a fascinating glimpse of lascar treatment on board ship, where Indians were addressed exclusively in the imperative, with phrases such as 'remain silent' and 'obey me'.[45]

Even after Salter had struggled to gain a strong grasp of Asian languages, he found that they lacked the means to express key Christian concepts such as 'sin' 'repentance' and 'regeneration'. He wrote:

> The language ... does not afford the faculty to express spiritual ideas which the languages of Europe do, because, until our missionaries entered the field of Labour, there never existed a motive to express these ideas, hence words for them have never been supplied by the native. For instance, in *Hindoostanee*, the word for conscience does not exist. If I wish to say 'conscience tells you so', I must say '[your] heart tells you so'.[46]

The word for 'convert', so essential for the missionary's vocabulary, presented even greater problems for Salter. He wrote, 'If I wish to ask a *Hindoo* Christian when he was converted, I must say. "When did you become a Christian". But if I wish to call on them to be converted to God, I am driven to another expedient equally remote. I can hardly make plain to my reader my difficulty in this respect'.[47] Salter's frustration stemmed from the fact Hinduism was not an evangelical creed. In order to develop a language of conversion, language itself had to go through a process of conversion, it had to be reformulated to voice new meanings and concepts.

Access and appropriation of language was just as important to lascars as missionaries. Opinions differed about levels of literacy among Indian seamen. J.C. Buckley, a vicar at St Luke's, who was involved with the establishment of the Lascar Mission, believed a fair proportion of lascars could read and write their own vernaculars, but not English.[48] Reverend Bhose, however, estimated 90 per cent illiteracy.[49] Whatever the actual rates of illiteracy, lascars had a great deal to gain from possessing a command of English, as well as a written knowledge of their mother tongues. Benefits included respect from peers and improved job prospects. One *serang* told a parliamentary committee that if he could understand English he would not be a lascar, but follow a more lucrative profession instead.[50] Lack of language skills made lascars vulnerable to unscrupulous men, from both within and outside their own community, who would rob and cheat them. Language barriers also isolated lascars from the local dock community in which they lived. This was compounded by the fact that lascars lived apart from the host population on ships. The wide range of dialects spoken by lascars prevented intercourse between men from different regions of India. Indeed several missionaries including T.R. Underwood, Bhose's successor at the Lascar Mission, noticed how seamen from different provinces of India refused to socialise with each other: 'If a party of Bombay men is in possession of the room and a party of Calcutta men arrives, the Bombay men leave playing their games and intimate it is time to go.'[51] As the majority of lascars were Muslim if would appear that language and regional loyalties were more divisive than religion. Although it is possible, as Underwood suggested, that Muslim seamen were split along Sunni/Shiite lines.

The cross transmission of language could be financially rewarding. Asian lodging housekeepers benefited greatly from English wives and partners who had learnt to speak Indian vernaculars. Women known as Mrs Peroo, Mrs Mohamed, Mrs Janoo, Lascar Sally and Calcutta Louisa were paid to interpret in court cases involving lascars.[52] But sometimes concealing knowledge of English could be more profitable, as in the case of one lascar, known as Shaik Boxshoo, a professional beggar, who had deserted ship and taken up residence in London. Boxshoo was quick-witted enough to realise that displaying fluency in English would not elicit the sympathy of his British patrons, clashing as it did with their view of romantic eastern mendicancy, as a result he pretended to have no knowledge of English. Arguably taking the deception a little too far by claiming to be deaf and dumb as well.[53]

Hostile Responses to Lascars

Apart from the practical difficulties of constructing a language of conversion, environmental obstacles also hindered evangelisation among London's lascar population. The ill treatment lascars received in the Docks throughout the nineteenth and early twentieth centuries did little to endear them to England, its inhabitants or its religion. The London City Mission's missionary to lascars at Tilbury, Abraham Challis, highlighted this when he wrote:

Effective evangelistic work among Orientals is most difficult. Those from distant lands meet with much that tends to close their hearts against Christian instruction. If at any time they encounter scorn, ill-treatment, or injustice from Englishmen, they are not likely to esteem highly the religious faith of those at whose hands they have suffered.[54]

Well-founded fear of assault and robbery at the hands of local men and women caused lascars to remain imprisoned in often cramped and crowded ships, afraid to venture outside the dock area. When lascars did venture out at weekends, they presented highly visible targets for youths, who frequently pelted them with stones.[55] The latent hostility behind these acts of violence is demonstrated by the testimony of one workhouse employee. Joseph Salter questioned him when a lascar was found dying in appalling conditions at Shadwell workhouse: 'He is one of the troublesome darkies: they are always coming here and we never treat them too kindly, for they don't understand it and we should never get rid of them again, if we did.'[56]

Evidence from missionary reports does not correspond with the stereotype of the submissive, uncomplaining lascar discussed earlier. On the contrary, lascars complained bitterly about the behaviour of locals towards them. They even told missionaries to write to the Queen, whom they (wrongly) believed owned the docks, informing her of the ill treatment they had received. Indian seamen contrasted the treatment of British people with the civility and kindness shown towards then by the 'common people' in other countries.[57] The police were singled out for the most scathing criticism: 'They say that in this respect London is the worst of all the countries they have been to, and express their surprise that the Queen, whose police in Bombay or Calcutta can maintain such excellent order, that no one may with impunity molest another in public streets should be powerless to prevent street ruffianism in her own country.'[58] Reverend Bhose agreed that 'the police can or will give them no protection', suggesting that the police were deliberately not acting to protect lascars from assault.[59]

Fifteen years later, in 1905, Reverend Underwood reported similar cases of stone throwing, theft, verbal abuse and bullying, as well as serious assault, where lascars had been subjected to beatings. However, Underwood also reported that the situation had improved with police claiming 30 convictions against youth in a one-month period.[60] It is important to stress that the Docks had a reputation for being lawless and dangerous at night.[61] But while crime was a fact of everyday life for the inhabitants of the docks, Indian seamen, through their ignorance of British life and language, were particularly susceptible to fraudsters and charlatans. On one occasion some men in a public house offered to change a lascar's notes into gold and, having got possession of the notes, refused to give them back. On another occasion a man passed off a theatre bill for a five-pound note.[62] The short duration of lascars' sojourn in Britain created difficulties in bringing cases to court.

Missionaries were concerned about the bad impression lascars received of Britain. One wrote: 'It is very much to be feared that most of them carry away a wrong impression of the people of this country from the degraded specimens of men and women they often see in the streets.'[63] In order to counteract this negative image Indian seamen were taken on trips to the West End of London. There is evidence that these trips made some impact. One lascar observed: 'The people here are quite gentlemanly. They don't stare at us, nor laugh at us as they do at the other end of London.'[64] The violence and hostility encountered by lascars in the London docks exposed the gap between the rhetoric of evangelical Christianity as expressed by missionaries and the reality of life in a Christian nation. By extension, it also cast doubts on Britain's imperial mission and its claims to civilisation and superiority. The missionary's natural enemy, 'sin', in its various forms, appeared to be manifestly present in the docks, where Christianity, from the lascar perspective, seemed to have made very little visible impact. Apart from the dock inhabitants and missionaries the only other Europeans lascars came into contact with were British officers on board ship. Here, too, evidence of ill usage by British naval officers served to undermine the lascars' perception of the value of Christianity. One lascar was asked by the ship's steward to assist in an act that he considered to be dishonest. When the lascar refused he was beaten. Salter wrote: 'The poor fellow came to me with a contused eye and complained that if Christianity had no better influence on Englishmen than that, it was unworthy of his acceptance.'[65] Salter was particularly annoyed, as he believed he had been making progress towards conversion with this man.

Overt Resistance to Conversion

The greatest barrier to the conversion of large numbers of lascars to Christianity in Britain came from the lascars, themselves. Although missionaries fought a slow war of attrition, trying to wear down resistance, ultimately they achieved very little success. Missionaries found that Indian seamen were less easy to manipulate than their reputation suggested. Lascars resisted conversion by both overt and covert means. Some, particularly Muslims, were extremely vocal in their opposition to Christianity. They were described as 'very fond of arguing and apt sometimes to lose their tempers'.[66] Any questioning of the gospels was viewed by Joseph Salter and later Ebenezer Bhose as examples of lascar bigotry and superstition.[67] Only Abraham Challis was prepared to acknowledge that lascars should not be dismissed as ignorant and easy fodder for conversion. He expressed his unconventional views in an article entitled 'Lascars as Critics and Heroes': 'The typical lascar is far shrewder a person than many people give him credit for and if he is not over-ready to embrace Christianity, he can, if called upon, give some forcible reasons for not doing so, and reasons that are not so easy to combat.'[68] Challis elaborated further about the difficulties he faced:

> They are very keen about knowing what kind of a foundation Christianity rests upon before they are willing even to give it friendly consideration. If one is not prepared to be criticised through and through and if one is not also prepared to submit to the criticism of all that we believe and the manner in which that belief is or is not lived out, it is not much good to expect their interest, even if we had twice as fine a Mission Institute as we possess.[69]

In stark contrast to Bhose and Salter, Challis admitted a sneaking admiration for the stand lascars took on 'what they believed to be the truth in religion'.[70] Salter cited 'the most determined antagonist' as lascars from Bombay and Upper India.[71] The following is an illustration of the type of opposition Salter faced. He was told, 'You Christians expect to live all your life-time in sin, and when you are about to die and to account to God for your misdeeds, you expect to roll all your transgressions on Christ, and stand before God as sinless'.[72]

The greatest theological objection to Christianity was the doctrine of the Holy Trinity or the divinity of Jesus Christ, whom Muslims recognised only as a prophet. They claimed Christians had tampered with the New Testament in order to bring it into agreement with Christian views. This was just one of the 'endless objections and difficulties' put forward by lascars.[73] Some Indian seamen claimed translations of the gospel were 'utterly untrustworthy' and insisted on hearing the original Greek, which was, of course, unintelligible to them. Lascars challenged missionaries to prove the superiority of Christianity. One *serang* called on a missionary to place his hand in a fire in the name of his faith, only then would he agree to convert.[74] According to Reverend Underwood, lascars would avoid theological debate unless an educated man could attend to defend Islam. Experience of missionary tactics had made lascars weary and suspicious, consequently they would only confront missionaries when fully prepared. This strategy enjoyed some measure of success as Underwood conceded: 'Some of the *serang*s are well read and argue quite cleverly.'[75] Criticism of Christian doctrine was not new, already by the middle of the nineteenth century Muslim teachers in India were debating with missionaries utilising philosophical arguments to undermine the scriptures.[76] Although it is unclear to what extent lascars would have been influenced by debates conducted by privileged members of India's Muslim community, contact is unlikely to have been substantial. Nevertheless Muslim lascars in Britain were feeding into this tradition of intellectual resistance, with its roots in the subcontinent.

Covert Resistance to Conversion

Just as British rule of India required an epistemological understanding of Indian society, missionary conquest of the 'heathen soul' in Britain also demanded similar breadth of knowledge, but this understanding was lacking. Consequently Indian seamen were able to exploit missionary ignorance of eastern theology and Indian cultural norms. For example, when Joseph Salter tried to convince Hindu lascars 'of the folly of worshipping material things instead of a supreme being' he was immediately corrected by a lascar who declared that 'he did not worship the image, but the *Dharam* or personal essence of the imaginary divinity'.[77]

Missionaries were encouraged by lascar friendliness and politeness, believing that such behaviour represented a willingness to convert. In fact, the warm welcome missionaries received on board ships was part of a strictly observed culture of hospitality, which is still practised today in many Asian countries. Although accommodation on board ship was overcrowded lascars took great pains to make sure the missionary was as comfortable as possible by providing him with the best of their meagre provisions.[78] Outward hospitality masked resistance. When Salter attempted to convert the Chinese owner of a Joss House – a place of worship attended by Chinese lascars – the man, in an act of supreme irony, tried to return the favour by offering incense sticks for Salter's ancestors. Salter plans had backfired, he found himself subjected to Chinese Buddhist ritual. By conveying the impression of an 'ignorant native' the Joss House owner had successfully subverted the act of conversion.[79] At times the 'mask of civility'[80] slipped and irritation towards the missionary became more apparent. Sook-dai came to Britain to appeal to

Queen Victoria to return his land. He was assisted by Salter when he became destitute in London. But when Salter started to preach the gospel, Sook-dai began to show signs of increasing exasperation: 'Why talk to me about an affair that took place so long ago? My *bigah* of land is only an affair of yesterday. Talk to me about that. It is time the other was forgotten.'[81]

Subtle and covert forms of opposition, which camouflaged lascar rejection of Christianity in a cloak of studied indifference were particularly effective in thwarting missionary ambitions, as is evident from Joseph Salter's failed attempts to engage Hindu seamen. Although they were polite and accepted the literature handed to them without complaint, Salter had problems reading their responses, observing: 'there is very little manifestation of any influence either pro or con.'[82] While some Indians felt the need to defend their faith, it was those who neither defended nor explained their religion that particularly baffled and frustrated Salter. He wrote, 'My remarks were unwelcome but received in that merry, indifferent spirit that seemed to say that words are only idle wind'.[83] Other Asian visitors to London also adopted the strategy of not responding to missionary overtures. The Buddhist contingency at the 1876 Indian exhibition in London ignored Salter, refusing to debate the merits of their beliefs, causing Salter to write: 'One of the Buddhists (not a priest) did not seem to consider his faith worthy of explanation or defence.'[84] Missionaries viewed Hindu and Buddhist refusal to participate in theological debate as passivity, which reinforced existing stereotypes of the placid lascar. But, as Ashish Nandy has argued in his book *Intimate Enemy*, the colonised Indian was able to harness passivity and perceived weakness as a weapon of resistance. Nandy writes, 'Seemingly he makes all-round compromises, but he refuses to be psychologically swamped, co-opted or penetrated … it might be sometimes better to be dead in somebody else's eyes, so as to be alive for one's own self'.[85] Thus it is possible to argue that adopting an indifferent stance was utilised by some Indian seamen, to frustrate the missionary enterprise.

The Lascar Mission's reports show that a few baptisms did take place. Five had taken place at St Luke's by 1910. A lascar called Yusuf Sayah, who took the name Luqa after baptism, was described as the 'most satisfactory convert the mission had ever had'.[86] Luqa had been a *Hafiz*[87] and a *moulvi* (priest) in a mosque in Bombay. As a result he was highly respected by his countrymen and assisted at the Lascar Mission. Despite his acceptance of Christianity Luqa, who had also been a physician in India, still rejected Western medication. He attempted to cure his tuberculosis with homeopathic drugs. Thus, even when the message of the gospel did secure rare conversions, other associated aspects of western civilisation were not accepted so readily.

The pluralistic and pragmatic approach many lascars adopted to religion clashed with the narrow unitary approach of missionaries. Salter was very disappointed to discover that a would-be candidate for conversion, Monshee Syed, was not progressing in quite the way he had hoped. Syed claimed no contradiction in worshipping Christ, the Gospel and the Koran. When Salter tried to explain that only the Gospel had any validity Syed rejected his argument.[88] Similar views were expressed by lascars at the turn of the century. An Indian seaman told Abraham Challis: 'Padri Sahib, when we are in Bombay we are Muhammedans, but when we come to London you are our religious teacher and we do not wish it to be otherwise.'[89] This statement shows the complex nature of lascar religious commitment. On the surface they appeared to have responded positively to Christianity, but on return to India they again took up their birth religion. This strategy enabled lascars to accommodate two distinct religions and adapt to the religious cultures of Britain and India. Joseph Salter viewed this flexible approach to religious identity, expanding and contracting to incorporate eclectic influences, as fundamentally flawed. He made his opinions known to a Hindu woodcarver at the 1876 Indian exhibition in London: 'You make your god and then worship him, you can make him to your own fancy and repair him when he is damaged.'[90]

For evangelical Christians like Salter, Jesus Christ was the only path to salvation, alternative prophets were viewed as Satanic and consequently a pluralistic attitude to religion was despised. This contrasts with the opinions voiced by European women who cohabited with lascars. When describing the death of a lascar one woman told Joseph Salter: 'He died quite like a Christian calling out Allah! Allah! Allah! before he died and they say that in his country that is the name of God!'[91] Thus in the mind of this woman Allah and Jesus had become indivisible, a different name for the same God. Notions of superiority and inferiority, fundamental to missionary Christianity were not evident.

Salter viewed the equal worth of different religions, as just one of the many delusions afflicting the 'heathen mind': 'He [the lascar] thought God had provided salvation for everyone in the world, but each must seek it through the medium of their respective prophets. He considered that his only way was through Mohamed. The Christian could succeed through Christ and the *Hindoo* through *Vishnoo*.' Salter concluded, 'They seemed to believe that Jonah's God was as good as their own'.[92] Thus lascars challenged the fundamental tenant of the missionary project – the assumed superiority of Christianity – by claiming parity of religious belief. Although missionaries frequently described lascars as bigots, evidence suggests they were open to a range of religious influences. For example, Salter was surprised when lascars asked to be remembered in his prayers.[93] This all-embracing conception of religion contrasted sharply with the inclusive and chauvinistic stance adopted by missionaries. Lascars' pragmatic approach meant that while very few embraced Christianity wholeheartedly, neither were they willing to reject the possible benefits which could accrue from contact with missionaries. Total rejection of missionary overtures jeopardised access to welfare facilities provided by missionaries. Indian seamen tantalised the missionary with the unspoken prospect of conversion, by taking on the role of a suggestible native, just long enough to take advantage of the many functions performed by the missionary in his capacity as secretary, social worker, translator and news provider.[94]

The following extract demonstrates particularly well, how lascars were able to benefit from contact with missionaries, while surrendering virtually none of their religious autonomy. Reverend Underwood described a typical visit to a warehouse in the London docks:

> When I make my appearance at the Godown [warehouse] they crowd round me to *salaam* and shake hands. Someone tells the *serang*, and he shouts from his corner: 'Oh! Ho! The *Padri Sahib* has come. He is my *Padri Sahib*'. Then he comes down with words of welcome, and leads me up to his bunk. I take off my shoes and sit on the top cross-legged. The *serang* orders the men to bring their pillows and several are pulled up for me to lean against. Then a man is told to make me a cup of tea and the rest sit round to hear the news. First of all they all want to know what ships are coming home, and when they will arrive, the dates of sailing, after that any Indian news; and, finally, anything of interest in the daily paper ... I have found it very difficult to give any direct Christian teaching ... If I begin to speak definitely about the truths of Christianity the *serang* shouts out: 'The *Padri Sahib* is tired, he has come a long way, and it is getting late. We must not keep him as he has a long way to go. Get his bicycle ready!' My shoes are handed to me and they very politely see me off.[95]

In their desire to convert lascars, missionaries viewed every act, which did not constitute outright hostility as a sign that their message was getting through. Indian sailors were able to exploit and manipulate the missionary's boundless optimism to great effect. While 'they carefully avoided religious subjects in conversation'[96] they were not slow to utilise the numerous facilities provided by the Lascar Mission. The Lascar Mission operated as a clubroom providing newspapers, board games, refreshments and instruction in English. As stated above, the missionary performed various duties such as addressing envelopes, reading aloud, directing lascars to other ships and taking messages. Figures for attendance are patchy, but climate may have been a decisive factor. In the summer months attendance was higher, but in the winter lascars were reluctant to venture out in the cold. The 1890 Lascar Mission report claimed highest attendance, on Sunday nights, averaging about 35.[97] An indication of the extent to which attendance fluctuated can be gauged by looking at figures for attendance for five consecutive weeks in the summer of 1907 and the same week, three years later, in 1910:

| 1907 | 99 | 97 | 93 | 31 | 61 |
| 1910 | 57 | 102 | 47 | 26 | 45[98] |

Indian seamen soon discovered functions for the home, which had not originally been intended. The building was used as a welcome hiatus in the long walk to Petticoat Lane Market,[99] as well as a place where they could rest and show off their purchases. It also enabled lascars to haggle effectively: a sailor would make an offer to a shopkeeper, then retreat to the Mission for half an hour before returning to make another offer, until a satisfactory price could be negotiated. Indian seamen would often check prices with the missionary to avoid being overcharged.

Imperial Mission and Lascar Politicisation

Missionaries who worked with lascars saw their role as political as well as evangelical. Conversion was inextricably connected to the imperial mission, but even on this issue missionaries faced some degree of resistance. Soon after the Lascar Mission was established in 1887 Reverend Bhose reported Indian loyalty to and interest in Queen Victoria, who was the subject of numerous enquiries.[100] But the Lascar Mission reports also reveal that lascars were voicing criticisms of British administration in India. The Queen was reproached for her inability to keep law and order in the docks.[101] Many Indian seamen complained to Reverend Bhose of the excessive taxation levied on Indian subjects. Bhose reported: 'They say that … they are … taxed so heavily that, in order to pay the Government duties, the poor are reduced to the point of starvation.'[102] Lascars also complained when duty was introduced on gifts taken for relatives in India. The enforcement of sanitation measures by the British authorities to check the spread of the plague in India provoked particular opprobrium from Muslim lascars, who objected to government intervention on religious grounds. Although Bhose vigorously refuted allegations made against the British authorities, lascars continued to believe 'that hundreds were forcibly removed to the hospital on mere suspicion and there given something to put them out of existence'.[103] Apart from parochial concerns, lascars also showed an interest in international politics, particularly the Russo-Japanese war and the Boer war, as well as social questions, such as the condition of women.

Missionaries regarded their work with lascars as crucial to British hegemony in India. Consequently they took every opportunity to extol the virtues of British rule. In 1893 the Lascar Mission report stated:

> We take advantage of every suitable occasion to point out to them blessings they enjoy under the Queen's rule and to say a few words to strengthen and stimulate their loyalty and allegiance and this is all the more necessary as occasionally one hears from the bazaar gossip of a possible Russian invasion of India and we have reason to believe that some think in such an event Russia will be successful.[104]

Although missionaries claimed lascar loyalty to Queen Victoria was unassailable, clearly they were not prepared to take any chances. Political revolt could not be ruled out. British fears were realised in 1883 when two crews of 120 Indian seamen were reported to be in revolt as a result of British suppression of a rebellion in Egypt. A London newspaper wrote: 'Fanatical Moslems have been on a mission to the docks, proclaiming as unholy the English crusade against the faithful in Egypt, and forbidding Lascars, under penalty of future torture, to take any part in the expedition.'[105] Evidently the British could not rely on lascar support at all times, especially when pan-Islamic sentiments were raked up. The growth of Indian nationalism also impacted on lascars in Britain. In the 1920s the *London City Mission Magazine* noted the presence of Indian agitators in the Tilbury docks, advocating 'Home Rule' for India.[106] Many lascars had already been approached by Indian National Congress activists in India, who highlighted the discrepancy between the rich produce passing out of India and the poverty of India's people.[107] This argument was particularly well received by lascars at a time of increasing economic hardship.[108]

Conclusion

In this study I have attempted to demonstrate the divergence between the public image of the docile and pliant lascar, stripped of agency in Britain, and the private reality of resistance to missionaries, who attempted to penetrate lascar belief systems. The structural-economic weakness and exploitability of the lascar masked his latent rebelliousness. Thus the lascar was able to manipulate the standard stereotype of inferiority to foil missionary designs on his religious and political consciousness.

'Survival strategies', the term employed by Norma Myers, to describe lascar initiatives in London, during the period 1780–1830, were driven by economic necessity – prerequisites for survival in a hostile society – whereas lascar resistance to religious and political encroachment by missionaries in late nineteenth and early twentieth century London reflects the exercising of agency and choice, above and beyond, basic survival instincts. Adherence to birth religions provided comfort and stability for Indian seamen, buffeted by the forces of capital, commerce and empire. It is testimony to the resilience and strength of indigenous habits of mind that more Indian lascars did not succumb to missionary rhetoric, even if the lascar often found it expedient to give the impression that he was open to persuasion.

Notes

1   For the purposes of this study the public/private model has been reconfigured so that private represents the spiritual/political world of the self rather than the home.
2   N. Myers, 'The Black Poor of London: Initiatives of Eastern Seamen in the Eighteenth and Nineteenth Centuries', in D. Frost (ed.), *Ethnic Labour and British Imperial Trade: A History of Ethnic Seafarers in the UK*, London, Frank Cass, 1995, pp. 7–21.
3   All references to the Lascar Mission at St Luke's, Victoria Docks come from St Andrew's Waterside Church Mission, hereafter referred to as *SAWCM Reports*. I am very grateful to the Mission to Seamen for allowing me to consult their records.
4   For details about these encounters see S. Lahiri, *Indians in Britain: Anglo-Indian Encounters, Race and Identity, 1880–1930*, London, Frank Cass, 1999.
5   For a definition of this term see preface of R. Guha, *Subaltern Studies 1: Writings on South Asian History and Society*, New Delhi, Oxford University Press, 1982.
6   In this study the term 'lascar' will be used to describe Indian seamen.
7   W.H. Hood, *The Blight of Insubordination: The Lascar Question and the Rights and Wrongs of British Shipmasters*, London, Spottiswoode & Co., 1903, p. 4.
8   G. Balachandran, 'Recruitment and Control of Indian Seamen: Calcutta, 1880–1935', *International Journal of Maritime History*, 9, 1, 1997 pp. 1–3.
9   Balachandran, op. cit., p. 1.
10   Hood, op. cit., p. 9.
11   C. Dixon, 'Lascars: The Forgotten Seamen', in R. Ommer and G. Panting (eds), *Working Men who got Wet*, Maritime History Group Memorial, University of Newfoundland, 1980, p. 270.
12   Ibid., p. 266.

13 Balachandran, op. cit., p. 6.
14 *Report of the Committee appointed by the Board of Trade into Questions Affecting the Mercantile Marine,* British Parliamentary Papers (BPP) Vol. 62, cd., 1608, pp. 303–4.
15 Balachandran, op. cit., pp. 10–11.
16 Sobriety was associated with the Muslim taboo against alcohol consumption.
17 Hood, op. cit., p. 49.
18 J. Walsh, 'The Empire's Obligation to the Lascar', *The Imperial and Asiatic Quarterly Review*, 30, 59–60, 1910, p. 346.
19 Hood, op. cit., p. 43.
20 *The Church and the Sailor*, 1 (1912), p. 132.
21 Hood, op. cit., p. 43.
22 *The Church and the Sailor*, 1 (1912), p. 134.
23 F.J.A. Broeze, 'The Muscles of Empire: Indian seamen and the Raj, 1919–1939', *Indian Economic and Social History Review*, 28, 1, 1981, p. 45.
24 Hood, op. cit., p. 87.
25 Most research on Indian seamen in Britain has focused on mendicancy. See Dixon, op. cit. and Myers, op. cit.
26 Hood, op. cit., p. 5.
27 Ibid., p.43.
28 *SAWCM 1890 Report*, p. 25.
29 David Arnold makes a similar point in his discussion of the colonial prison in India: 'The body of the "oriental" might be disciplined, but his "soul" remained out of reach.' D. Arnold, 'The Colonial Prison: Power, Knowledge and Penology in Nineteenth Century India', in D. Arnold and D. Hardiman (eds), *Subaltern Studies, viii, Essays in Honour of Ranajit Guha*, New Delhi, Oxford University Press, 1994, p. 175.
30 B. Stanley, *The Bible and the Flag: Protestant Missions and British Imperialism in the Nineteenth and Twentieth Centuries*, Leciester, Appollos, 1990, p. 157.
31 *Report of the Meeting for the Establishment of the Strangers Home for Asiatics, Africans and South Sea Islanders and others occasionally residing in the Metropolis*, London, 1855, p. 6.
32 Unfortunately this information is very brief and no names are given. W.H. Harris, *Lascars and Chinese: A Short Address to Young Men, of the Several Orthodox Denominations of Christians*, London, Tower Hill, 1814.
33 *Sailors Magazine*, 50 (1843).
34 J. Salter, *The Asiatic in England: Sketches of Sixteen Years Work among Orientals*, London, Seely, Jackson Halliday, 1873 and J. Salter, *The East in the West or Work Among the Asiatics and Africans in London*, London, S.W. Partridge, 1896.
35 Information concerning Reverend Bhose was obtained from *Crockfords Directory* and the *Clergy List*. I am grateful to Catherine Wakeling of the United Society for the Propagation of the Gospel for all her assistance. Despite lengthy searches in the USPG archives I have not been able to locate any additional information on Reverend Bhose. For information on other Indian Clergymen who established independent missions for lascars in Glasgow and Birkenhead see Lahiri, op. cit.
36 *Sailors Magazine*, 50 (1843).
37 Salter, op. cit. 1873, p. 125.
38 *SAWCM Report*, 1893.
39 G. H. Mitchell, *Sailortown*, London, Jarrolds, 1917, pp. 87–91.

40   *SAWCM Report*, 1902, p. 22.

41   B.S. Cohn, 'The Command of Language and the Language of Command', in R. Guha (ed.), *Subaltern Studies iv: Writings on South Asian History and Society*, New Delhi, Oxford University Press, 1985, p. 278.

42   Salter, op. cit. 1873, p. 43.

43   Harris, op. cit., pp. 5–8. The perceived superiority of Sanskrit and it derivative, Bengali, stemmed from their connection with European languages.

44   Salter, op. cit. 1873, p.22.

45   S.C.S.G.C. Parry, *Lascar Hindustani for Ship-Surgeons*, London, W.J. Clarke & Co., 1930.

46   *London City Mission Magazine* (LCM), 25, 1860 p. 151.

47   Ibid.

48   *SAWCM Report* 1887, p. 19.

49   *SAWCM Report* 1902, p. 22.

50   *BPP 1903*, Vol. 62, cd. 1608, p. 338.

51   *SAWCM Report* 1906, p. 27.

52   T.R. Underwood, 'Work among the Lascars in London', *The East and the West*, 4, 1906, p. 454.

53   Ibid., p. 457.

54   *LCM Magazine*, 89, 1914, p. 143.

55   *SAWCM Report*, 1894, p. 33; *Report* 1890, p. 26; *Report* 1887, p. 19.

56   Salter, op. cit. 1873, p. 72.

57   *SAWCM Report*, 1890, p. 27.

58   *SAWCM Report*, 1891, p. 28.

59   Ibid.

60   *SAWCM Report*, 1905, p. 18.

61   Missionaries working with lascars were also subject to assault. See *LCM Magazine*, 25, 1860, p. 151.

62   *SAWCM Report*, 1915, p. 21.

63   *SAWCM Report*, 1887, p. 19.

64   *SAWCM Report*, 1912, p. 36.

65   *LCM Magazine*, 62 (1877) p. 172.

66   *SAWCM Report*, 1887, p. 20.

67   Ibid., p.19. See also *Report* 1888, p. 24, *Report* 1891, p. 28 and *Report* 1897, p. 20.

68   *LCM Magazine*, 74, 874, 1909, p. 200.

69   Ibid.

70   Ibid.

71   Salter, op. cit. 1896, p. 272. Suratis were described as 'very intelligent and the best educated Asiatics on board, but the most difficult to deal with in spiritual matters'. Ibid., p. 71.

72   Salter, op. cit. 1873, p. 260.

73   *SAWCM Report*, 1887, p. 20.

74   *SAWCM Report*, 1888, p. 23.

75   *SAWCM Report*, 1905, p. 19. Lascars were not the only group of South Asians who grew weary of missionary attention, middle-class Indians also resented it. See Lahiri, op. cit.

76   A.N. Porter, 'Empires in the mind', in P.J. Marshall (ed.), *A Cambridge Illustrated History of British Empire*, Cambridge, Cambridge University Press, 1996, p. 211.

77   *LCM Magazine*, 51, 1886, p. 183.

78   See *SAWCM Report,* 1890, p. 25; *Report* 1906, p. 28; *Report* 1909, p. 25.

79   Salter, op. cit. 1896, pp. 44–5.
80   See Homi. K. Bhabha, *The Location of Culture*, London, Routledge, 1994.
81   Salter, op. cit. 1896, p. 121.
82   *LCM Magazine*, 51, 1886, p. 182.
83   Salter, op. cit. 1873, p. 91.
84   Salter, op. cit. 1896, p. 147.
85   A. Nandy, *The Intimate Enemy: Loss and Recovery of Self under Colonisation*, New Delhi, Oxford University Press, 1988, p. 111.
86   *SAWCM Report*, 1917, p. 21.
87   *Hafiz* is the title given to a person who knows the Koran by heart.
88   *LCM Magazine*, 1, 1858, p. 363.
89   *LCM Magazine*, 65, 1900, p. 171.
90   Salter, op. cit. 1896, p. 145.
91   Salter, op. cit. 1873, p. 142.
92   Ibid., p. 136.
93   Ibid., p. 91.
94   Indian seamen's responses to missionaries partly resemble the experience of Jews in the East End. See discussion of the 'conversion business', in W.J. Fishman, *East End Jewish Radicals, 1875–1914*, London, Duckworth, 1995, p. 120.
95   *SAWCM Report*, 1912, p. 35.
96   *SAWCM Report*, 1911, p. 33.
97   *SAWCM Report*, 1890, pp. 26–7.
98   *SAWCM Report*, 1917, p. 21.
99   *SAWCM Report*, 1913, p. 25.
100 *SAWCM Report*, 1901, p. 22. Some Indian seamen visited her grave in 1901.
101 *SAWCM Report*, 1891, p. 28.
102 *SAWCM Report*, 1895, p. 37. Lascar criticism of British taxation and inflationary food prices reflected Indian nationalist economic critique of British rule based on the 'Drain of Wealth' theory. For a brief summary of this complex subject see S. Sarkar, *Modern India, 1885–1947*, London, Macmillan, 1989, p. 248. Lascars also questioned the disparity between English and Indian wages. See *SAWCM Report*, 1906, p. 28.
103 *SAWCM Report*, 1897, p. 21.
104 *SAWCM Report*, 1893, p. 32.
105 *LCM Magazine*, 68, 1883, p. 178.
106 *LCM Magazine*, 89, 1924, p. 64.
107 *LCM Magazine*, 87, 1922, p. 123. See 'Drain of Wealth' theory above.
108 Growth in Trade Union activity in India after the First World War also served to radicalise Indian seamen. See Balachandran, op. cit., p. 9.

9 From Shandong to the Somme: Chinese Indentured Labour in France During World War I

PAUL BAILEY

In the autumn of 1919, as Chinese delegates gathered in France for the Versailles Peace Conference, one of their number, a legal councillor at the Chinese Ministry of Foreign Affairs, wrote the words to a stirring song in honour of the nearly 150,000 Chinese labourers who had been recruited by the French and British governments in 1916 and 1917 to undertake war-related work in France. The song was recorded and 5,000 copies were made, to be distributed throughout the Chinese labour camps in France:

> Marching, marching ever onwards,
> Unencumbered by heavy baggage,
> Our long route lit by auspicious stars,
> We fear not the cold, heat or weapons of war.
> Since leaving our motherland
> We have crossed seas and mountains.
> Whether metal, stone, earth or wood, we can work it,
> The devastation of war we can repair.
> We, the children of sacred China whose fate lies with Heaven,
> Esteem the farmer and favour the artisan, but never resort to force.
> Marching, marching, ever marching.
> All within the four seas are brothers.
> We are an army of workers devoting ourselves to labour
> In order to build peace for you, humanity.[1]

These words intriguingly capture official Chinese perceptions of their contribution to the victory of the entente powers in World War One by placing it within the context of an altruistic dedication to world peace by a peace-loving and hard working Chinese labouring class.[2] As will be noted later,

179

Chinese officials were to be cruelly disabused of their immediate hopes that such a contribution would be rewarded by a new approach to international relations by the powers, whereby China would be treated as an equal and foreign privileges gained by 'unequal' treaties imposed on China during the nineteenth century dismantled. Nevertheless, the recruitment of Chinese indentured labour during World War One was a significant episode in the history of Chinese migration in terms of the extent to which it differed from the previous unregulated 'coolie' trade of the nineteenth century, how it was represented by Chinese official and intellectual élites as an integral component of Sino-French cultural interaction in the first two decades of the twentieth century, and the actual experiences of Chinese workers themselves during their sojourn in France.[3]

Chinese Labour Overseas Before 1914

The recruitment of Chinese indentured labour during World War One was a significant departure from the unregulated and illegal 'coolie' trade of the nineteenth century, when over 300,000 Chinese were recruited mainly to work on sugar plantations in Peru, Cuba and British colonies in the Caribbean and South America (i.e. British Guiana).[4] The trade was illegal because the ruling Qing dynasty had officially proscribed emigration in 1712 (reflecting a traditional fear that migrants were potential troublemakers who might participate in rebellion or engage in piracy along China's coastal frontiers). Nevertheless, between 1847, a few years after the forcible opening of China's first treaty ports to foreign residence and trade, and 1873, when the 'coolie trade' was formally ended, indentured labourers were recruited (often forcibly or by deception) by foreign agencies in the treaty ports not subject to Chinese law because of the privilege of extraterritoriality, and their Chinese collaborators. The appalling conditions and treatment suffered by these labourers finally convinced the dynasty that strict official supervision of recruitment practices and conditions had to be implemented. After the military invasion by Britain and France in 1860, the Chinese were compelled to recognise the right of their subjects to emigrate. In 1866 the Qing government drafted regulations on the recruitment of Chinese indentured labour, and the 1712 ban was formally lifted in 1893. Since such regulations limited the term of employment to five years and clearly specified that labourers were to be guaranteed free passage home after the expiry of their contracts, the British and French governments refused to recognise their validity.[5]

With growing demand for labour to mine gold deposits in the Transvaal at the turn of the century the British government reached an agreement with China in May 1904 to recruit Chinese workers on the basis of the 1866 principles. According to the Anglo-Chinese Convention the text of the indenture had to be published in the Chinese press and to specify clearly the location and duration of the employment, wage rates, and the number of working hours per day. The right to free medical assistance during employment was also guaranteed, as well as paid passage home after the expiry of the contract. Chinese officials and inspectors were to be present at embarkation ports and Chinese consuls appointed in South Africa to oversee the labourers' welfare. Finally, the indenture provided for an 'allotment system' whereby a portion of the labourers' wages was to be used for the support of their families back home. Between 1904 and 1906 just over 63,000 Chinese labourers went to the Transvaal gold mines. The principal recruitment centre was opened in Britain's leasehold territory (obtained in 1898) of Weihaiwei in the northern province of Shandong, and of the 63,695 labourers eventually recruited 62,000 came from northern provinces (most of China's previous migrants and indentured labourers had originated from southern provinces such as Fujian and Guangdong). Although originally provision had been made for renewal of the contract for a further three years, recruiting was stopped in November 1906 as a result of growing hostility amongst white workers in the Transvaal to the import of 'cheap Asiatic labour'.[6]

Chinese Labour in Wartime France and its Wider Agenda

What distinguished the recruitment of Chinese labour in France during World War One from even that in South Africa in 1904–1906 was the enthusiastic support provided by Chinese official and intellectual élites who invested the project with wider political, social and cultural agenda. As soon as World War One broke out in Europe, Yuan Shikai, who had emerged as president of the new Chinese republic in 1912, proposed China's military participation on the side of the entente powers, mainly to forestall Japanese action in China. Yuan feared, correctly as it turned out, that as Britain's ally Japan would declare war on Germany and thereby gain justification for its seizure of the German concession area (obtained in 1897) centred on the port of Qingdao, Shandong province.[7] On two further occasions, in 1915 and 1917, the Chinese government even proposed sending Chinese troops abroad to gain favour with the entente powers; on the former occasion Yuan suggested the Dardenelles, an idea rejected by Japan,[8] while on the latter occasion Duan Qirui, who had emerged as military strong man following Yuan's death, proposed sending Chinese troops to the Western Front. The French government was initially enthusiastic, but the idea was quickly dropped because of Britain's disdainful response, the lukewarm attitude of the USA, and the scarcity of convoy ships.[9]

Although the idea of Chinese military participation was eventually rejected, the use of Chinese labour was not. As early as 1915 the French government was considering the option of employing Chinese workers to make up for acute labour shortages. Even before the advent of war a decline in the French birth rate[10] had resulted in the growing presence of foreigners, of whom there were over one million by 1911.[11] Immigration before the war, however, had been mostly unregulated and involved the free movement of peoples adjacent to France. During the war the French government was to become more actively involved in the recruitment and organisation of immigrant labour, which was now centred in major cities such as Lyon and Rouen as well as in smaller centres of war production such as Bourges, Brest and Le Havre. For the first time, also, large numbers of non-European workers were recruited, principally from French colonies in North Africa and Indochina. During the course of the war France was to recruit over 660,000 foreign workers, of whom over 132,000 were from Algeria, Morocco and Tunisia, and 49,000 from Indochina.[12]

It was against this background that, in late 1915, a mission led by Lieutenant-Colonel Truptil was sent by the French Ministry of War to China to open negotiations. Since China was still officially neutral Truptil described himself as an 'agricultural engineer' to avoid German suspicions and dealt with the ostensibly private Huimin Company. In reality the Huimin Company was a quasi-government organisation since it was under the control of Liang Shiyi, a government minister and close confidant of Yuan Shikai.[13] Liang, like other Chinese officials, was enthusiastic about the project; he believed that Chinese workers in France would learn skills that might in future contribute to China's industrial development, as well as assuming that supplying labourers for the entente cause would enhance China's status at a future peace conference.[14] By May 1916 a contract had been signed between Truptil and the Huimin Company (which came under the control of the Bureau for Overseas Chinese Workers when China officially entered the war in August 1917),[15] and the first group of Chinese workers, totalling 1,700, arrived in France in August 1916. At the same time the British government reached agreement with Chinese authorities to recruit Chinese workers initially to replace British dockyard and transportation workers in France, and hence release them for military service or work back home.[16] The first group under

British employ (totalling 1,000) arrived in Plymouth in April 1917 before being transported to France. While the French government after 1915 mainly recruited through the Huimin Company, Britain, employing Chinese agents, recruited directly from its leasehold territory of Weihaiwei, just as it had done in 1904-1906. Recruiting centres for those employed by the French were established in Tianjin, Qingdao and Pukou; a number of skilled artisans were also recruited from the French Concession area in Shanghai. Eventually, there were to be nearly 100,000 Chinese workers under British control and over 35,000 under French control.[17] Most came from impoverished peasant families in the north, particularly Shandong province, although one observer was later to note that students, former minor officials and those who had obtained lower level degrees under the old civil service examination system, which had been abolished in 1905, also enlisted.[18]

Interestingly, while Chinese labourers were referred to by the pejorative term 'coolies' in the English version of the contract, the Chinese text used the term *huagong* (Chinese workers), symbolising the positive contribution Chinese officials anticipated such labourers would make to the future enhancement of China's international standing.[19] Those employed by Britain were officially called the Chinese Labour Corps and had three year contracts, notices of which, in Chinese, were posted in a wide variety of public places such as teahouses. After passing a medical examination and signing the contract – usually by means of a thumbprint since many potential recruits were illiterate – the indentured worker was awarded an embarkation payment of 20 Mexican dollars (approximately US$10.8); identification tags recording a worker's allotted number, name and next of kin were attached to the worker's wrist. While in France workers were to be paid one franc (US 19.3 cents) for a ten hour day, this was about half the daily wage of a British army private. Foremen were to receive two to five francs a day. During their sojourn a monthly payment of 10 Mexican dollars (US$5.4) was to be awarded their next of kin in China. There was no provision for sick pay other than continued free food and lodging; more drastically still, if a worker was sick for more than six months the monthly allotment payment was to cease. Although the contract specifically stated that workers were not to be involved in 'military operations' they were still subject to martial law. Billeted in camps that were located along France's western coast as well as in the northwest (some of which comprising more than 3,000 men), the Chinese Labour Corps by 1918 was engaged in trench digging, burying war dead, and building aerodromes from Arras to Cambrai. Significantly, the Chinese Labour Corps was to form the largest contingent of foreign workers employed by Britain during the war, others included 48,000 Indians, 21,000 black South Africans, 15,000 Egyptians and 8,000 West Indians.[20]

Workers recruited by the French government had five year contracts, and unlike those employed by Britain, had the option of staying on, in which case their return home would not be paid. A report by a French military official in 1925 was to note the continued presence in France of 3,000 Chinese workers and apprentices.[21] Initially under the control of the Colonial Labour Service (*Service d'organisation des travailleurs coloniaux*) established by the War and Colonial Ministries, and later of the Labour Ministry, these workers, unlike their compatriots under British control, were more widely dispersed throughout the country in smaller camps situated near rural settlements. From Brest in the north to Marseille in the south French-employed Chinese labourers were sent to work in government munitions factories as well as in privately owned metallurgical, chemical and construction firms. In contrast to those under British employ, these Chinese workers constituted a smaller proportion of the total number of foreign workers recruited by France during the war (36,941 out of a total of 662,000).[22] Also, in order to pre-empt the accusations of French trade unions that their government was importing cheap labour, French-employed Chinese workers were paid more than their compatriots in the Chinese Labour Corps; in addition to the provision of food, clothing and lodging, they were paid 2.5 francs a day. Whereas the highest wage a British-employed Chinese worker could earn was five francs a day, as a Class One interpreter, machinists recruited by the French in Shanghai could earn 8.25 francs a day. Furthermore, it was stipulated that French-employed Chinese workers were to receive the same amount of bonuses as their French counterparts in the same occupations. They were also to receive 50 centimes daily sick pay for up to six weeks. Interestingly, although both British and French-employed Chinese workers were entitled to one day off per week, in addition to French national holidays, the latter were also entitled to have time off for *Chinese* national holidays. In the event of death or permanent disablement both the British and French contracts stipulated a payment of 150 Mexican dollars to the worker's family.[23]

Although the contracts stipulated that Chinese workers in France were not to be considered as combatants, they were still exposed to considerable risk. Some of the earlier groups were transported via the Suez Canal and the Mediterranean where the transport ships were vulnerable to German submarine attacks. One such ship, the *Athos*, was torpedoed in the Mediterranean in February 1917, resulting in the deaths of 540 Chinese workers.[24] After August 1917, when China declared war on Germany, Chinese workers in French employ were expected to work near the battle lines, exhuming and reburying war dead. An article in *The Times*, which appeared on 28 December 1917, reported that Chinese workers were actually bringing up ammunition to the front line and that they remained in the trenches repairing dugouts and keeping machine gun emplacements in order. By the end of the war nearly 2,000 Chinese workers had perished as a result of illness or enemy attack. Those working in Calais and Dunkirk, for example, were especially vulnerable to air attack.[25]

The recruitment of Chinese labour for work in France was not only welcomed by Chinese officials. Since the turn of the twentieth century a group of Chinese Francophile educators, scholars and reformers, with extensive contacts with both Chinese political figures and French official and intellectual circles, had been promoting Sino-French cultural relations and the importance of Chinese overseas study in France.[26] The most prominent among them was Li Shizeng (1881–1973), the son of a Qing court official who had studied in France during the early years of the century. Li became a fervent admirer of French culture and praised the ideals of the French secular republic, which he defined as freedom, creativity and pacifism and contrasted with those of Germany, which he associated with autocracy, utilitarianism and militarism. He established a wide network of contacts with French politicians and intellectuals, including Paul Reclus, the nephew of the geographer and utopian anarchist Elise Reclus. In the following years in Paris, Li and other Chinese intellectuals published an anarchist journal and opened a night school for Chinese workers whom Li had recruited after 1908 for employment in a bean curd factory he opened just outside Paris in Garenne-Colombes.[27] For Li and his colleagues, France was a republic *par excellence*, free of the baleful influences of monarchy and religion, and hence an ideal environment for study. In 1912, following the establishment of a republic in China, Li founded the Association for Frugal Study in France (*Liufa jianxue hui*), which sent nearly 100 Chinese students to France before 1914, most of them enrolling at Montargis College, whose principal was a personal acquaintance of Li's.

At the time of Truptil's negotiations with the Huimin Company in 1916, Li Shizeng confidently predicted that enormous benefits would accrue to China as a result of France's recruitment of Chinese labour. Not only would the unemployment problem in China be solved, but also, according to Li, Chinese labourers in France would form the nucleus of an educated workforce contributing to the diffusion of industrial skills and the reform of society on their return.[28] Li argued that Chinese workers would also become 'civilised' during their sojourn in France, allowing them to abandon their superstitious, irresponsible and spendthrift behaviour. The obsessive concern with the reform of popular customs and behaviour that preoccupied Chinese intellectual élites after the turn of the century[29] was the product of two interrelated concerns. Firstly, the Boxer uprising of 1899–1900 had been a rude shock for many officials and scholars, convincing them of the essential 'backwardness' of the Chinese people; and secondly, Chinese élites were anxious that future overseas Chinese avoid the fate of Chinese migrants to North America, who had been the target of scorn and abuse since their arrival in the mid-nineteenth century.

In 1916, Li Shizeng opened a Chinese workers school in Paris to teach French, Chinese and science. The first group of students were those Chinese workers already in France before 1914, and it was hoped some of them could be trained as interpreters for those beginning to arrive at the end of 1916. Lectures given at the school drew attention to the 'unsavoury' habits of the Chinese people, which included extravagance, uncivil behaviour in public and adherence to superstitious beliefs. Chinese labourers about to arrive in France were to be encouraged to adopt Western customs such as politeness, a sense of decorum – an example of which was to cede one's seat to a woman on public transport – a love of animals and concern with the public welfare.[30] In a journal especially aimed at Chinese labourers in France – the *Huagong Zazhi* (*Chinese Worker*) – Li and others drew up elaborate guidelines for daily living. Chinese workers were advised to wipe their shoes before entering any premises, to refrain from opening the window in the morning if still dressed in nightclothes, to knock and wait for a reply before entering a room, and to desist from spitting in public, throwing rubbish out of the window, gesticulating and shouting in public, and picking a fight if pushed or shoved in a crowd. Lastly, they were urged to read newspapers on a Sunday![31] Such concerns were shared by the Chinese Minister to France, who in 1917 warned that Chinese workers would have to be seen to be frugal and industrious if China's reputation were not to be impaired; he particularly bewailed the 'unkempt' and 'shabby' appearance of Chinese paper-flower sellers on the streets of Paris and the ridicule they aroused amongst passers by.[32]

Another example of the way in which the recruitment of Chinese labour was invested with a wider agenda involved the creation of the Sino-French Education Association (*Zhongfa jiaoyu hui*) in 1916. Founded jointly by prominent French intellectuals, such as the historian Alphonse Aulard, and Francophile Chinese reformers such as Li and Cai Yuanpei (1868–1940)[33] as an umbrella organisation to promote and develop Sino-French cultural and educational relations, the Association aimed to encourage part-time education amongst Chinese labourers in France, to support the establishment of French language schools and colleges in China, and to oversee a work-study movement that would bring nearly 1,500 Chinese students to France in 1919–20.[34] For Li and his colleagues, such a movement would not only enable Chinese students to acquire manual skills as well as intellectual knowledge but also, because of the continuing presence of Chinese workers in France after 1918, would be part of a massive social experiment in which Chinese students would interact with their worker compatriots and thereby eliminate the gulf between intellectual and manual labour which they believed had always characterised traditional Chinese culture.

The Chinese Worker Experience

French opinion, too, detected a wider significance in the recruitment of Chinese labour. Thus Marius Moutet (1876–1968), the socialist politician and wartime Colonial Minister, welcomed the idea in 1916, claiming that Chinese workers on their return home after service in France would become 'the best agents for French propaganda in their own country'.[35] Moutet's grandiose hope that the indentured Chinese workers might in the future become the instruments for the enhancement of France's cultural and economic influence in China, however, did not alter the fact that, as with Chinese migrants in North America, Chinese labourers once in France were often described by their western hosts in stereotypical terms that ranged from the virulently racist to the excruciatingly condescending. For the most part they were referred to as naive, docile and obedient – if 'handled properly'. A 1917 report in *The Times*, after having noted that the Picardy landscape might contain 'a squad of Chinamen in blue or terracotta blouses and flat hats, hauling logs or loading trucks, always with that inscrutable smile of the Far East upon their smooth, yellow faces', went on to declare: 'The Chink, like the Kaffir, has to be kept under ward when he is not working. He gives little trouble if rightly managed, gambles a good deal, but does not get drunk or commit violence and is docile and obedient.'[36] An article on the Chinese Labour Corps published in the *North China Herald* in 1918 insisted that:

> Not a man will return the same as he came out ... After all, they are only great big boys, and whatever their age may be, they are none of them older than ten years in character ... very amenable, easily managed with kindness and firmness, and loyal to the core if treated with consideration ... They bear nothing but dislike for anyone who is afraid of them. A dog is the same.[37]

The assumption that Chinese workers were childlike was well captured by instructions issued by the French Ministry of War on how employers should deal with them: 'The Chinese have a lot of self pride. It is therefore appropriate to treat them with kindness and not to hesitate in giving them a reward, no matter how small, every time they try and do something well.'[38]

On the other hand, some observations betrayed a curious defensiveness. Thus included in the instructions issued by the Ministry of War was a warning to French employers not to lose their temper since the Chinese believed that for one 'to give way to external expressions of anger symbolised a lack of self control, thereby [in the mind of the Chinese] remaining a barbarian'. A report on a labour camp near Rouen criticised the general demeanour of Chinese workers because they 'retained towards us [i.e. the French] their condescending and arrogant superiority'.[39] Fears were also expressed from time to time that Chinese workers might fraternise with German prisoners and even join with them to commit sabotage; although on at least one occasion Chinese workers attacked German prisoners after an air attack had killed some of their number. Such fears were linked to the suspicion that Germany, from the beginning, had attempted to disrupt the recruitment process in China. A pamphlet, in Chinese but thought to be of German origin, discovered on one transport ship warned of the life-threatening conditions Chinese labourers would face in France, as well as exploiting racist fears that they would have to associate with African blacks, Vietnamese and other 'remnants of dead nations'.[40]

In fact Chinese workers were neither as docile nor as compliant as their British and French employers assumed or wanted them to be. They often protested against breaches in their contracts, the dangerous nature of their work, and the harsh treatment they at times received. Scuffles between French and Chinese workers occurred at war plants in Le Creusot in 1916 and in the gasworks of Saint-Denis in 1917. Companies employing Chinese dockworkers in Bordeaux and Nantes complained that they were intractable. In September 1917 a strike amongst Chinese workers in Dunkirk protesting against their exposure to German air attack led to armed clashes with French guards during which two workers were killed. Between 1916 and 1918 there were twenty-five disturbances, riots and strikes, involving Chinese workers.[41] Significantly, after May 1918, Chinese workers under French employ were made subject to military discipline.[42]

As equally significant as these displays of militance was the enthusiasm shown by many Chinese workers in France for self-improvement. In places such as Montargis, Caen and Clermont-Ferrand, they organized 'self-governing associations' (*zizhi hui*) which drew up rules of etiquette and daily behaviour and proscribed gambling and fighting amongst their members.[43] Fines were also imposed on members for such unseemly behaviour as getting drunk. Spare-time and night classes were organised, often taught by Chinese members of the YMCA or work-study students who arrived in France in 1919. Such classes taught over 700 Chinese workers near Toulouse in 1917, while in 1918–19 night schools were opened in Lyon, Toulon and Rouen; the latter catering for up to 900 workers. At a factory in Fargniers, 400 Chinese workers set up their own school in 1920 and invited nearby work-study students to help with the teaching. A report on the progress of Chinese workers' education at a match factory in Vonges between May 1917 and March 1919 noted that, by the latter date, nearly a quarter of the 930 Chinese workers there were attending lectures, while 50 per cent of them were studying in their spare time and reading copies of the *Huagong zazhi*.[44] A compelling incentive for worker literacy was the desire to read letters from home without having to depend on more literate colleagues, and to be able to read notices and instructions in French. The consequences of being unable to do so could be rather dramatic; one worker, for example, not understanding the significance of his bread ration ticket, did not take it with him when he visited a local bakery. When he was refused bread he proceeded to smash up the premises.[45]

At all times Chinese workers were exhorted to fulfil their patriotic duty by saving money and studying. There is clear evidence that an emerging *national* consciousness, transcending more parochial loyalties to province or region, began to develop amongst Chinese workers at this time. When news of General Zhang Xun's ultimately abortive attempt in 1917 to revive the Qing monarchy reached France protesting telegrams were sent in the name of 'Chinese workers, merchants and students residing in France'.[46] Two years later, in October 1919, workers at a factory in Capdenac, in southern France, embroidered a national flag to celebrate the anniversary of the outbreak of the 1911 Revolution. Perhaps most revealing of all was the response to widespread floods that engulfed the metropolitan province of Zhili in northern China in 1918. Hundreds of Chinese workers in France contributed funds for famine relief; 500 at Le Creusot, for example, donated 557 francs, while 1,000 at Vonges donated 2,070 francs.[47]

Epilogue

The Chinese workers recruited by Britain were repatriated in 1920, while many of those under French employ returned home in 1922. Their role during the war was fulsomely praised by some contemporary observers. Thus Manico Gull, the British commander of the second group of workers transported to France as part of the Chinese Labour Corps, commented in 1918 that 'their emigration from the shores of Shandong will take its place certainly as one of the most important aspects of the Great European War',[48] while Marius Moutet later observed that:

> What is worth remembering of this experience is the undoubted good will of the Chinese government to take an active part in the conflict in which the very existence of France was at stake. This assistance was valuable. Thousands of Chinese workers in our factories allowed us to spare an equal amount of French workers for military service.[49]

Nevertheless, the hopes Chinese delegates had at the 1919 Versailles Peace Conference that the contribution of Chinese indentured labour to the allied war effort might bring about an improvement of China's international position went unrealised. Except for the minor concessions granted China after it had declared war on Germany in 1917 (i.e. Boxer indemnity payments were postponed for five years and import tariff levels were allowed to be raised to an effective rate of 5 per cent), the unequal treaty system imposed on China by the powers in the nineteenth century was not dismantled. Japan was allowed to retain the former German leasehold territory of Qingdao, along with its mining and railway concessions, that it had appropriated in 1914; Weihaiwei was to remain a British leasehold territory until 1930.[50] Also, hostility to Chinese immigration that had emerged in the latter half of the nineteenth century in places such as North America continued unabated after 1918. In Canada, for example, the severe restrictions on immigration dating from the 1880s and 1890s remained in place, culminating in the 1923 Immigration Act which effectively halted further Chinese immigration until after World War Two. The United States government likewise passed an Exclusion Act in 1924 ending further Chinese immigration.[51] Moutet's praise notwithstanding, even the French government soon lost interest in the episode. When, in April 1925, the General Association of Chinese Workers, which was created in 1919 and representing those workers who had remained after 1922, petitioned the French government to mark the contribution made by Chinese workers during World War One by erecting a commemorative monument and establishing a national cemetery for those who had died in France – it also suggested that Boxer indemnity funds owed by France might be used to finance repatriation of Chinese workers still living in France – it was politely, but firmly, rebuffed.[52]

Furthermore, a kind of historical amnesia has set in. Although in 1920 Chen Duxiu, the radical intellectual and founder of the Chinese Communist Party in 1921, cited the efforts of Chinese labourers in France as an example of the diligence and courage of the Chinese working class,[53] and Gu Xingqing, in a book published in 1936 detailing his experiences as an interpreter for a Chinese labour battalion in France, underlined the contributions Chinese workers had made to world peace and the enhancement of China's international reputation,[54] the episode has subsequently attracted little interest amongst Chinese historians.[55] Perhaps more surprisingly, to date there exists no substantial monographic study in French on the recruitment and experiences of Chinese workers in France during and after World War One.[56]

Nevertheless, the episode is highly significant in two ways. Firstly, it demonstrated the, potentially, *political* use which Chinese official and intellectual élites attached to overseas Chinese labour, that is as a marker of China's international commitment and its right to be accorded equal standing in the international system. This was a phenomenon that was to occur in the 1960s when the sending of Chinese workers to help build the Tanzania railroad was represented by the People's Republic of China as a symbol of its commitment to the nonaligned world.[57] Secondly, the episode intriguingly reveals the extent to which Chinese élites were *active participants* in the recruitment as part of a simultaneous promotion of Sino-French cultural interaction.[58] Two little known events add a further nuance; in 1919 the Chinese government donated 50,000 francs towards the restoration of education in war-torn Verdun, while in 1922, at the height of the postwar economic depression in France, the Chinese government sent food relief in the shape of 400 tons of eggs.[59] Clearly, the conventional view of China at this time as merely the bankrupted and hapless victim of imperialism incapable of playing an autonomous role on the world stage needs to be questioned.

Notes

1   *La Politique de Pkin*, 22 February 1920, 8, p. 128, gives the text in Chinese and French. I have translated directly from the Chinese. On the other side of the record was the Chinese national anthem.

2   It should be noted that between 1915 and 1917 Russia also recruited Chinese indentured labour, the total numbers varying from 50,000 to 100,000. Many worked on the repair of the Murmansk railroad in the north, while others were sent to the oil fields at Baku and the coal mines of the Donets basin in the south. See Li Yongchang, 'Zhongguo jindai fu'E huagong shulun' ('An account of Chinese workers in Russia in the modern period'),

Jindaishi yanjiu, 2, 1987, p. 225, He Ping,'Eguo yuandong dichu huagong wenti zhi chutan' ('A preliminary exploration of the Chinese worker question in the Russian Far East'), *Haiwai huaren yanjiu,* 3, 1995, pp. 97–8; Chen Sanjing, *Huagong yu Ouzhan (Chinese Workers and WW1),* Taibei, 1986, p. 33.

3   A recent overview of indentured labour in the nineteenth and early twentieth centuries makes only one brief reference to the episode. D. Northrup, *Indentured Labor in the Age of Imperialism 1834–1922,* Cambridge, Cambridge University Press, 1995, p. 59. Unfortunately, there is virtually no reference at all to Chinese workers (or indeed to any foreign workers recruited from Africa, South and Southeast Asia) in two recent works on the mobilization of labour and society during World War One. See J. Horne, *Labour At War,* Oxford, Clarendon Press, 1991 and J. Horne (ed.), *State, Society and Mobilization in Europe During The First World War,* Cambridge, Cambridge University Press, 1997. For other references and information in English and French, see Chen Ta, *Chinese Migrations, with Special Reference to Labor Conditions,* Washington, US Dept. of Labor, Bureau of Statistics, 1923, pp. 142–58; H. McNair, *The Chinese Abroad,* Shanghai, Commercial Press, 1933, pp. 235–8; P. Wou, *Les Travailleurs Chinois et la Grande Guerre,* Paris, 1939; J. Blick, 'The Chinese Labor Corps in WW1', *Harvard Papers on China,* August 1955, pp. 111–45; N. Griffin, 'The Use of Chinese Labour by the British Army 1916–1920: The "Raw Importation", its Scope and Problems', unpublished PhD thesis, University of Oklahoma, 1973; A. Kriegel, *Communismes au Miroir Francais,* Paris, Editions Gallimard, 1974, pp. 61–73; M. Summerskill, *China on the Western Front,* London, Michael Summerskill, 1982; P. Bailey, *Reform the People: Changing Attitudes Towards Popular Education in Early Twentieth Century China,* Edinburgh, Edinburgh University Press, 1990, pp. 233–6. To date, there has been no study in English that makes use of Chinese language sources. Chinese Foreign Ministry archival materials on the recruitment of Chinese labour during World War One have recently been published by the Institute of Modern History, Academia Sinica in Taiwan. See *Ouzhan Huagong Shiliao (Historical Materials on Chinese Workers in the European War),* Taibei, 1997 (hereafter *OHS*).

4   D. Northrup, op. cit., pp. 25, 37, 38, 61. In Peru Chinese indentured workers also mined guano deposits.

5   Yen Ching-hwang, *Coolies and Mandarins: China's Protection of Overseas Chinese During the Late Ch'ing Period 1851–1911,* Singapore, Singapore University Press, 1985, pp. 32–71, 102–11.

6   P. Richardson, 'The Recruiting of Chinese Indentured Labour for the South African Gold Mines 1903–1908', *Journal of African History,* 18, 1977, 1 pp. 85–108; P. Richardson, *Chinese Mine Labour in the Transvaal,* London, Macmillan, 1982, pp. 104, 166.

7   M. Chi, *China Diplomacy 1914–1918,* Cambridge, Mass, Harvard University Press, 1970, pp. 20, 72; Lo Hui-min (ed.), *The Correspondence of G.E. Morrison,* Cambridge, Cambridge University Press, 1976, 2, 559–61. Morrison, a former *Times* correspondent in China from 1898 to 1911, became Yuan Shikai's political adviser in 1912.

8   M.Chi, op. cit., pp. 129–30; T. LaFargue, *China and the World War,* New York, Howars Fertig, 1973, pp. 83–4, 157–9.

9   See Archives du Ministre des Affaires Etrangres (Paris), Srie E:Asie 1918–1929 (Chine), (Hereafter cited as AMAE), E-22-14, Telegrams from the French Minister in China to Paris, 2 January and 31 March 1918. He reported that Duan Qirui was ready to send 10,000 troops immediately. Both the French Minister and the French Military Attaché in Beijing enthusiastically welcomed the idea, seeing it as an opportunity to enhance French

military influence in China. Although the Chinese government *did* declare war on Germany in August 1917 the principal advantage of this as far as Britain was concerned was that German property and ships in China could now be requisitioned.

10 The excess of births over deaths per thousand dropped from a peak of 5.8 in 1821–30 to a low of 0.7 in 1891–1900. Also, while the population rose by nine million between 1801 and 1860, it increased by only 2.5 million between 1860 and 1913. G. Cross, *Immigrant Workers in Industrial France*, Philadelphia, Temple University Press, 1983, pp. 6–7.

11 G. Cross, 'Towards Social Peace and Prosperity:The Politics of Immigration in France during the Era of WWI', *French Historical Studies*, 11, 4, 1980, p. 610; J. Horne, 'Immigrant Workers in France During WWI', *French Historical Studies*, 14, 1, 1985, p. 57. As Horne notes, by the 1920s France was 'second only to the US as an industrialized immigrant society'.

12 J. Horne, ibid., p. 59. The largest contingent of foreign workers comprised Spaniards, who totalled 230,000. It is interesting to note that before 1914 some French enterprises (e.g. in the iron industry) were already calling on the government to assist with recruitment of foreign workers. G. Cross, op. cit. 1980, p. 614.

13 For reports on the negotiations, see AMAE,E-110-2/E-22-15, Telegrams from the French Minister in China to Paris, 4 February 1916, 5 February and 1 March 1916. See also *La Politique de Pkin*, 25 August 1918, No. 34.

14 Cen Xuelu (comp.), *Sanshui Liang Yansun xiansheng nianpu (A Chronological Biography of Liang Shiyi)*, 1, Taibei, 1962, pp. 271–2, 299–300; Bai Jiao, 'Shijie dazhan zhong zhi Huagong' ('Chinese workers during WW1'), *Renwen Yuekan*, February 1937, 8, 1, p. 2.

15 The text of the contract is in *OHS*, pp. 184–95. It is also reprinted in Chen Sanjing, op. cit., pp. 191–203. For the English version, see Chen Ta, op. cit., pp. 207–10. The first director of the Bureau was Zhang Hu, a member of Liang Shiyi's official clique. Branches of the Bureau were also set up in a number of Chinese provinces, while an official was attached to the Chinese Embassy in France specifically to represent the interests of Chinese workers once they arrived in France. Chen Sanjing, op. cit., pp. 107, 110. Instructions sent by the Foreign Ministry to the Guangdong provincial government in February 1917 reminded local authorities that the recruitment process was to be strictly supervised in order to avoid the deception and exploitation involved in the 'coolie' trade of the nineteenth century. *OHS*, p. 256.

16 N. Griffin, op. cit., pp. 33–43. As early as July 1916 the Army Council raised the possibility of recruiting Chinese labour. Originally, it was envisaged using such labour in both Britain and France, but concern with potential opposition from British trade unions prompted a final decision in August 1916 to use Chinese labour solely in France.

17 *OHS*, pp. 216, 355–6; Chen Sanjing, op. cit., pp. 27–8.

18 *Jiaoyu yu Minzhong (Education and the Masses)*, 2, 7, March 1933, p. 3. Figures provided by the French Ministry of War in 1922 on the Chinese workers under French employ stated that 31,409 came from northern China, 4,024 from the south, 1,066 from Shanghai and 442 from Hong Kong. Chen Ta, op. cit., p. 144. See also the report by the Bureau for Overseas Chinese Workers on 25 November 1918 in *OHS*, pp. 413–6.

19 In Chinese official texts the term used for the 'coolies' of the nineteenth century was *zhuzai* (lit:'swine').

20 M. Summerskill, op. cit., p. 163. Chinese workers were also employed in the repair of railway lines and the maintenance of engines and carriages. Chen Sanjing, op. cit., p. 90; N.Griffin, op.cit., p.117.

21   Archives du Ministre de l'Intrieur: F7 1348, Report by General Brissaud-Desmaillet addressed to the Ministry of War, 26 June 1925.

22   G. Cross, op. cit., pp. 35–6.

23   *OHS*, pp. 184–95.

24   Chen Sanjing, op. cit., p. 72. Subsequent groups were also transported across the Pacific, then overland across Canada, and finally shipped across the Atlantic to England. A Chinese interpreter who accompanied one group of 3,000 workers noted that his ship left China on 17 April 1917, reached Nagasaki in Japan on the 19 April before leaving Yokohama on the 24 April. The ship arrived in Vancouver, British Columbia on the 9 May. After a week travelling across Canada (during the journey British troops were stationed in each carriage to ensure the Chinese labourers did not abscond), the group left Canada on the 18 May and arrived at Liverpool on the 1 June. A train then took them to Folkestone and the group finally arrived in Boulogne on the 7 July. Gu Xingqing, *Ouzhan Gongzuo Huiyi Lu* (*A Recollection of Experiences in the European War*), Changsha, 1938, pp. 4–16.

25   Between August 1917 and April 1918 131 Chinese workers were killed in Calais and Dunkirk as a result of German air attacks. Chen Sanjing, op. cit., pp. 106–7. Gu Xingqing, op. cit., pp. 21–2 reported that his group was vulnerable to German air attack at Abbeville-Noyelles and, later, at Pomperinghe in Belgium.

26   P. Bailey, op. cit, pp. 227–33; see also my chapter 'The Sino-French Connection 1902–1928', in D. Goodman (ed.), *China and the West: Ideas and Activists*, Manchester, Manchester University Press, 1990, pp. 72–102.

27   Li recruited 30 workers from his native district in Gaoyang, Zhili province. In 1913 about 48 Chinese workers had also been directly employed by the French at an artificial silk factory in Arques-la-Bataille in Normandy. See the report by Li Jun, the official in charge of overseas Chinese workers attached to the Chinese embassy in Paris, to the Chinese Foreign Ministry on 4 December 1917 in *OHS*, p. 352. The French Commissioner of Police in Dieppe reported on the 'sober industriousness' of the Chinese workers at Arques-la-Bataille in February 1914. See Archives du Ministre de l'Intrieur, F7 1348.

28   *Lu'Ou Jiaoyu Yundong* (*The Educational Movement in Europe*), Tours, 1916, pp. 82–3. Other articles Li wrote in 1917 elaborated on the same theme. See *Li Shizeng Xiansheng Wenji* (*Collected Writings of Li Shizeng*), Taibei, 1, 1980, pp. 220–5; and *Lu'Ou Zazhi* (*Journal for Chinese Students in Europe*), 1 February 1917, No. 12.

29   What one might refer to as 'behavioural modernization', an expression used by one commentator to describe the campaigns launched by the Chinese Communist Party in the 1980s to promote 'civilised' behaviour amongst the public. See H. Harding, *China's Second Revolution: Reform After Mao*, Washington DC, Brookings Institution, 1987, p. 187.

30   Many of these lectures were given by Cai Yuanpei, another Francophile reformer and educator, who had joined Li Shizeng in France. For examples, see *Cai Yuanpei Xiansheng Quanji* (*The Collected Works of Cai Yuanpei*), Taibei, 1969, pp. 197, 202–5, 210–20.

31   *Huagong Zazhi* (*The Chinese Worker*), No. 2, 25 January 1917 and No. 3, 10 February 1917.

32   *Dongfang Zazhi* (*Eastern Miscellany*), 14, 7, *neiwai shibao*, 1917, p. 172.

33   Cai Yuanpei had been the first Education Minister of the Chinese Republic in 1912, and later went on to become Chancellor of Beijing University.

34   On this, see my article 'The Chinese Work-Study Movement in France', *China Quarterly*, No. 115, September 1988, pp. 441–61.

35 Archives Nationales: Section Outre-Mer, NF 269 (1), Letter from Marius Moutet to the Ministry of War, January 1916. For a discussion of French attitudes towards China in a larger context in this period, see my article 'Voltaire and Confucius:French Attitudes Towards China in the Early Twentieth Century', *History of European Ideas*, 14, 6, 1992, pp. 817–37.

36 'An Army of Labour', *The Times*, 27 December 1917.

37 M.Summerskill, op. cit., p. 132.

38 'Les Travailleurs Chinois en France', *Le Temps*, September 1919, pp. 13–14.

39 A. Dupuoy, 'Un Camp de Chinois', *La Revue de Paris*, November–December 1919, pp. 161–2. A British missionary, writing on the Chinese Labour Corps in 1920, also referred to the Chinese proclivity for dressing up in foreign garments and caricaturing the 'funny' foreigners. E. Thompson, 'The Chinese Labour Corps, and the Effect of its Sojourn Here as a Possible Help to Missionaries', *East and West: A Quarterly Review for the Study of Missionary Problems*, Oct.ober 1920, p. 316.

40 N.Griffin, op. cit., p. 71 (fn. 120); M. Summerskill, op. cit., p. 57. There were reports of scuffles between Chinese and Arab workers at Bassens in January 1917, and between Chinese and black workers at Le Mans in July 1918. On the other hand, the French apparently segregated conscripted Vietnamese workers from their colony in Indochina and the Chinese workers out of fear the former would fall under the latter's subversively 'nationalist' influence. See Li Jun's second report to the Chinese Foreign Ministry on 10 June 1918 in *OHS*, p. 381. See also Chen Sanjing, op. cit., p. 145. The extent to which racial notions existed in China before the coming of the West, and how such notions interacted with a Western discourse of scientific racism in the late nineteenth and twentieth centuries has been explored by F. Dikotter, *The Discourse of Race in Modern China*, London, Hurst, 1992.

41 Chen Ta, op. cit., pp. 150–1; Chen Sanjing, op. cit., pp. 117–18, 145. Workers often protested over limited food rations, such as the two hundred who went on strike in Calais in May 1918. They also protested at having to eat horsemeat, which the French substituted for pork and lamb. The practice was subsequently abandoned.

42 Those under British employ had been subject to military law from the start. Chen Ta, op. cit., pp. 146–7.

43 *Lu'Ou Zhoukan* (*Weekly Journal for Chinese Students in Europe*), 15 November 1919, No. 1; *Huagong Zazhi*, No.19, 25 February 1918; No. 28, 25 November 1918; No. 35, 25 June 1919. Gambling was apparently a serious problem. One worker in Le Creusot committed suicide after losing all his savings in a gambling spree.

44 *Jiaoyu Gongbao* (*Bulletin of Education*), No. 4, April 1919, *jizai*, pp. 22–5.

45 *Huagong Zazhi*, No. 17, 10 January 1918.

46 *Lu'Ou Zazhi*, No. 20, 15 July 1917.

47 *Huagong Zazhi*, No. 18, 25 January 1918; No. 20, 25 March 1918; No. 21, 25 April 1918; No. 22, 25 May 1918; No. 24, 25 July 1918. Chinese workers in Boulogne, Alencon and Suresnes also donated money. Gu Xingqing, op. cit., pp. 50–1, also noted that after the war the British army organised an international athletics meeting in Belgium; nearly 6,000 Chinese workers turned up to participate but withdrew when they saw no Chinese flag being displayed.

48 M. Summerskill, op. cit., p. 7.

49 See Moutet's preface to P. Wou, *Les Travailleurs Chinois et la Grande Guerre*, pp. 7–8.

50   For a study of the Weihaiwei leased territory, see P. Atwell, *British Mandarins and Chinese Reformers:The British Administration of Weihaiwei (1898–1930) and the Territory's Return to Chinese Rule*, Hong Kong, Oxford University Press, 1985.

51   For the history of the Chinese in Canada, see E.Wickberg (ed.), *From China to Canada:A History of the Chinese Communities in Canada*, Toronto, McClelland and Stewart, 1982; and P. Li, *The Chinese in Canada*, Toronto, Oxford University Press, 1988. For the Chinese experience in the USA, see M. Hunt, *The Making of a Special Relationship:The United States and China to 1914*, New York, Columbia University Press, 1983; Shih-san Henry Tsai, *China and the Overseas Chinese in the US 1868–1911*, Lafayetteville, University of Arkansas Press, 1983; Shih-san Henry Tsai, *The Chinese Experience in America*, Bloomington, Indiana University Press, 1986. There is also much useful information in L. Pan (ed.), *The Encyclopedia of the Chinese Overseas*, Singapore, Chinese Heritage Centre, 1998, pp. 234–9, 261–6.

52   AMAE, E-544-1. The letter by the General Association of Chinese Workers in France was written on 21 April 1925 and addressed to the French Foreign Ministry and President of the Council of Ministers. The reply from the French authorities was sent in October 1925.

53   Chen Duxiu, 'Huagong' ('Chinese Workers'), *Duxiu Wencun (Writings of Chen Duxiu)*, Anhui renmin chubanshe, 1987, p. 596. Chen asserted that Chinese labourers had contributed to the opening up the whole world (particularly America and Australia) and that they represented China's only concrete contribution to the allied cause in World War One.

54   Gu Xingqing, op. cit., pp. 4,16. One of the prefaces to the book, written by Zhu Jingnong, also argued that the contribution of Chinese workers proved the superiority of the Chinese vis-à-vis the whites when it came to endurance and hard work, and that China was the match of the western powers in working for 'righteousness and justice'.

55   A number of comprehensive documentary collections, nevertheless, have been published on both overseas Chinese workers and the Chinese work-study movement in France. See, for example, *Huagong Chuguo Shiliao Huibian (Collection of Historical Materials on Chinese Workers Overseas)*, Beijing, 1984; *Fufa Qingong Jianxue Yundong Shiliao (Historical Materials on the Work-Study Movement in France)*, Beijing, 1979–81.

56   Certainly, there is nothing to match M. Michel, *L'Appel l'Afrique*, Paris, Publications de la Sorbonne, 1982, an exhaustive study of the role played by black workers and military conscripts from French West Africa during World War One.

57   For Chinese policy in Africa, see B. Larkin, *China and Africa 1949–1970*, Berkeley, University of California Press, 1971; and A. Ogunsanwo, *China's Policy in Africa 1958–1971*, Cambridge, Cambridge University Press, 1979.

58   A recent work on China's international diplomacy during this period, which aims to demonstrate China's growing autonomy on the international stage, strangely makes no mention at all of the recruitment of Chinese labour in World War One. See Zhang Yongjin, *China in the International System 1918–1920*, London, Macmillan, 1991. It might also be noted that the active political and cultural agendas of the 'host' country (i.e. from where indentured labour was recruited) are not taken into account by historians who debate the significance and nature of indentured labour in the nineteenth and early twentieth centuries simply in terms of whether it represented a 'disguised' continuation of slavery or whether it had more in common with 'free' European migration of the nineteenth century. See D. Northrup, op. cit., pp. ix–x.

59   *La Politique de Pkin*, 7 September 1919, and 11 June 1922.

10 It's Not Working: Refugee Employment and Urban Regeneration

ALICE BLOCH

Refugees[1] have long been a feature of British society and in some inner London areas they make up a significant proportion of the total population. In the London Borough of Newham, estimates place the number of refugees at around 20,000 which is more than 9 per cent of the total population. Refugees in Newham, like refugees generally, come from diverse backgrounds and therefore bring with them a range of pre-migration characteristics and experiences. However, once within Britain, refugees experience many of the same disadvantages when it comes to settling in the host society. Some of the difficulties faced by refugees are associated with the experience of exile, some are the result of national policies and some are due to racism and discrimination.

This chapter will explore the experiences of language learning, education, training for work and employment among refugees in the London Borough of Newham within the context of urban regeneration. Although the settlement of refugees is affected by a number of factors, there is some consensus that fluency in host society language skills and paid employment are both crucial for the successful resettlement of refugee people.

The acquisition of host society language skills has been identified as the first stage in the acculturation process, as it enables new migrants to gain access to social and economic institutions within the host society.[2] Those without language skills are likely to remain isolated.[3] Employment is also crucial in the settlement process as those who are working are able to adjust more easily to the host society. Employment provides economic independence, it is crucial for self-esteem and it can facilitate social contacts with members of the host society, all of which can help refugees to settle in the new country. However, refugees experience higher levels of unemployment than any other groups. Research carried out by the Home Office[4] found that only 27 per cent of refugees who were considered to be economically active were in paid

197

employment while the Refugee Council[5] has estimated that 70 per cent of refugees in London are unemployed. The minority of refugees who are working are usually employed in unskilled jobs which are often sporadic in nature such as private security work, porters and fast-food assistants.[6] The work that refugees find tends not to reflect their skills and previous experience. The reasons why refugees are unemployed and underemployed will be explored in this chapter.

One of the strategies which has been operationalised in an effort to reduce the high levels of unemployment experienced by some communities was the Urban Programme. Urban regeneration strategies set out to alleviate the disadvantages which are experienced by certain groups, including ethnic minority people, through skills training and education.

This chapter will first contextualise the situation of refugees in Newham by providing some background information about the local economy and urban regeneration policies. It will then provide an overview of the skills and experience that refugees bring with them on arrival to Britain. The role of urban regeneration policies in the reskilling of disadvantaged communities and refugee people's experiences of, and participation in, language learning, training and employment will then be explored.

The data presented in this chapter is from a survey of refugees from the Somali, Tamil and Congolese communities in the London Borough of Newham. A total of 180 interviews were carried out: 60 with members of each of the three communities. Interviews were in the mother tongue and quotas were set for age, gender and length of residence in the United Kingdom (UK) to ensure that the survey included a range of different experiences.

Background: the Local Economy in Newham

In the last few decades, the whole employment structure of London East, including Newham, has changed due to the decline in the manufacturing industries and the closure of the docks.[7] Among those who are employed, the main areas of employment are in public administration, education and health (26.5 per cent), distribution, hotels and restaurants (21.8 per cent), banking, finance and insurance (17 per cent) and manufacturing (14.7 per cent).[8] Although some sectors of the economy have experienced growth, overall there has been a decline in the number of jobs available in Newham since the 1970s. Not surprisingly, unemployment rates in Newham are disproportionately high. In June 1998, rates of employment in Newham were 12.3 per cent compared to a Greater London average of 6.7 per cent and a United Kingdom average of 5.3 per cent.[9]

Rates of employment differ between different ethnic groups and gender. Nationally, Bangladeshis experience the highest levels of unemployment followed by Black Africans and Pakistanis while women are generally less likely to be unemployed than men.[10] Table 10.1 shows that in Newham the national patterns of unemployment were reflected locally.

Table 10.1 Total percentage unemployed in Newham by ethnic group and sex

Total population: 212,170

	Male	**Female**	**All**
White	18.6	10.9	15.4
Black Caribbean	22.4	14.0	18.2
Black African	42.7	35.5	39.6
Black (other)	25.8	19.8	22.9
Indian	18.5	19.5	18.9
Pakistani	35.0	36.9	35.4
Bangladeshi	41.3	48.5	42.8
Chinese	13.9	10.0	21.1
Other Asian	27.8	17.5	23.3
Other	26.8	22.4	25.1
All (percentages)	22.1	15.1	19.3

Source: 1991 Census.

Levels of unemployment do not tell us anything about the type of work that those who are employed are engaged in or about their levels of pay. There is a great deal of diversity between different ethnic groups although what is consistent is the relative disadvantage experienced by both men and women from the Bangladeshi and Pakistani communities. Some ethnic minority women have higher levels of pay than their white counterparts, most notably Caribbean, African Asian and Indian women. Among the men, African Asians and Chinese earn the same as white men while others earn less.[11]

Longitudinal work has shown that after an initial period of downward occupational mobility, some ethnic minority groups are now experiencing upward occupational mobility. This trend has been especially noticeable among

East African Asians, many of whom came to the UK as refugees in the late 1960s and early 1970s. Many of the East African Asians were well qualified and had excellent English language skills on arrival in Britain as well as a community network which could provide help and support to new arrivals.[12] Self-employment has been a route successfully taken by East African Asians and it has also provided family members and co-ethnics with employment.[13]

Not all refugees bring with them English language skills, business acumen or have access to an already established ethnic community to turn to for help and assistance. These factors will be relevant when assessing the economic activity and the aspirations of refugees in Newham. The urban programme sets out to reduce inequalities by creating opportunities for reskilling and retraining unemployed people in the areas where there are skills shortages in any given locality.

Urban Regeneration

Although levels of unemployment in Newham are above the national average, there are still growth areas in the locality although most of the employment vacancies are for the least desirable occupations like catering, security, cleaning and cashier work. The most notable exception being the inability to fill jobs for primary school teachers. In terms of future needs, London East Training and Enterprise Council (LETEC) forecasts that the growth areas in East London will include: computer literacy, management, information technology, languages and personal skills like flexibility and motivation.[14]

One of the patterns in East London is the tendency for the higher skilled jobs to be filled by people from outside the area. The 1991 Census found that 63 per cent of employed East London residents worked in East London, while 37 per cent commuted to work. Conversely, 29 per cent of local jobs were taken by people commuting to East London from outside the area, mostly from Essex. According to LETEC: 'Generally inward commuters take a higher proportion of well qualified jobs within the area, while residents working locally take a higher proportion of unskilled and semi-skilled jobs.'[15] At the moment there is a skills mismatch between what is needed locally and what local residents can provide. If the skills gap is not closed then the better paid jobs in East London will continue to be filled by inward commuters rather than local residents. One of the criticisms made by LETEC is that training provision does not reflect the demands of local employers and that training is preparing people for low grade, low skill occupations.[16] This is in direct conflict with urban regeneration policy which sets out to combat high levels of unemployment through capacity building so that the most disadvantaged are in a position to obtain the well paid jobs in any given locality.

Development of the Urban Programme

Successive governments have set out to tackle the problems faced by inner city areas, such as economic, social and environmental decline, through an urban programme concerned with regeneration.[17] The Urban Programme was initiated in the 1960s in response to urban uprisings and the disadvantage experienced by ethnic minority people. Up until March 1996, money was allocated specifically to projects concerned with ethnic minorities under three schemes: Section 11 funding, the Ethnic Minority Grant (EMG) and the Ethnic Minority Business Initiative (EMBI). These schemes have been gradually incorporated under the Single Regeneration Budget (SRB) which came into effect in April 1994.

Three dimensions of the urban programme have been criticised. First, it evolved in a piecemeal fashion rather than through the formulation of strategies and targets.[18] Secondly, under the SRB, money is allocated to specific geographical areas and focuses on economic and environmental regeneration rather than the social and community needs of local residents, especially those who experience disadvantage like refugee groups. Thirdly, the way in which funds are allocated has also been criticised because they disadvantage ethnic minority communities. The main source of funding is the SRB which is administered by the Department of the Environment. Other sources of funding available for regeneration come from the European Union, the City Challenge programme and City Pride. What these schemes have in common is their concern with structural regeneration as well as the promotion of access to jobs for local people.

Funding programmes for regeneration emphasise the role of local partnerships between the statutory, voluntary and private sectors and match funding is a prerequisite for some of the regeneration initiatives. The funding arrangements mean that ethnic minority organisations may find themselves disadvantaged when bidding for grants. First, most funding now requires an element of match funding from local partners. Groups working with minority ethnic communities may not have as many 'mainstream' contacts as other groups which make it more difficult to establish viable partnerships.[19] Secondly, newer organisations tend to lack information about the bidding process and many missed out on the first round of SRB bids because they were not aware of the change in funding. As a recent report recorded:

> In the absence of pro-active and strategic allocations, a competitive bidding system is likely to benefit larger, white-led or 'ethnic-elder' voluntary organisations ... To encourage newer groups, and in particular ethnic minorities under-represented in UP [Urban Policy] activity, authorities should explore further ways of providing 'capacity building' assistance.[20]

Thirdly, the shift from capital to revenue funding impedes minority ethnic organisations as they are less able to capitalise on public resources and have always relied on revenue based programmes which makes it harder to match fund.[21]

The disadvantage experienced by ethnic minority organisations in terms of getting access to funds means that there are fewer resources to help some of the most disadvantaged groups, which includes refugees, when it comes to training and employment. The data to be explored in the following sections will firstly examine the skills and qualifications that refugees bring on arrival to Britain and secondly, the barriers that refugee people face gaining access to training programmes, to the labour market and in getting jobs which utilise their skills.

Refugees on Arrival to Britain: Language, Education and Employment

English Language

Refugees arrive in Britain with vast differences in their knowledge of the English language. Figures 10.1 and 10.2 show that country of origin and gender were the main factors which affect proficiency in the English language.

Refugees from Somalia and Sri Lanka, both of which had colonial links with Britain, were much more likely to speak English than were Congolese who had no colonial links with Britain. Moreover, men had higher levels of English language skills than women; a reflection of differences in literacy levels, especially among Somali women, prior to exile. Data from a world survey of women shows that in 1995, 16 per cent of women in Somalia were literate compared to 41 per cent of men. Levels of literacy were much higher among Sri Lankans and people from the former Zaire (now Congo). In 1995, 87 per cent of women from Sri Lanka were literate while among men the

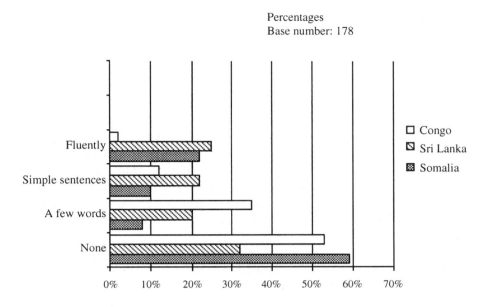

Figure 10.1 Spoken English on arrival in Britain by country of origin

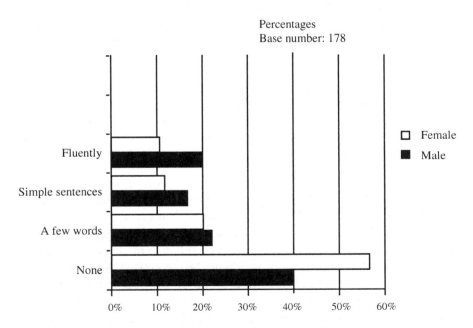

Figure 10.2 Spoken English on arrival in Britain by gender

proportion was 93 per cent. Among Congolese the gender differentials were greater than among Sri Lankans. Literacy levels among women in the former Zaire stood at 68 per cent compared to 87 per cent among men.[22]

Education

Refugees tend to be among the most educated in their country of origin. Three-quarters of all respondents had a qualification on arrival to Britain. Eleven per cent had a degree, 4 per cent had a postgraduate qualification, 5 per cent were qualified teachers and 41 per cent had 'A' level qualifications or their equivalent. There were differences in levels of education and academic qualifications by gender and community. Somalis were less well educated than were others, especially Somali women who for the most part had received no formal schooling.

Refugees generally arrive in Britain with higher academic qualifications than that obtained by people educated in Britain. In fact refugees are more likely to have a higher degree, a degree or an 'A' level or equivalent qualification that their white or ethnic minority counterparts.[23] However, refugee's qualifications remain largely unused. Transferring qualifications obtained overseas to their UK equivalents can be problematic as some are not recognised or are not transferable.[24] Less than a quarter of those who had qualifications on arrival to Britain said that their qualifications were recognised. One Tamil woman described her own experience in the following way:

> I finished my degree in Sri Lanka and I was about to get a teaching job. Because I came here I couldn't get a professional job like teaching. I wanted to train myself for teaching in Britain but I was told that I would have to do further education which involved a long period so I decided to do some other jobs like cashiering, shop assistant etc.

Among those who had qualifications that were not recognised, only 16 per cent had tried to get them recognised. Table 10.2 shows the reasons why refugees had not attempted to get their qualifications recognised.

The most frequently mentioned reason for not trying to get qualifications recognised was due to a lack of information, although in nine cases there was an assumption that qualifications would not be recognised. According to one Somali respondent: 'I have been told by the Somali community that such qualifications would not be recognised.' In some circumstances, refugees were not able to bring their certificates with them and so they are unable to provide the evidence which would enable the conversion of qualifications.

Table 10.2 Reasons for not trying to get qualifications recognised

Frequencies ·
Base number: 80

Reason	Frequencies
Lack of information	25
No need/not necessary	14
Assumed that it would not be recognised	9
No particular reason	8
Do not have certificate	6
Due to language barrier	3
No time to do it	2
Want to continue with other studies	2
Other*	5

Missing: 6

* Other included just arrived in Britain, do not have the motivation and not interested.

Employment

Before coming to Britain, 32 per cent of refugees were employed, 11 per cent were self-employed and 33 per cent were students. Table 10.3[25] shows the variation and diversity of employment that refugee people had before coming to Britain.

Table 10.3 shows that people brought skills for which there were shortfalls in East London, especially teaching. One Tamil respondent described his own situation in the following way: 'I have nearly 25 years of experience, 15 years teaching and ten years as a school principal, but without British training I can't get into teaching.' Thus refugees come to Britain with a range of qualifications and employment experience which, as we shall see, remain largely unused in the British economy.

Language Training in Britain

There are no formal reception and resettlement programmes for refugees who arrive in Britain spontaneously. Spontaneous refugees are those who come to Britain and seek asylum either at the port of entry or once within Britain. It is

Table 10.3   Number of people in different types of job

Base number: 68[26]

Frequencies

Teacher	13
Clerk/admin/accounts	10
Cashier	5
Secretary/typist	4
Mechanical/engineering	4
Shop keeper	4
Market trader	4
Civil servant	4
Farmer	3
Business person	2
Statistical researcher	1
Computer analyst	1
Sales person	1
Meteorologist	1
Carpenter	1
Nurse	1
Army colonel	1
Banker	1
Broadcaster	1
Postman	1
Dressmaker	1
Factory worker	1
Caterer	1
Marketing executive	1
New technology	1

only quota refugees, who arrive in a group and have refugee status on arrival to Britain, such as the Chileans and the Vietnamese, who have been part of an organised reception programme. One component of the reception programmes has been English language training. Most spontaneous refugees attend English for Speakers of Other Languages (ESOL) classes in order to learn or improve their English language skills. In total, 69 per cent of refugees had attended English language classes in Britain. Many of those who had not attended English classes were Somali women who did not speak any English on arrival in Britain. Some were lone parents whose child care responsibilities made attendance difficult and there were also cultural and religious constraints which could affect participation in language classes.

The reasons for studying English varied. Not surprisingly, most people attended language classes to simply communicate better (86 per cent) and/or to increase the chance of getting a job (67 per cent). However, 19 per cent also said that they attended language classes to meet new people. Most of those who attended language classes to meet people were Congolese, a reflection of the fact that they are a newer community, without former links with Britain, and therefore without an established social network to turn to for support and help; ESOL classes was one way of meeting new people. ESOL is funded by a number of different sources, including urban regeneration programmes. ESOL is often taught in conjunction with other subjects such as information technology and maths. More than half of those who had studied English had learned the language in conjunction with other subjects and the majority received free training which was funded by the local authority or the further education college which in turn receives urban regeneration money. Only 9 per cent of those who had attended language classes had financed themselves.

The number of hours which students attended varied from less than five hours to 21 or more hours a week. Policy changes, enacted in September 1996, mean that any courses at further education colleges which involve more than 16 hours of study a week are now deemed to be full time and, as a result, students taking these courses will no longer be entitled to any social security benefits. This will have an adverse affect on rapid language learning for new arrivals without English language proficiency. A number of different organisations provide ESOL, these include: the further education college, community organisations and the local authority. On the whole, people were satisfied with their English language classes although Table 10.4 shows that there were some aspects of language learning which did not meet the needs of refugee people.[27]

The areas where there was the most dissatisfaction expressed were also the areas which were highlighted as problematic by service providers. Service providers were aware that they did not have the resources or the facilities to meet the diverse and often complex needs of refugee students. The problems faced by refugee students were exemplified by the fact that nearly a third of students who had started a course had been unable to complete their studies. The reasons for not completing course varied. Reasons stated included needing the time to look for work, the course was not suitable and problems which arose with housing and immigration.

Table 10.4   Satisfaction with different aspects of English language provision

Percentages

	Satisfied	Neither satisfied nor dissatisfied	Dissatisfied	Total number*
Course content	75	19	6	117
Teaching methods	72	16	12	121
Awareness of refugee experience	59	16	25	115
Student support	58	23	19	120
Class sizes	84	7	8	107
Information about progression	66	16	19	116

*   The base number varies as there were a lot of 'don't knows' recorded for some of these questions.

Those who had attended ESOL classes were asked to state all the ways in which English language provision could be improved. The most frequently mentioned strategies were: teachers from their own community (44 per cent), different level classes which better reflected language learning needs (42 per cent), more hours of study (33 per cent) and longer courses (22 per cent). Although there were areas of language provision where people were dissatisfied and where improvement could be made, Figure 10.3 shows that English language skills had improved markedly while in Britain.

There were variations by gender and country of origin. In terms of gender, most of those who did not speak any English at the time of the survey were Somali women. Moreover, at the time of the survey, more than a third of Somali women understood not a word of English. The continued disadvantage experienced by refugee women has been noted by others: 'Refugee women … arrive … with lower levels of English language proficiency than men … Yet refugee women's lower initial level of English proficiency is compounded by less access to training classes and by relative social isolation through staying at home.'[28]

Not speaking English is very problematic for refugee women. Not only does it affect access to social and economic institutions within the host society, it also makes women dependent on others for help and assistance when it comes to dealing with agencies and service providers. Moreover, lack of host

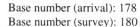

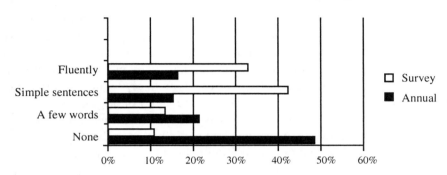

Figure 10.3 Change in spoken English from arrival until the time of survey

society language skills can affect family relationships because children can often find themselves acting as interpreters and therefore privy to information which they would not normally have access to. This can create a power imbalance between women and their children.

In terms of country of origin, refugees from Congo showed the most dramatic improvements in English language. On arrival to Britain, more than half the Congolese respondents spoke no English. However, the number speaking no English at the time of the survey had dropped to just one person. Conversely, while only two per cent spoke English fluently on arrival to Britain, the proportion who spoke fluently at the time of the survey had risen to a third. This impressive language learning among Congolese reflects, in part, their high levels of education but also their tendency to be multilingual. It may also reflect the fact Congolese refugees are a relatively new refugee group without much community organisation to turn to for help and support in the early stages of resettlement so it was extremely important for members of this community to learn English as soon as possible.

Education in Britain

At the time of the survey, 36 per cent of those interviewed had either studied in Britain or were studying. Participation in education was influenced by a number of variables. Men were more likely to have studied than women and length of residence was also influential. The longer people had been resident in Britain, the more likely it was that they had studied. One of the reasons for this is the grant regime. Those with refugee status are entitled to mandatory local authority awards for education while others have to wait for three years before they are entitled to a student grant. Because many refugees are young and have had their education interrupted, the delay in gaining access to grants can be problematic as it adversely affects their lives in exile. In addition, those who felt more settled in Britain were more likely to have studied than those who definitely wanted to return to their country of origin. The desire to return home and the 'myth of return' has been identified as an indicator of segregation which affects investment and participation in the host society.[29]

Those who were studying or had studied in the past were most likely to have studied for a degree than any other qualification. Six respondents had successfully completed a degree since living in Britain while 11 were studying for a degree at the time of the survey. In addition to degree level qualifications, refugees had either obtained, or were studying for, a diverse range of academic and vocational qualifications since arriving in Britain, which included 'A' levels, NVQs and GNVQs. There was a high rate of course non-completion among refugees with 15 per cent starting a course and not being able to complete. The most frequently mentioned reasons for non-completion were difficulties concentrating and child care problems. Others did not complete due to financial problems, some found the courses too difficult and some found that their level of English language was insufficient to meet the demands of academic work.

Training for Work

Training for work is provided at many locations in Newham and sets out to provide people with the skills and experience necessary to enter the labour market. In Newham, 16 per cent of refugee people had participated in training courses. Low levels of participation in training, relative to high levels of unemployment, is a pattern which has been identified for people from minority ethnic communities in general. This is because ethnic minority people are disadvantaged when it comes to getting onto training courses in the first place.[30]

One of the reasons for the lack of participation is the funding regime. First, the level of funding has declined, especially the proportion aimed at the long term unemployed, of whom refugees and people from minority ethnic communities form a disproportionate group.[31] Secondly, 25 per cent of funding for Employment Training and Employment Action is linked to outcomes in terms of qualifications gained, progression to further education or higher education and positive employment and self-employment outcomes. Under the Training for Work scheme, 75 per cent is paid to trainers on the successful demonstration of agreed outputs. Research on the effectiveness of the Training and Enterprise Councils (TECs) in achieving jobs and qualifications for disadvantaged groups which include members of refugee communities maintained that: 'Concern has been expressed that output related funding (ORF) provides an incentive for TECs and training providers to practice "creaming", by selecting the most "able" of the unemployed who are likely to achieve a job or a vocational qualification in a short period.'[32] There is a propensity for training providers to 'screen out' members of groups who may be less likely to achieve job outcomes or are more likely not to complete the training. This includes people with English language needs as well as those who have family commitments or religious or cultural influences which might affect outcomes. Moreover, in the case of refugees, some may experience more fundamental anxieties which may result in non-completion.[33]

The incompletion rates among refugees in Newham was high: nearly a quarter of all courses started were not finished. Reasons for not finishing courses varied although training providers felt that refugee people needed advice provision and self-help discussion groups to help them complete their courses. Moreover, the vocational training that refugees had been involved in did not build on their previous professional or educational experience. For example, a degree educated and experienced teacher from Somalia had taken a catering course while a degree educated mechanical engineer had taken a course in welfare rights.

Research on the employment outcomes of the training schemes found that there were differences in training outcomes by ethnic community.[34] On Network schemes, which are schemes for 16–18 year olds, 14 per cent of trainees from minority ethnic communities got a job on completion compared to 40 per cent of white trainees. On Advance schemes, which provide training for unemployed adults, 18 per cent of people from minority ethnic communities got a job compared to 21 per cent of white trainees. Language was found to be a key variable in terms of employment outcomes as Table 10.5 shows.[35]

In spite of the difficulties that refugees might experience getting onto training and completing courses, there was evidence to suggest that participation in training was helpful in terms of future employment although

Table 10.5 Job outcome by white/non-white and whether English is first language

Percentages

	Non-white English first language	Non-white English not first language	White All
Got job	38	22	65
Did not get job	62	78	35

the data must be interpreted cautiously as the numbers were so small. A larger proportion of people who had done training for work courses had also worked as compared with those who had not done training for work. Half of those who had done training had been involved in the labour market compared to 35 per cent of those who had not done any training. However, there was little evidence of any relationship between the training done and the type of future employment. For example, one person trained in carpentry and joinery and worked, for a couple of months, as a kitchen porter.

One of the reasons for the lack of correlation between training and future employment for refugees could be the attitudes of placement employers. Research carried out by the Policy Studies Institute identified employer discrimination as a problem in terms of positive training outcomes:

> Employer discrimination was identified as a problem by respondents in most of the TECs, both against the long-term unemployed in general and against particular groups including disabled people, ethnic minorities and people in deprived areas. Employer attitudes towards disadvantaged trainees were frequently seen by TECs as a major constraint on the placement of trainees and on achieving job outcomes.[36]

The problem of employers' discrimination is clearly demonstrated by the fact that only a few trainees from minority ethnic communities went on to get employment from their placement employer compared to just over half of the white trainees.[37]

Although training did not appear to be providing refugee people with access to the better paid jobs in the area, most people still wanted to do training (62 per cent). The sort of training that people wanted was very diverse. Clerical, office and business administration was the most popular (24 out of 111) followed by information technology (20 out of 111) then retail and service sector skills (19 out of 111). Thirteen respondents said that they would like training in 'anything useful'. Moreover, the majority of those looking for work still thought that training would help them to get the sort of job they wanted The training that people wanted most often was in clerical and office work, business administration, retail, service sector information technology, mechanical and electrical work and teaching. Some of the training that respondents said they could do to help them get a job reflected areas where there were skills gaps in the local economy such as information technology and teaching. However, as shown earlier, there is little correlation between training and employment outcomes especially among those who do not speak English as a first language. What is striking is that many refugees seemed resigned to the fact that any training and subsequent employment would mean downward occupation mobility. There was definitely a sense of resignation among refugees about the reality of their situation.

Labour Market Participation in Britain

Labour market participation was very low among refugees. Only 14 per cent (or 25 respondents) were involved in work as either employees or as self-employed people while 46 per cent were unemployed. Thus levels of unemployment were higher among refugees than among people from ethnic minority groups (see Table 10.1). Those who were employed tended to be Tamils (18 out of 25), they all spoke English either fluently or at the level of simple sentences, were male, had lived in Britain for longer and were more secure about their immigration status. Moreover, there was a strong correlation between employment activity in Britain and immigration status.[38] People with refugee status or exceptional leave to remain (ELR) were more likely to be working than those on temporary admission. In contrast, those on temporary admission were much more likely to be unemployed. One of the reasons for this is the insecurity associated with temporary admission which makes it very difficult for people to invest in their future or even to get on with their everyday their lives.

There are a number of reasons why refugees experience such high levels of unemployment. First, qualifications might not be transferable. Secondly, English language skills may not be commensurate with the skills and qualifications that refugees bring with them. Certainly the research in Newham mirrored the findings of research carried out by the Home Office: refugees who were working were the most proficient in English.[39] Thirdly, some refugees, for example, from rural areas, do not have skills which can be directly transferred to the British labour market.[40] Fourthly, methods of job seeking and the practices of employers can affect access to the labour market. There is a propensity for employers to fill posts without advertising; this practice adversely affects refugees as they do not have enough host society contacts and are effectively excluded. Linked to this is the fact that refugees tend to rely on informal contacts due to their orientation towards people from the same community. Indeed, research among refugees from Iraq showed that a lack of contacts with members of the host society meant that refugees had little knowledge about the organisation of occupations and the structure of the local economy.[41]

A fifth reason relates to national policy. In Britain, existing legislation hinders equal access to the labour market for some asylum seekers. On arrival to Britain, asylum seekers cannot apply for a work permit until they have been resident for six months. The process of obtaining a work permit might be a slow one. Research carried out by the Home Office found that 86 per cent of those who had applied for a work permit had waited between six months and a year for a decision to be made while 14 per cent had waited for a year or longer.[42] Finally, employer discrimination will affect access to the labour market for refugees.[43] There is a concern that discrimination might have increased as a result of the 1996 Immigration and Asylum Act which contained a clause relating to employment. The Act specifies that employers taking on a member of staff without the appropriate documentation will be fined. According to Morris:

> ... internal policing will tend to focus suspicion on the 'visibly different' minorities and having the effect of eroding their legitimate rights ... the requirement of employers to police the legality of their workers ... common in Europe and known to discriminate against legally present minorities, has been introduced in Britain by the 1996 Asylum and Immigration Act.[44]

Figure 10.4 shows that refugees identified discrimination as the main barrier to employment.[45]

Lack of employment experience and language were also key barriers to employment. The following quotes by two Tamil refugees illustrate these problems:

> I would like more on the job training to people who have studied for qualifications in Britain. Though I have enough qualifications to do an office job I am unable to get one because I have no work experience.

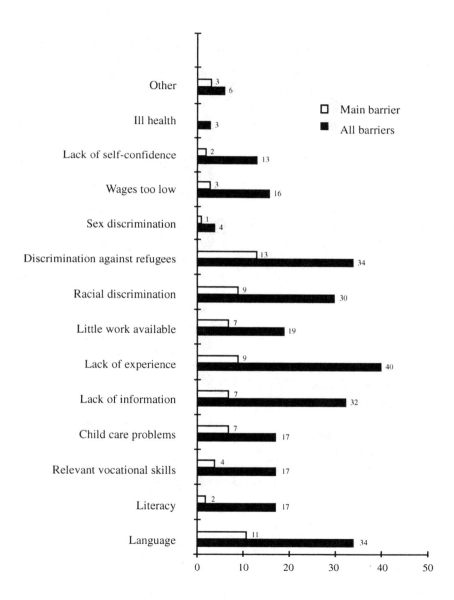

Frequencies
Base number: 78

□ Main barrier
■ All barriers

Figure 10.4 Barriers to employment

> Language is a great barrier to finding a suitable job. In my case I have done a
> degree in commerce back in Sri Lanka but I did it in the Tamil medium so I
> could not get a good job here.

The minority of refugees who had worked in Britain found themselves
employed almost exclusively in the secondary labour market, one which is
characterised by poor terms and conditions of employment, evening and
weekend work and low pay. Data from the Labour Force Survey found an
average hourly rate of £7.44 among the white population and £6.82 among
people from ethnic minority communities.[46] In contrast, refugees were earning
an average of less than £4 an hour.

Figure 10.5 shows the type of employment that those who were working
or had worked in Britain in the past were, or had been engaged in.

Figure 10.5 shows that there is a lack of diversity in terms of types of jobs
that refugees find. Lack of diversity in the area of employment among refugees
is something that has been identified in research among Vietnamese refugees
in Manchester where more than half of those interviewed were employed in
the catering industry.[47] Nearly half of those who had been employed in the
past but were not working at the time of the survey had been in their last job

Frequencies
Base number of those working: 25

Base number of past employment: 38

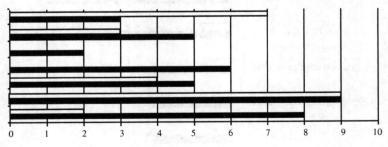

☐ Current employment

■ Last job among those who have worked in Britain in the past

*   Other includes sorting at the post office, English language teacher and community worker.

**Figure 10.5 Last paid job for those who have worked in Britain but are
not currently working and current job among those
working at the time of the survey**

for less than a year and for those in cleaning and security it had been a matter of weeks or months. Table 10.6 shows the reasons why refugees had left their last job.

Table 10.6   Reasons for leaving last job

Base number: 39

	Frequencies
Redundant/job finished	11
Personal reasons	7
Return to education	6
Look after home	3
Low pay	3
Ill health	2
Unsociable hours	1
Racism in workplace	1
Immigration restriction	1
Got sacked	1
To look for full time job	1
Got arrested for working illegally	1
Petrol garage business went down	1
Total	39

In some cases the reasons for leaving a job merely reflected the nature of refugee employment, which was sporadic, with low pay and with poor terms and conditions of service. However, nearly two in 10 had left their last job for personal reasons, which suggests that refugees can have serious problems to deal with which might affect their capacity to maintain employment.

Refugees are not able to use their skills and experience in the UK labour market. For example, teachers found work in shops or as cleaners while engineers found work as security guards or in shops. Indeed, among those who were working, seven in 10 said that they felt that there were other jobs which would suit them better and the reason they gave was that there current job did not reflect their professional experience.[48] Even refugees who had obtained degrees while in the UK were, for the most part, not employed in graduate type jobs. Instead graduates tended to be working in factories and shops although it should be stressed that five out of six graduates were employed – a much higher ratio than that found among those who had not graduated in Britain. Nevertheless, it is of great concern that refugee people are unable to obtain well paid jobs. Certainly within this context, the effectiveness of training for work, language learning and education, some of the key components of urban regeneration, must be brought into question.

Conclusion

Many refugees arrive in Britain with high levels of education and qualifications. Nevertheless, they seem unable to use their skills in paid employment and levels of unemployment among refugees exceeded that of any other group. Those who were working tended to be employed in low paid work with poor terms and conditions of employment. There was a positive attitude towards training, as the majority said that they would like to take a training course. However, by and large, those respondents who wanted training were seeking training for relatively low skilled jobs, given the skills and qualifications that they had on arrival in Britain. Employment aspirations were low among refugees and many seemed resigned to the fact that they would not be able to use their skills and experience and instead looked for low paid, and often temporary, employment. Those who had participated in training did not find employment, for the most part, which related to the training they had done. Nevertheless, a higher proportion of those who had done training had worked in the UK than those who had never participated in training.

Moreover, funding regimes and lack of support for students with special needs means that refugees experience problems getting accepted on courses and where they do get on courses they can find it hard to complete as the necessary support structures are not in place. Even the handful of students who had obtained degree level qualifications from British universities were, for the most part, engaged in semiskilled and unskilled work.

Some refugees did have difficulties completing training courses or sustaining employment due to a range of personal reasons and stresses which may be directly related to being a refugee and living in exile. Indeed, it was recognised by some service providers that for refugees to be successful, many required support through their courses and the funding was not there to provide the necessary level of support.

The skills and experiences that refugees bring with them remain largely unused in a locality where there is a skills gap between the needs of the local economy and the skills that many of the population are able to offer. Urban regeneration schemes, in spite of their remit, have not succeeded in reducing the inequality and disadvantage which exists between different ethnic groups.

Refugees bring skills that could easily be utilised within the local economy but remain unused for a variety of personal and structural reasons. If urban regeneration is to be effective in reskilling people to meet the labour market demands of the locality in which they live, then assessments need to be made at a more micro level. For example, in this small study there were 13 qualified teachers unable to get work in their profession while there was a demand for ESOL teachers from refugee communities and primary school teachers. It would be a much more efficient use of resources if refugees' skills were utilised by offering fast track conversion courses rather than training courses which led to unrelated semiskilled or unskilled work or continued unemployment. Given the importance of employment in relation to refugee settlement, this is a matter that needs to be addressed with some urgency.

Notes

1   Unless otherwise specified, the term refugee is used as a generic one to describe refugees, people with exceptional leave to remain on humanitarian grounds and asylum seekers waiting for the Home Office to make a decision on their case.

2   C.K. Bun and T.C. Kiong, 'Rethinking assimilation and ethnicity: The Chinese in Thailand', *International Migration Review*, 1993, 27 (1) pp. 140–68.

3   D. Thomas, 'The social integration of immigrants in Canada', in S. Globerman (ed.), *The Immigrant Dilemma*, Vancouver, Canada, 1992.

4   J. Carey-Wood, K. Duke, V. Karn and T. Marshall, *The Settlement of Refugees in Britain*, Home Office Research Study 141, London, HMSO, 1995.

5   Refugee Council, 'Sanctuary on the streets', *Exile*, London, Refugee Council, 1992.

6   A. Sivanandan, *Communities of Resistance: Writings on black struggles for socialism*, London, Verso, 1990.

7   V. Rix, 'Industrial decline, economic restructuring and social exclusion in London East, 1980s and 1990s', *Journal of East London Studies*, 1997, 1 (1), pp. 118–41.

8   London East Training and Enterprise Council (LETEC), *London East Economic Assessment*, London, LETEC, 1996.

9   London East Training and Enterprise Council, *Economic Bulletin, Issue 23*, LETEC, London, July, 1998.

10   See F. Sly, 'Ethnic groups and the labour market: Analyses from the Spring 1994 Labour Force Survey', *Employment Gazette*, June, pp. 251–62, The Employment Department, London, HMSO, 1995 and F. Sly, 'Ethnic minority participation in the labour market: Trends from the Labour Force Survey 1984–1995', *Labour Market Trends*, 104 (6), pp. 259–70, London, HMSO, 1996.

11   T. Modood, 'Ethnic diversity and racial disadvantage in employment', in T. Blackstone, B. Parekh and P. Sanders (eds), *Race Relations in Britain: A Developing Agenda*, London, Routledge, 1998.

12   V. Robinson, 'Marching into the middle classes? The long-term resettlement of East African Asians in the UK', *Journal of Refugee Studies*, 1993, 6 (3), pp. 230–47.

13   H. Metcalf, T. Modood and S. Virdee, *Asian self-employment: The Interaction of Culture and Economics in England*, London, Policy Studies Institute, 1997.

14   London East Training and Enterprise Council, *Economic Assessment 1996–1997*, London, LETEC, 1997.

15   London East Training and Enterprise Council, *Economic Assessment*, London, LETEC, 1995, p. 5.

16   London East Training and Enterprise Council, 1996, op. cit.

17   Central Office of Information, *Urban Regeneration*, London, HMSO, 1995.

18   B. Robson, M. Bradford, I. Deas, E. Hall, E. Harrison, M. Parkinson, R. Evans, P. Garside, A. Harding and F. Robinson, *Assessing the Impact of Urban Policy*, Inner Cities Research Programme for the Department of Environment, London, HMSO, 1994.

19   J. Crook, *Invisible Partners: The Impact of the SRB on Black Communities*, London, Black Training and Enterprise Group, 1995.

20   V. Hausner and Associates, *Economic Revitalisation of Inner Cities: The Urban Programme and Ethnic Minorities*, Inner Cities Research Programme for the Department of Environment, London, HMSO, 1992, p. 12.

21   B. Robson et al., op. cit.

22   R. Leger Sivad, *Women ... A World Survey*, Washington, World Priorities, 1995.

23   London East Training and Enterprise Council, *Household Survey 1995*, London, LECTEC, 1995.

24   J. Gambell, *Welcome to the UK*, National Association of Citizens Advice Bureaux, London, 1993.

25   A. Bloch, *Beating the Barriers: The Employment and Training Needs of Refugees in Newham*, London, London Borough of Newham, 1996, Table 18, p. 46.

26   The total number of responses is less than the number of people who were working before coming to Britain because in nine instances respondents provided insufficient detail about their job before coming to the UK.

27   Bloch, 1996 op. cit., Table 10, p. 27.

28   R.L. Bach and R. Carroll-Seguin, 'Labour force participation, household composition and sponsorship amongst Southeast Asian Refugees', *International Migration Review*, 1986, 20 (2) p. 388.

29   Robinson, op. cit.

30   J. Payne, S. Wissenburgh, and M. White, *Employment Training and Employment Action*, London, Department of Education and Employment, 1996.

31   J. Carey-Wood et al., op.cit.

32   H. Rolfe, A. Bryson and H. Metcalf, *The Effectiveness of TECs in Achieving Job Outcomes for Disadvantaged Groups*, London, Policy Studies Institute, 1996, p. 10.

33   Ibid.

34   Local Economic Policy Unit (LEPU), *Improving Work Placements and Positive Outcomes for Trainees from Minority Ethnic Groups and Trainees with Disabilities*, LEPU, London South Bank University, 1996.

35   Ibid.

36   H. Rolfe, op. cit., p. 10.

37   LEPU, op. cit.

38   A. Bloch, 'Refugees in the job market: a case of unused skills in the British economy', ch. 10 in A. Bloch and C. Levy (eds), *Refugees, Citizenship and Social Policy in Europe*, Basingstoke, Macmillan, 1999.

39   J. Carey-Wood et al., op. cit.
40   R. Parkinson, *Survey of Refugee Needs in Hackney for theHackney Refugee Training Consortium*, Cardiff, Research Consultancy Training, 1998.
41   M. Al-Rasheed, 'The Iraqi community in London', *New Community*, 1992, 18 (4), pp. 537–50.
42   J. Carey-Wood et al., op. cit.
43   D. Joly, L. Kelly and C. Nettleton, *Refugees in Europe: The Hostile New Agenda*, London, Minority Rights Group, 1997.
44   L. Morris, 'A cluster of contradictions: The politics of migration in the European Union', *Sociology*, 1997, 31 (2), pp. 241–59.
45   Bloch, op. cit. 1996, Figure 24, p. 60.
46   F. Sly, op. cit.
47   C. Girbash, *Manchester Vietnamese Employment and Training Survey*, The Centre for Employment Research, Manchester, Manchester Polytechnic, 1991.
48   Bloch, op. cit. 1999.

11 Are the UK's Ethnic Minorities at a Disadvantage When They Get Older?

MAHMOOD MESSKOUB

Introduction

For decades a 'silent' change has been taking place in the population structure of most European countries. The population of Europe has been ageing. As a consequence of a declining fertility and rising life expectancy, one in seven people in Europe were over 65 in 1996, a ratio that is going to increase to one in five by 2020. This ageing population is not a homogenous mass but differentiated by social class, gender, ethnic background and race; factors that by all accounts shape the social and physical ageing of individuals and largely determine their well being in old age.[1] Such differences have to be taken on board if social and economic policies are to be successful in their objective of providing reasonable living standards for the mass of the elderly population in the twenty-first century.

This chapter is concerned with the situation of elderly non-white immigrants, some of whom came to the United Kingdom in the early 1950s, and who form the bulk of what the Office of Population Census and Surveys (OPCS) designate as 'ethnic' in its enumeration of the non-white British population.[2] A distinction should be drawn between the concept of 'ethnic' and 'immigrant' as these have a tendency to overlap. An immigrant community usually forms a distinct ethnic group but the reverse is not always true – not every ethnic group is necessarily borne out of immigration. For the purpose of this study, however, the overlap between non-white 'ethnic' and non-white 'immigrant' is large enough to use these terms interchangeably.

This chapter will build on the literature on ageing in Europe that has been conducted under the EU's Programme of Actions for the Elderly, and EU Observatory On Ageing and Older People, and will also draw on the wider literature on the economics of ageing.[3] The research agenda of the Observatory provides a useful starting point for the setting up of our comparative study of ageing among migrant communities. The Observatory covered the following topics for its country studies:

- living standards and way of life;
- employment and the labour market;
- health and social care;
- the social integration of older people in both formal and informal settings.[4]

Here we deal with the first two areas of the above list and also attempt to answer the following question by looking at present and future entitlement to pensions and other social security provisions: 'Do ethnic minorities face a more uncertain economic future than others when they age in Britain?'

Ethnicity and Ageing

Defining ethnicity is fraught with difficulty. Ethnicity could be read as a demarcation line between different groups who would give its defining characteristics. From the point of view of the majority group it is the 'otherness' that becomes the defining characteristic of an ethnic minority. The 'white' majority population may perceive all the non-whites as an ethnic group. For example it is common in the USA to refer to the non-whites as 'ethnic', whilst in Australia those whose first spoken language is not English are referred to as 'ethnic'. In these examples colour and language of the majority are used as demarcation lines which indirectly assign the title ethnic to the 'other' groups.

The same categories of colour and language as well as religion, culture, country of origin and national background, have been used to provide a direct definition of an ethnic grouping. This approach could be refined further by relying on self-definition rather than on an outsider's view of who is a member of an ethnic group. Though this is a much more democratic way of defining a group as ethnic than defining them indirectly and with reference to the majority, it still has the problem of masking socioeconomic differences within ethnic groups, differences which reflect and determine the present and future standards of living of individuals. Self-definition could also be approached from 'above' or 'below'. In the former case the upper echelon within an ethnic group could define who belongs to that group and thus use this as a means of social control, whereas in the latter case groups and individuals could locate themselves within an ethnic grouping. The British Population Census of 1991 uses this latter approach to identify different ethnic groups that in published results are consolidated under broad categories.[5]

No matter how we define an ethnic group the question remains 'who are the old?' within ethnic groups. In defining who the 'old' are we should draw a clear distinction between biological ageing, which closely correlates with chronological age, and socially constructed notions of ageing such as retirement age. Evidence on biological ageing suggests that there are no marked differences among people of different ethnic backgrounds and races. Ageing is attributed to a combination of genetic and environmental factors.[6] The life expectancy indicator shows that longevity has for decades been on the increase around the world.

Once we distinguish between mortality and ill health effects of ageing some differences are observed among ethnic groups and between these groups and the white population. Mortality rate due to cancer is significantly lower among the blacks and Asians, but mortality due to coronary heart disease, diabetics, tuberculosis and infectious diseases are higher among the Asians despite their lower rate of smoking and alcohol consumption. The Caribbean migrants, on the other hand, are more at risk of dying from strokes and cardiovascular problems, liver cancer, diabetics and accidents than the whites.[7] Some rare diseases like thalassaemia and sickle cell have only been observed among certain ethnic groups. Such differences in the cause of mortality call for targeted policies to increase life expectancy among the ethnic minorities. On balance one might conclude that the ethnic minorities do not suffer from higher rate of mortality because of their ethnic origin.

As far as ill health, measured by health service access and use and self-reporting, is concerned the situation of ethnic communities appears to be worse than the white population, in particular in the industrial areas of West Midlands and Yorkshire and Lancashire, whilst in the more affluent areas of Leicester and London no such differences have been observed, which implies that in the latter case socioeconomic background is more important than ethnic origin as a cause of ill health.[8] The importance of socioeconomic status is also observed among the whites living in the inner cities industrial areas who have had health problems above national average. In short differences which exist in health conditions of both ethnic and non-ethnic population are a combination of social-economic background and health problems related to life long working conditions and poor health earlier in life, as well as minor genetic differences among ethnic groups.

When it comes to social ageing the matter gets complicated. At the official level it is retirement or pensionable age which is used as a cut off point for referring to people as old. At the time of the 1991 Census the pensionable age, i.e. the minimum age at which people could claim and receive a state retirement pension, was 65 for men and 60 for women. Unless otherwise stated we use these cut off years in this paper to refer to people as 'old'.[9] More often than not the functional age goes well beyond the official chrono-logical retirement age, and many people can be, and are in fact, productive beyond their official retirement age. The retirement age in the word of some commentators has the 'function of clearing jobs for the younger generation'.[10]

A number of points are in order in relation to the 'age of ageing ... [that is] the average age the individual passes the invisible frontier of failure to cope with the expected work load or responsibilities of the indigenous culture'.[11] In this respect any society's treatment of ageing is closely related to the way in which it organises its productive activities.

With more control over productive activities and building up of reserves care of the elderly becomes easier. At the same time development of property rights and control over resources grant certain power to older generations giving them status in the community. In short, ageing is much more graceful if you have accumulated knowledge and economic resources (financial and otherwise) or have access to a pool of resources provided by the community. Being old is also related to the society's evaluation or perception of one's contribution and of one's role. The rich and the powerful usually age 'later' than the poor, in part because of the control that they keep over the assets of their community and society.

Gender aspects of the notion of 'old', are closely related to the economic power of women and society's perception of their social role. If motherhood is seen as a major role for women, then menopause is often used as a popular cut off point for referring to a woman as 'old.' However, in general, control over economic resources and the organisation of power within the household and in society at large would have a strong bearing over the attribution of old to an individual. Her Majesty the Queen (who turned 73 in 1999) is rarely referred to as an 'old woman'.

With the development of the modern educational system with its systematic intergenerational transfer of knowledge and information, the older generation not only has lost some of its advantages over the young but in fact is being disadvantaged by the development of economic activities requiring some basic level of literacy. Technological change that has always been a source of skill obsolescence has affected older workers more than young ones. Most employers with access to a large pool of younger workers prefer to retrain the younger generation for the new skills.

The use of retirement age as a cut off point to define 'old' is a twentieth century development. In the UK the depression and mass unemployment of the 1930s led to the adoption of a retirement policy to increase labour demand for the younger workers. It was argued that it is better to pay *retirement benefit* to the older workers, to ease them out of employment than pay *unemployment benefit* to the young.[12]

In short the concept of ageing is historically determined, varies across different societies and it is closely related to gender relations and to an individual's economic and social position within them.

Age, Ethnicity and Poverty

Most of the causal factors of poverty in old age are common to all the aged, irrespective of their race. Poverty in old age is due to low levels of savings, assets, and pension entitlement, that are often due to low pay and low skill and social class background earlier in life. In other words if you do not pull out of poverty when young most probably you will be poor in old age. But that is not the end of the story. There are strong tendencies for the elderly to be *structurally* poor once they have been thrown into a situation of *conjunctural* poverty as a consequence of unforeseen problems, like a stock market crash which would reduce the value of their annuities and assets. *Structural* poverty is the long term poverty of individuals due to their personal or social circumstances, and the *conjunctural* poverty is the temporary poverty into which ordinarily self-sufficient people may be thrown by crisis.[13] The question then is how to ensure that the non-working elderly do not fall into a poverty trap.

Strategies designed to ensure the entitlement of the non-working elderly to a reasonable standard of living are not fundamentally different from those designed for other non-working and dependent sections of the population. The key policy issue is not only how to tackle the welfare needs of the present elderly generation, but how to help the future generation of the elderly, who are potentially more numerous, to maintain their standard of living. Welfare of any age group depends on their claim over the resources of the society they are living in. Claims that are mediated through income earning opportunities (employment or self-employment), ownership of income bearing assets (e.g. financial assets, real estate, shares), social and family support. Accumulation of assets is at the heart of how we individually create claim over future resources. Such accumulations would depend on our current income, assets and what we inherit. In the absence of any inheritance or redistributive measures, inequality in ownership of asset and income among the younger generation will be carried over into the future generation of the elderly.[14]

As far as people from ethnic minorities are concerned it has been argued that they have to bear the double burden of age and race, a double jeopardy, as they get older. They suffer from economic, social and psychological disadvantages not only because they are old but also because they live in societies with deeply entrenched cultural views on the inferiority of some races.[15] Research has shown that it is not always easy to separate the effect of race on poverty and inequality in old age, from the effect of social class, profession, or gender on poverty. What is needed are longitudinal studies of individual experiences in order to isolate the effect of race on poverty in old age.[16] This is beyond the scope of this chapter but we can ask questions about for example social security and pension regulations (that do not necessarily discriminate on the basis of race) but might well disadvantage one section of the society more than others. For example, if qualification for a full pension is 40 years of working life, an immigrant who has started work later than most of the indigenous population will not qualify for a full pension, and will be on a downward slope to poverty on retirement if s/he has not been able to build up enough assets to compensate for low pension entitlement.

Transfer of assets through inheritance could be an important way for one generation to support another. First generation migrants may well have problems with the transfer of such assets from their country of origin to their new home. Even if we set aside legal restrictions on capital movement, exchange rate and differences in price levels between the two countries could reduce the value of their inheritance substantially. Last but not least is the sense of belonging and attachment to a culture and the psychological support that it provides, something which many first generation migrants would be lacking by growing old in an unwelcoming and racist culture and society.

A Socioeconomic Profile of Ethnic Groups in Britain

This section provides a detailed account of the socioeconomic profile of the ethnic communities, including age structure, dependency, and employment that have important implications for the present and future generation of ethnic elderly.

Table 11.1 presents a summary of the basic information about the UK's ethnic population. According to the 1991 Census people belonging to ethnic minority groups numbered 3.1 million,[17] forming a small proportion (5.5 per cent) of the total population in the UK.[18] Compared with the estimated figures in 1981, the ethnic population had grown by 585,000 (a 28 per cent increase) by 1991.[19]

Indians are the largest ethnic group, numbering 845,000 and forming 1.5 per cent of the total UK population. It is important to note that a large percentage of ethnic minorities were born in the UK, e.g. 42 per cent of Indians and 53.7 per cent of Black-Caribbeans. A further interesting characteristic of the ethnic minorities is the variation in balance between male and female population. The ratio of male to female in each ethnic group varies from 0.90 for Asian – other to 1.09 for the Bangladeshi group, as compared with 0.94 for the white. Last but not least is the difference between median age of the white and the ethnic groups. The latter have a lower median age than the former, a reflection of the ethnics' younger age structure (for further detail on age structure see below and Table 11.3).

As far as the geographic concentration of ethnic population is concerned Table 11.2 shows that southeast region of the UK is home to over half (56.2 per cent) of the ethnic population except for the Pakistani ethnic group – only 29.9 per cent of whom live in the southeast. For the Black-African group the figure is as high as 83.5 per cent. The great majority of ethnic people living in the southeast are concentrated in the Greater London area. The other major concentrations are West Midland metropolitan counties (12.4 per cent), northwest which also includes Greater Manchester (8.1 per cent), East Midlands (6.2 per cent) and West Yorkshire (5.4 per cent).

This pattern of residence has evolved over the years and closely follows the regional pattern of demand for migrant labour. For example, the Caribbeans were employed in public services in London while the Pakistanis were employed in the textile industry in West Yorkshire. Another factor has been the UK government's settlement policy, which sent a great number of Asian immigrants to London and the East Midlands' city of Leicester following their expulsion from East Africa.

The Age Structure of Ethnic Groups

It has already been noted that ethnic minorities have a younger age structure than their white peers. However, there are variations among the ethnics' median age. For example the Black – other group has the youngest median age for both sexes (male: 15.6 years, female: 16.8 years), while the Black-Caribbeans have a median age (male: 29.6 years, female: 30) which is closer to that of the whites' (male: 34.9 years, female: 38.6) (see Table 11.1).

Table 11.1   Number, sex ratio, median age and percentage UK born of ethnic population, UK, 1991

| | White | Minority ethnic groups | | | | | Black | | |
		Indian	Pakistani	Bangladeshi	Chinese	Asian – other	African	Caribbean	Other
Population: M	25,216	423	246	85	78	94	107	239	87
(1000) F	26,948	417	231	78	79	104	106	260	91
T	52,164	840	477	163	157	198	213	499	178
% of UK pop.	94.5	1.5	0.9	0.3	0.3	0.4	0.4	0.9	0.3
% UK born* (in each ethnic group)	95.8	42.0	50.5	36.7	28.4	21.9	36.4	53.7	84.4
M/F ratio	0.94	1.01	1.06	1.09	0.97	0.9	1.01	0.91	0.96
Median age: M	34.9	27.8	19.9	17.3	27.5	28.8	26.7	29.6	15.6
(years) F	38.6	27.8	19.7	16.9	29.4	30.7	25.9	30	16.8

*   For example 42 per cent of the Indian ethnic group were born in the UK.

Source: compiled from OPCS, 1996, Vol. 1, tables 4.8 (p. 112), 4.10 (p. 117) and 6.1 (pp. 154–5).

Table 11.2   Major concentrations of ethnic population, UK, 1991[1]

| Region | White | Minority ethnic groups | | | | | | Black | | Other |
		Indian	Pakistani	Bangladeshi	Chinese	Asian – other	African	Caribbean	
Proportion living in:										
Greater London	10.3	41.3	18.4	52.7	36.1	57.1	77.1	58.2	45.2
West Midlands MC[2]	4.2	16.8	18.5	11.1	3.9	4.5	1.9	14.4	8.8
East Midlands	7.3	11.8	3.7	2.6	4.8	3.7	1.6	4.9	6.0
West Yorkshire	3.6	4.1	16.9	3.7	2.5	2.3	1.2	3.0	3.7
Greater Manchester	4.5	3.5	10.4	7.0	5.3	2.5	2.5	3.4	5.2
Wales	5.4	0.8	1.2	2.3	3.1	1.9	1.3	0.7	1.9
Scotland	9.5	1.2	4.4	0.7	6.7	2.3	1.3	0.2	1.5
Total	44.8	79.5	73.5	80.1	62.4	74.3	86.9	84.8	72.3

Notes

1   Only the largest concentrations of ethnic populations have been included in this table, the rest live in other parts of the country.
2   MC: Metropolitan County.

Source: compiled from OPCS, 1996, Vol. 1, table 4.4, p. 91.

Table 11.3 Age structure (percentage distribution) by sex and dependency ratios of ethnic groups, UK, 1991

Age group	White M	White F	Indian M	Indian F	Pakistani M	Pakistani F	Bangladeshi M	Bangladeshi F	Chinese M	Chinese F	Asian–other M	Asian–other F	Black-African M	Black-African F	Black-Caribbean M	Black-Caribbean F	Black–other M	Black–other F
0–14	19.4	17.3	28.2	27.6	40.4	40.7	44.0	45.3	22.7	20.8	24.6	21.8	28.1	27.9	21.9	19.7	49.9	47.1
15–29	22.3	20.9	24.6	26.5	24.9	27.4	24.7	27.2	32.4	30.2	26.8	26.1	31.6	35.2	27.7	29.7	31.3	34.3
30–44	21.9	20.6	26.8	26.1	18.8	19.8	12.9	16.9	27.2	31.6	30.7	35.1	27.1	26.3	17.8	22.0	12.3	21.8
45–59	17.5	16.5	14.4	13.2	11.4	9.2	13.7	9.1	12.5	11.4	13.9	12.8	9.9	8.6	20.0	19.3	4.3	4.0
60–74	13.8	15.3	6.0	5.4	4.1	2.4	4.6	1.4	4.6	4.7	3.3	3.5	2.9	1.7	11.4	8.0	1.7	1.5
75 +	5.2	9.4	1.1	0.9	0.4	0.4	0.2	0.3	0.7	1.4	0.6	0.7	0.4	0.4	1.1	1.2	0.4	0.4
Total[1]	100	100	100	100	100	100	100	100	100	100	100	100	100	100	100	100	100	100
Dependency ratios:[2]																		
Child[3]	31.7		45.1		76.7		91.2		31.9		33.5		41.7		30.8		103.0	
Elderly[4]	31.4		8.0		4.3		3.0		6.0		4.4		2.7		10.9		3.3	

Minority ethnic groups

Notes

1 Percentages may not add up to 100 because of rounding.

2 Dependency ratios are not sex-specific.

3 Child dependency ratio = (number of persons aged 0–15/men aged 16–59) x 100.

4 Elderly dependency ratio = (men aged 65 and over plus women aged 59 and over/men aged 16–64 plus women aged 16–59) x 100.

Source: compiled from OPCS, 1996, Vol. 1, tables 4.11 (p. 118) and 6.2 (p. 158).

Being younger also means that ethnic minorities have a smaller proportion of their population in age groups over 60 than the white population, the respective percentage figures are: male 6.5/female 5.3 for ethnic minorities, and male 19/female 24.7 for the white population (see Table 11.3). But there are wide variations among the ethnic minorities that are concealed in the aggregate figures (see age pyramids, Figure 11.1).

As far as the population of pensionable age (over 60 for women and over 65 for men[20]) is concerned there were 119,000 ethnic people in 1991 – 73,000 women and 46,000 men – comprising a small proportion (1.15 per cent) of the UK's total population of pensionable age.[21] We can estimate the number of ethnic elderly of pensionable age in the next millennium by assuming that all women and men who would have reached the age of 60 and 65, respectively, and that all the present elderly would be alive by 2001. Accordingly there will be 100,000 more men and 106,000 more women of pensionable age by 2001, when the total male and female ethnic population of pensionable age would reach 146,000 and 179,000, respectively. The rates of increase for men is almost 300 per cent and for women 68 per cent, that are much higher than those for the white population. These substantial rises are due to the younger age structure of the ethnic population.[22]

A glance at the age pyramids of the UK population by ethnic background reveals that Pakistani, Bangladeshi and Black – other groups have the youngest age structures – the base of their respective pyramids are wider than others, whilst other ethnic minorities distinguish themselves by having larger sections of their populations in the 15–44 age groups. Another salient feature of the age structure of different ethnic groups is the balance between the sexes – there are more women than men in the 45–59 age group among the Black-Caribbeans, and Asian–other. The Black-Caribbeans also distinguish themselves by having more women than men in the age group 30–44. A more detailed picture of the age structure of each ethnic group is presented in Table 11.3.

What emerges from Table 11.3 and Figure 11.1 is evidence that not all ethnic groups age at the same pace, and with similar sex ratios. The Black-Caribbeans are the fastest ageing ethnic groups in which there are more men than women in the current elderly population of 60–74 years of age. This will be reversed in the future with the balance heavily tilted towards women, this is also the trend for the Asian–other group. The Indian, Chinese and Black-African ethnic groups have younger age structures than the Black-Caribbeans, and with relatively balanced sex ratios across all age groups and with their future age pyramids resembling those of the total population. The Pakistani, Bangladeshi and Black – other groups have the youngest age structures, their

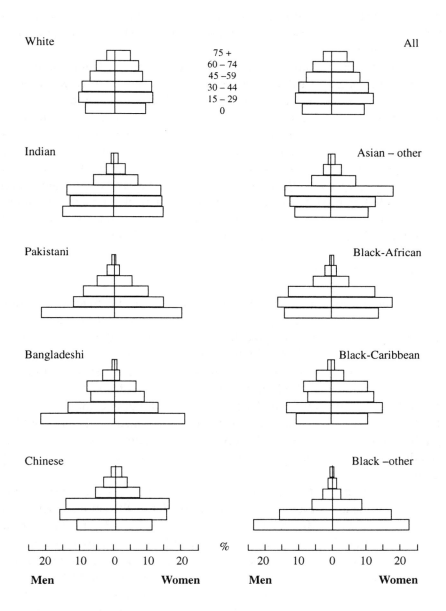

Figure 11.1 Age structure of the white and ethnic population

Source: compiled from OPCS, 1996, Vol. 1, Figure 6.1, p. 157.

future age structure being similar to the total population, with an important difference, the Bangladeshi group will have more men among its elderly in the next 10 years.

Several factors account for the current age structure of ethnic minorities. The most important ones are: (a) the history of migratory flow (whether migrants came with their families or alone, and if and when their family joined them); (b) age at which different cohorts entered UK; (c) the rate of turnover by age and sex; and (d) return migration and retirement. Fertility patterns may well differ across ethnic communities but it is wrong to attribute the young age structure of, for example, the Black – other group to their higher fertility. The category of Black – other is mostly composed of first generation blacks, including mixed race black, from different black ethnic backgrounds, in fact 84 per cent of the Black – other group was born in the UK (the highest percentage of UK born among all ethnic groups, see Table 11.1).

The Dependency Issue

One of the important issues in the debate over the macroeconomic consequences of an ageing population is the relative size of the old to working age population. This ratio is typically calculated by dividing the number of those above the age of 60 or 65 by those of the working age (16–60 or 65). A similar ratio could be constructed to measure young dependency ratio by dividing the number of children (those below the age of, say 16) by those of the working age. In measuring dependency ratios for ethnic communities we should bear in mind that the dependency ratio is a macro indicator, and has usually been applied to the whole population of a country in order to provide an indicator as to the relative burden of the young and the old on the working age population.

The dependency ratios are presented in Table 11.3. It is not surprising that given the young age structure of the ethnic population the young dependency ratio (52.1 per cent) is far greater than that for the old (6.7 per cent). For the white population these ratios are almost equal (31.7 for the young and 31.4 for the old). Obviously the social cost of investing in, and caring for, the dependent population – children or elderly – is shared by all white and non-white ethnic groups. Children (0–15 years) from ethnic backgrounds comprise nine per cent of total population of children in the UK, the corresponding figure for the share of ethnic elderly (65 years and over) is 1.3 per cent.[23] These figures imply that children from ethnic minority backgrounds would put a higher demand (compared with the share of the ethnic population in the total population) on the social support system than the total ethnic population, that however is compensated by the lower demand of the ethnic elderly. A further implication of a young age structure is that the future working age population is going to be large, that will improve the economic potential of caring for an ageing population. In other words, in the not too distant future it is the ethnic minorities who are going to carry a larger economic and social responsibility of looking after the elderly of the UK population.

Applying this macroeconomic relationship between the working and old population (which by implication is non-working) to the debate on the ageing of ethnic population raises several interesting questions. Are the aged going to be cared for within the family? What are the future family structures of different ethnic groups? Do families have the necessary means to care for their elderly? Let us shed some lights on these questions.

There is overwhelming evidence that there are more ethnic elderly people living with their families than elderly white in what is commonly known as extended households (note that the ethnic families are also typically larger than the white families), but there are sharp differences within ethnic groups. Data from a 1 per cent sample taken from the 1991 Census indicate that the elderly blacks are similar to their elderly white counterparts in their living arrangements – by the age of 75 about half of the black and white groups live alone. The corresponding figure for the South Asian group is 15 per cent.[24]

Differences also emerge among ethnic groups when we consider households with three generations (parents, children and grandparents). Such households comprise a larger proportion of ethnic households (varying from 4 to 17.5 per cent depending on the ethnic group) than those among the white households (2.5 per cent). The Indian group has the highest percentage of three generation households: 17.5 per cent (one in six households), followed by the Pakistani/Bangladeshi group: 11.2 per cent (one in nine households), Chinese and Asian – other: 5.8 per cent (one in 17 households), and blacks (including Caribbean, African, and Blacks – other): 4 per cent (one in 25 households). Among the white, only one in 40 households is three generational.[25]

A further difference is that the great majority (about 75 per cent) of the 'secondary' families living in 'complex'[26] white or 'complex' black households are lone parents – typically young daughter of the head of household – as compared with an average of 15 per cent for the others. These proportions are reversed when we look at figures which provide a more direct indicator of the living arrangement of the elderly. On average 25 per cent of the 'secondary' family living in 'complex' households of Indian, Pakistani/Bangladeshi or

Asian – other groups are parent/parent-in-law of the head of the household compared with 10 per cent among the whites and only 5 per cent among the blacks.

But are these living arrangements matters of choice or are they the result of economic necessity and what has been termed as a 'coping strategy'? If it were to be a matter of choice then these differences between ethnic groups of Asian origins (including Chinese) and others should hold irrespective of the level of income and social status of the head of the household.[27] But data suggest otherwise, information on the social class distribution of the heads in single family and two-plus families households shows that 'in every group, those higher up the social scale are more likely to be in a single-family home, with relatively little difference in the patterns between groups [including the white]'.[28] For example, 40 per cent of the households of the Indian ethnic group living in one family households come from the salaried social classes, that is comparable with that for the white – 37 per cent; and Asian – other (including Chinese) groups – 44 per cent. The corresponding figure for the Black is 32 per cent and for the Pakistani/Bangladeshi, 27 per cent.[29] In other words the higher propensity of some ethnic groups to have extended families is more a reflection of their poorer social and economic position than choice. A similar pattern also exists in USA where it has been suggested that 'if the distribution of income for minority groups were the same as for whites, most of the variations in living arrangements would disappear'.[30]

If the living arrangements of the elderly are more a matter of their economic position than choice should we assume that the younger generation has the necessary means to look after their elders? The answer is no, since it is the poorer households who have extended family structures. On other measures of poverty, like unemployment and quality of housing the poorer ethnic groups, most notably the Pakistanis and Bangladeshis, also have the worst records. In 1991 these two groups had the highest rates of unemployment among all ethnic groups (29 per cent and 32 per cent respectively). As for housing, eight per cent of the Pakistani and 20 per cent of the Bangladeshi households lived in overcrowded accommodations (defined as houses or flats with more than 1.5 person per room). The corresponding figures for the white population is 0.4 per cent, Black Caribbean 1.3 per cent, Black – other 1.9 per cent, Indian 2.7 per cent, Asian – other 3.6 per cent, and Black-African 6 per cent.[31]

Finally, it cannot be assumed that family loyalties and customs are not going to change. In short it is far from certain that the family is going to be the dominant or a viable institutional framework for the care of elderly among ethnic minorities.

Employment and Labour Market

A study of employment situation of the working age population is important for understanding what potential there is for poverty or prosperity when they age.

The ethnic minorities have a lower economic activity rate[32] (male: 80 per cent, female: 57 per cent) than the white population (male: 87 per cent, female: 68 per cent), this in part reflects the ethnics' younger age structure plus the fact that a larger proportion of their population are of school age. Similar factors also account for differences among various ethnic groups with the Black-Caribbean having the highest participation rate (male: 86 per cent, female: 73 per cent), and Pakistani group (male: 71 per cent, female: 28 per cent) and the Black-African group (male: 70 per cent, female: 61 per cent) having the lowest rates for men, and Bangladeshi group having the lowest rate for women (male: 74 per cent, female: 22 per cent).[33] The relative positions of white and ethnic groups are reversed when one considers the 'inactive' population – the proportion of 'inactive' among the ethnic groups is less than that among the white, this again is a reflection of the ethnics' younger age structure. But such aggregate comparisons mask the differences that exist at different age groups, especially the older age groups which interest us.

Table 11.4 provides information on the 'inactive' population by age-group, sex, ethnic group and reasons for inactivity. In the older age groups a higher proportion of the ethnic group as a whole is inactive than the white population. On average, 63.6 per cent of the ethnic men were inactive because of permanent sickness compared with 55.2 per cent of the white men. The corresponding figures for women are: 26.3 per cent (ethnic) and 21 per cent (white). There is as usual a wide variation across different ethnic groups. For example, the lowest percentage of inactivity because of permanent sickness among men is observed in the Chinese group – 37.1 per cent, while the highest is that of the Pakistani group – 73.9 per cent, closely followed by the Bangladeshi group – 71.5 per cent. These differences have been attributed to these groups' employment history. Most of the Pakistani and Bangladeshi men were employed in the declining industries of textiles, clothing and engineering, which provided them with little employment opportunities once they were made redundant, or led to their poor health.[34]

As for women, the difference between the white (21 per cent) and ethnic groups (26.3 per cent) attributable to permanent sickness is low. The variation among women of different ethnic groups is much larger than that for men. The lowest percentage of inactivity because of permanent sickness among

Table 11.4   **Percentage distribution of economically inactive population by sex, age and ethnic group, UK, 1991**

| | | Minority ethnic groups | | | | | | Black | | | All ethnic |
	White	Indian	Pakistani	Bangladeshi	Chinese	Asian – other	African	Caribbean	Other	minorities
Sex and age										
Men (16–24):										
Students	92.9	96.7	93.3	93.9	98.1	95.1	89.2	85.6	89.9	93.8
Other inactive	2.3	1.6	3.3	4.0	1.3	3.8	8.9	7.1	4.7	3.6
Women (16–24):										
Students	61.6	75.5	46.7	45.1	90.9	79.8	74.4	63.1	61.9	66.1
Other inactive	35.4	22.9	50.5	53.6	8.6	19.3	24.3	33.5	35.1	32.0
Men (50–64):*										
Permanently sick	55.2	65.2	73.9	71.5	37.3	51.3	50.6	62.4	59.5	63.6
Other inactive	3.2	7.3	8.8	11.6	12.0	13.3	13.0	5.5	8.6	8.4
Women (50–59):*										
Permanently sick	21.0	27.8	13.8	8.1	8.5	19.2	30.6	51.9	37.0	26.3
Other inactive	65.6	64.8	82.2	87.2	77.8	71.9	55.6	34.7	51.6	65.3

*   Percentages do not add up to 100. The balance is accounted for by the percentage of inactive people who have retired.

Source: adapted from ONS (1997), Vol. 4, table 3.10 (p. 48).

women is observed in the Bangladeshi group – 8.1 per cent – while the highest is that of Black-Caribbean group – 51.9 per cent. Here both labour market conditions and the physical demand of the jobs were the suggested reasons for these differences. The high volume of economic inactivity among women from the Bangladeshi and Pakistani groups has been attributed to their 'domestic responsibilities'.[35]

Employment is one of the factors affecting the entitlement of individuals to a pension, the other important factor is whether they are employed full-time or part-time. Full-time workers have a more secure employment and normally accumulate more pension rights. As far as percentage of fully employed men is concerned there is not a big difference between the white (77.7 per cent) and ethnic (73.1 per cent) groups, whilst the variation among the ethnic groups ranges from 61.7 per cent for the Chinese to 83 per cent for the Black-Caribbeans, which mirrors the incidence of self-employment among these two groups, 27 per cent of the Chinese were self-employed compared with six per cent of the Black-Caribbeans. The other important difference is that between ethnic men and women with regard to part-time employment, a higher proportion of women (21 per cent) are in part-time employment than men (4.5 per cent). In this respect the white and ethnic groups are similar, though the difference between men and women is bigger among the white (3.4 per cent of men and 36.7 per cent of women were in part-time employment).

Let us now consider the problem of unemployment, which depending on the type of pension scheme, age and length of unemployment has important effects on the entitlement to pensions. Furthermore, long-term unemployment, especially from a young age, would seriously reduce one's potential to accumulate assets. In general unemployment reduces one's pension under any scheme which relates the level of entitlement to the period and level of contribution. Obviously entitlement to a non-means tested statuary state pension is not affected by a pensioner's employment history. These problems are not the sole concern of ethnic minorities and apply equally to all sections of unemployed population. However, ethnic minorities may well be at a higher risk of unemployment, partly because of their low skills and education, racial discrimination in employment practice, and the industries that they work in. Unemployment rate is much higher among the ethnic minorities than it is among the whites.

In 1991 the rate of unemployment among the ethnic men and women across all age groups was substantially higher than that of the white population. For example the unemployment rate among the ethnic men in the 16–64 age group was 20.3 per cent compared with 10.9 per cent for white men in the same age group. The corresponding figures for women (16–59 years) were 15.6 per cent for the ethnic group and 6.5 per cent for the white.[36] Despite the fact that the unemployment rate comes down for both ethnic and white groups as they age, the gap between the two groups does not narrow.

There are large variations in unemployment among the ethnic minorities, with the unemployment rate being particularly high among the 16–24 years old black and Pakistani men (about 37 per cent) compared with for example 15 per cent among Chinese or 20 per cent among Bangladeshis of the same age group. A similar variation exists among ethnic minority women. For example, Black-African, Pakistani and Bangladeshi women in the 16–24 age group have unemployment rates of 36 per cent, while most other ethnic groups have rates which are closer to 25 per cent. Ethnic women however, have a lower average unemployment rate than ethnic men.

What are the future prospects for ethnic minorities when it comes to their occupations and the industries that they are working in? According to the 1991 Census, ethnic minorities as a whole are *not* concentrated in the *declining* occupations (e.g., plant and machine operatives) and industries (e.g., transport and communication, textiles clothing) but the overall picture conceals notable variations among the ethnic minorities. Black men (particularly Black-Caribbeans) and South Asian men (particularly Pakistanis) are over-represented in the declining industries and occupations, but the overall picture conceals notable variations among the ethnic minorities. South Asian women are over-represented in declining industries, and occupations; 31 per cent as compared with an average of 15 per cent for other groups including the white. As for occupations, 59 per cent of them were working in declining occupations compared with 50 per cent of other ethnic and white women.[37] We should, however, bear in mind that some of these jobs are low skilled and part-time.

When it comes to type of work in terms of number of hours worked per-week a smaller percentage of ethnic women (21 per cent, which is typical of all ethnic groups) are in part-time employment[38] than white women (37 per cent).[39] But there is not a large difference between men from ethnic and white backgrounds, 4.5 per cent of the former and 3.4 per cent of the latter are in part-time employment. Self-employment is an important source of income for a large section of ethnic minorities, particularly among the Asian and Chinese ethnic groups. In 1991, about 20 per cent of Indian, Pakistani and Bangladeshi ethnic groups and 27 per cent of the Chinese were self-employed, compared with about 7 per cent among the blacks and 13 per cent among the whites.[40]

What is the situation of the self-employed when it comes to providing for their old age? To answer this question we need to distinguish between those who run businesses and those who are contracted to work for others on a self-employed basis. The former, as well as some of those in the latter groups, such as doctors, lawyers, accountants and people in the building and construction trade who have reasonable and secure incomes, can accumulate assets and purchase private pension plans. Among those who work for others, are those who work in activities which were contracted out by both the public and private sectors in the 1980s. The self-employed in this category are often former employees of the same concern who, after contacting out, work 'for themselves'.

With contracting out the responsibility for national insurance contribution passes from the employers to the, now, 'self-employed' workers, thus reducing the employers' labour costs. These 'self-employed' people maintained their entitlement to a minimum state pension, and retained their membership of their former occupational pension schemes if they continued to pay their full contribution (including what was contributed by their former employer). Some decided to withdraw their savings from occupational pensions and join private pension schemes, which usually have had higher administrative costs than occupational pension schemes.[41]

The 1991 Census does not provide detailed information on the number of people in different categories of self-employed, nor are there readily available data on self-employment segregated by sex. However it is possible to shed some light on the relative size of different types of self-employment among ethnic minorities, a large percentage of whom run small businesses employing others as well as family members. Bangladeshis have the highest percentage of self-employed with employees (74 per cent) followed by Chinese (58 per cent), Indian (43 per cent) and Pakistanis (38 per cent). The corresponding figures for the black and white population are, respectively, 24 and 33 per cent.[42]

It is difficult to establish whether or not self-employment among ethnic minorities is due to the positive effect of taking advantage of business opportunities or the negative effect of lack of employment opportunities. Whatever the motive for self-employment the question remains as to their standard of living. Under the most optimistic assumption that those who employ others have a reasonable living standard, it leaves a large section of the self-employed whose living standards have to be explained. If we further assume that at most 5 per cent[43] of the ethnic self-employed are engaged in well paid professional occupations, we can estimate the number of self-employed people who have ended up self-employed because of contracting out in the 1980s and thus have, in the main, low paying and insecure employment. Under these estimates we get the following percentages of self-employed people among the ethnic minority groups who are on low income: 70 per cent of all the black groups, 50 per cent of Indian and Pakistani groups, 20 per cent of the Bangladeshi group, and 35 per cent of the Chinese group. The corresponding figure for the white is 60 per cent.

There are other aspects of self-employment that are important for old age security. A recent study showed that: the unemployed had a high rate of entry to self-employment, the service sector attracted a disproportionately high share of the new self-employment with a high concentration in the low value added/income end of the personal services.[44] It is therefore *not* surprising that the 1995 General Household Survey revealed that 39 per cent of the self-employed never had a personal pension with another 10 per cent who had stopped contributing to personal pension schemes. The self-employed, however, are similar to those who are employed by others, 37 per cent of whom have never had a personal pension nor have been in an occupational pension scheme.[45] Several reasons have been put forward for the self-employed not taking a personal pension, some of which are business based decisions such as viewing pensions as having low returns compared to investing in their business or viewing their business as the source of their pension. Other reasons are to do with low, insecure and unpredictable incomes which make financial planning difficult. It has, therefore, been suggested that self-employment could increase the risk of being poor in the old age.[46] It is clear that self-employment is not going to offer much of a protection for the great majority of the ethnic minorities who are stuck in poorly paid and insecure occupations.

Do the second generation ethnic minorities have a better prospect than the first generation? Is the ethnic penalty, defined as 'all the sources of disadvantage that might lead an ethnic group to fare less well in the labour market than do similarly qualified whites',[47] going to continue to disadvantage the second generation minorities, who have mostly been born and brought up in Britain? The answer to this question is, regrettably, in the affirmative. Heath, and McMahon[48] divided the British population of the *same educational background* into different groups of salariat, petty bourgeoisie, and working class (broken down further by ethnic groups) and found that chances for second generation ethnic men and women to move up the social ladder by securing access to the salariat, self-employed or own account occupations, or avoiding unemployment were *not* different from the first generation.

Conclusion

As stated at the beginning of this chapter, the ageing population of the UK is not a homogenous mass but is rather stratified by constituents of social class, gender, ethnic background and race that have to be taken on board if social and economic policies are to be successful in their objective of providing reasonable living standards for the mass of the elderly population in the twenty-first century.

This chapter has been concerned mainly with the economic position of the elderly among the non-white immigrants who have settled in the UK since the Second World War. Using the 1991 Census we have observed that in general the ethnic groups in the UK have a younger age structure than the white population. But there are variations among the ethnic groups with the Black – other group having the youngest median age, whilst the figure for Black-Caribbeans is close to that for the white. These differences in age structure reflect more migration and life histories of various groups than differences in biological ageing that by all accounts do not vary greatly across races and ethnic groups. The Census also showed that the great majority of the ethnic people, and their elders, live in London, Greater Manchester, West Yorkshire and the metropolitan counties of Midlands.

As far as the health profile of the aged is concerned there are differences among ethnic groups and between them and the white group, that are due to a combination of socioeconomic background and health problems related to lifelong working conditions and poor health earlier in life, as well as minor genetic differences.

The question of poverty in old age is related to low levels of savings, assets, and pension entitlement, that are often due to low pay, and low skill and social class background earlier in life. The 'double jeopardy' thesis suggests that people from ethnic minorities suffer from the problems associated with old age as well as racial discrimination. Whilst on an *a priori* basis the 'double jeopardy' thesis is more relevant to the case of poor non-white ethnic minorities, for the rest it is not always easy to separate the effect of race on poverty and inequality in old age, from the effect of social class, profession, or gender. However, it may well be argued that there are structural reasons for the first generation ethnic minorities to become poor when they age, because as immigrants they have usually started work later than the indigenous people and therefore have less claims on any pension scheme which relates benefits to years of service. A similar argument could be made about pension schemes which relate benefits to contributions; immigrants who are in low paid jobs with low pension contributions end up with low pension entitlement. Both pension schemes are also affected by periodic unemployment. Immigrants from poor countries are also at a disadvantage when it comes to the intergenerational transfer through inheritance from their origin to their new home. International price differences, particularly property prices, and exchange rates could substantially reduce the value of their inherited assets in their new home.

Census data do not lend themselves to a comprehensive examination of the above issues but they do provide an indication as to potential, and actual, poverty among the large sections of ethnic elderly. For example, among most ethnic groups a higher percentage of men in the 50–64 age group leave the job market and become economically inactive than their white counterparts because of permanent sickness due to the concentration of ethnic men in declining industries. Unemployment also has been higher among ethnic groups as compared with white, though self-employment is higher among the Asian and Chinese ethnic groups. However a large percentage of the ethnic population are stuck in low income self-employed activities, and in this respect they are not different from their white counterparts. Is the extended family system going to be much of help in alleviating poverty in old age? If by poverty alleviation we mean sharing the meagre resources of a poor household, the answer is yes, otherwise it is the poorer households among ethnic minorities who have to share the overcrowding and care of the elderly – in the main the responsibility of women in the household.

It is important to point out that there are no major differences between the ethnic and white population when it comes to fundamental causes of poverty in old age, i.e. low lifetime income and low social class background, with the latter determining intergenerational transfer of assets within household. In this respect, the distributional role of state pension policies has to be strengthened. Second, pension entitlement rules with regard to period and amount of contribution need to be changed to take account of shorter, and interrupted, working life and low contributions. Financing of such a measure would be an issue, in particular with regard to occupational and fully funded pension schemes. One approach would be for state, and employers and employees to share the cost.

Notes

Acknowledgement: the first draft of this chapter was presented as a paper at the third conference of QMW's Centre for the Study of Migration, held on 14 November 1998. I am grateful to Anne Kershen and John Grahl for their support and encouragement in presenting the paper. This chapter also benefited from the comments of Anne Kershen and Malcolm Sawyer. Alas, I am solely responsible for any errors.

1   J. Bond, P. Coleman and S. Peace (eds), *Ageing and Society: an Introduction to Social Gerontology*, 2nd edn, London, Sage, 1993.

2   In 1996 OPCS (Office of Population Census and Surveys) and Central Statistical Office (CSO) merged to from the Office for National Statistics (ONS) which has since been responsible for the full range of functions of OPCS and CSO.

3   See, for example, A. Walker and T. Maltby, *Ageing in Europe*, Buckingham, Open University Press, 1997; A. Walker, A.-M. Guillemard and J. Alber, *Older People in Europe: Social and Economic Policies*, Brussels, CEC, 1993; R. Clark, J. Kreps and J. Spengler, 'Economics of Ageing: A Survey', *Journal of Economic Literature*, XVI, September 1978, pp. 919–62; R. Clark and J. Spengler, *The Economics of Individual and Population Ageing*, Cambridge, Cambridge University Press, 1980; M.D. Hurd, 'Research on the Elderly: Economic Status, Retirement, and Consumption and Saving', *Journal of Economic Literature*, XXVIII, June 1990, pp. 565–637; P. Johnson, and J. Falkingham, *Ageing and Economic Welfare*, London, Sage, 1992; R. Disney, *Can We Afford to Grow Older? A Perspective on the Economics of Ageing*, Cambridge, Mass., MIT Press, 1996.

4   Walker and Maltby, op. cit., p. 4.

5   For further details see OPCS, *Ethnicity in the 1991 Census. Volume One – Demographic Characteristics of the Ethnic Minority Populations*, eds D. Coleman and J. Salt, London, HMSO, 1996, table 2.2, p. 49. For a concise and very useful theoretical discussion of socio-logical concept of ethnicity and race see F. Anthias, *Ethnicity, Class, Gender and Migration: Greek-Cypriots in Britain*, Aldershot, Avebury, 1992, ch. 2. See also C. Barresi, and D. Stull (eds), *Ethnic Elderly and Long Term Care*, New York, Springer, 1993 and D.T. Rowland, *Pioneers Again: Immigrants and Ageing in Australia*, Canberra, AGPS, 1991.

6   See C.S. Bergman, *Ageing: Genetic and Environmental Influences. Individual*, Differences and Development Series, Vol. 9, London, Sage, 1997, ch. 1.

7   K. Blakemore and M. Boneham, *Age, Race and Ethnicity*, Buckingham, Open University Press, 1994, ch. 4; J. Askham, L. Henshaw and M. Tarpey, *Social & Health Authority Services for Elderly People from Black and Ethnic Minority Communities*, London, HMSO, 1995, ch. 1.

8   Blakemore and Boneham, op. cit., ch. 4.

9   Since 1992 the pensionable age for women has been 60 if they were born on or before 5 April 1950 or 65 if they were born on or after 5 April 1955. For women who were born after 5 April 1950 but before 6 April 1995, pensionable age is 60 plus one month for each month (or part month) that their date of birth fell after 5 April 1950. Note that the change in the pensionable age for women will be phased in from 2010 to 2020. For further details, see Benefits Agency Communications and Customer Liaison Branch, *A Guide to Retirement Pensions*, Leaflet NP 46, 1997.

10 S. Ekpenyong, O.Y. Oyeneye and M. Peil, 'Reports on Study of Elderly Nigerians', Centre for West African Studies, University of Birmingham, 1986, quoted in K. Tout, *Ageing in Developing Countries*, Oxford, Oxford University Press, 1989, p. 8.

11 K. Tout, *Ageing in Developing Countries*, Oxford, Oxford University Press, 1989, p. 5.

12 C. Phillipson, *Capitalism and the Construction of Old Age*, London, Macmillan, 1982.

For further discussion of these and other points related to historical ageing see Tout, op. cit., pp. 8–10 and references therein.

13 See J. Iliffe, *The African Poor: a History*, Cambridge, Cambridge University Press, 1987, p. 4.

14 This is based on entitlement theory developed by A.K.S. Sen, *Poverty and Famines: An Essay on Entitlement and Deprivation*, Oxford, Oxford University Press, 1981.

15 J.J. Dowd and V.L. Bengston, 'Ageing in Minority Populations – an Examination of the Double Jeopardy Hypothesis', *Journal of Gerontology*, 1978, 33, pp. 427–36.

16 Blakemore and Boneham, op. cit.

17 For a discussion of the 1991Census approach to questions about and enumeration of ethnic groups see OPCS, Vol. 1, 1996, ch. 2.

18 Ibid.

19 Ibid., p. 85.

20 These were pensionable age at the time of the 1991 Census, that has since changed: see note 9 for details.

21 OPCS, op. cit., table 6.1, pp. 154–5.

22 Calculations based on ibid.

23 Ibid., p.117. Compare these figures with the share of ethnic minorities in the total population of UK – 5.5 per cent.

24 M. Murphey, 'Household and Family Structure Among Ethnic Minority Groups,' in ibid., p. 229.

25 Ibid., table 8.10, p. 234. Note that Pakistani/Bangladeshi is treated as one group here.

26 A 'complex' household is one in which 'at least two distinct families' live together (Murphy, ibid., p. 228).

27 The 1991 Census categorises the population into the following social classes: 1. Higher Salariat, 2. Lower Salariat, 3. Routine Non-manual Class, 4. Petty Bourgeoisie, 5. Foremen and Skilled Working Class, 6. Semi- and unskilled Working Class, and 7. Unemployed. (For further detail see ONS, *Ethnicity in the 1991 Census. Volume Four: Employment, Education and Housing Among the Ethnic Minority Populations of Britain*, ed. Valerie Karn. London, HMSO, 1997, pp. 92–3.

28 Murphy, op. cit., p. 235.

29 Ibid., table 8.13, p. 236.

30 B. Soldo, and P. Lauriat, 'Living Arrangements Among the Elderly in the United States: a Loglinear Approach', *Journal of Comparative Family Studies*, 7 (2), 1976, pp. 351–66, referred to in Murphy, ibid., p. 236.

31 C. Peach, 'Introduction,' in ONS, *Volume Two*, 1996, table 11, p. 21. No overcrowding figures were reported for the Chinese group.

32 Activity rate is normally defined as the ratio of those who are officially working or seeking work to working age population.

33 D. Owen, 'Labour Force Participation Rates, Self-Employment and Unemployment', in ONS, *Volume Four*, 1997, pp. 29–66.

34 Ibid.

35 Ibid., p. 49.

36 Among the younger age group of 16–24 again the Ethnic group has a higher unemployment rate (men: 30.9 and women: 24.9 per cent) than the white (men: 17.4 and women: 11.4 per cent). For the age groups above 50 similar patterns exist, the rate of unemployment is among the ethnic groups (for both men and women) is at least twice than that among the

white. For example, the unemployment rate for ethnic men in 55–59 age group was about 21 per cent compared with 11 per cent among the white (see ONS, *Volume Four*, 1997, table 3.13, p. 54, and figure 3.4, p. 55.

37 A. Green, 'Patterns of Ethnic Minority Employment in the Context of Industrial and Occupational Growth and Decline', in ONS, *Volume Four*, 1997, tables 4.4, p. 74, and table 4.6, p. 80.

38 Part-time employment is defined as 30 or less hours of work per week: see Green, op. cit., p. 82.

39 Owen, op. cit., table 3.11 p. 51.

40 Ibid., table 3.12 p. 53.

41 Many of these private pensions schemes have proved to be totally unsuitable for people who took their money out of occupational pension schemes. In the past few years there have been many reports of these pension misselling in the press.

42 Owen, op. cit., table 3.12, p. 53.

43 This assumption is based on the percentage of first generation men from ethnic population who were in the salariat (high and low) class. According to a two per cent sample of 1991 census 12 per cent of Black-Caribbbeans, 27 per cent of Black-Africans, 21 per cent of Black – other, 29 per cent of Indian, 14 per cent of Pakistanis, 10 per cent of Bangladeshis, and 30 per cent of Chinese were in this class, compared with 33 per cent of the white (A. Heath and D. McMahon, 'Education and Occupational Attainments: the Impact of Ethnic Origins', in ONS, *Volume Four*, 1997, pp. 92–5.) On average about 20 per cent of the first generation ethnic men are in the salariat class with relatively secure employment, incremental salary scale, various fringe benefits (including occupational pension schemes) and significant promotional chances (ibid.). In this chapter I make the generous assumption that a quarter of these 'salariat' people are self-employed professionals.

44 N. Meager, G. Court and J. Moralee, *Self- Employment and the Distribution of Income*, Institute of Manpower Studies, Report 270, Brighton, IMS, 1994.

45 Stationary Office, *We All Need Pensions – The Prospects for Pension Provision*, London, Stationary Office, 1998.

46 For further discussion see ibid., pp. 73–6, 116.

47 Heath and McMahon, op. cit.

48 Ibid.

Index